Year 3
Textbook 3A

Ash

Ash is curious.

He likes to help if you get stuck.

flexible → **Flo**

brave → **Astrid**

helpful → **Sparks**

determined → **Dexter**

Series editor: Tony Staneff
Lead author: Josh Lury
Consultants (first edition): Professor Liu Jian and Professor Zhang Dan
Written by Tony Staneff and Josh Lury

Contents

Your teacher will tell you which page you need.

Unit 1 – Place value within 1,000 — 6
Represent and partition numbers to 100 — 8
Number line to 100 — 12
100s — 16
Represent numbers to 1,000 — 20
Partition numbers to 1,000 — 24
Partition numbers to 1,000 flexibly — 28
100s, 10s and 1s — 32
Use a number line to 1,000 — 36
Estimate on a number line to 1,000 — 40
Find 1, 10 and 100 more or less — 44
Compare numbers to 1,000 — 48
Order numbers to 1,000 — 52
Count in 50s — 56
End of unit check — 60

Unit 2 – Addition and subtraction (1) — 62
Use known number bonds — 64
Add/subtract 1s — 68
Add/subtract 10s — 72
Add/subtract 100s — 76
Spot the pattern — 80
Add 1s across 10 — 84
Add 10s across 100 — 88
Subtract 1s across 10 — 92
Subtract 10s across 100 — 96
Make connections — 100
End of unit check — 104

Unit 3 – Addition and subtraction (2) — 106
Add two numbers — 108
Subtract two numbers — 112

2

Add two numbers (across 10)	116
Add two numbers (across 100)	120
Subtract two numbers (across 10)	124
Subtract two numbers (across 100)	128
Add a 3-digit and a 2-digit number	132
Subtract a 2-digit number from a 3-digit number	136
Complements to 100	140
Estimate answers	144
Inverse operations	148
Problem solving (1)	152
Problem solving (2)	156
End of unit check	160

Unit 4 – Multiplication and division (1) — 162

Multiplication – equal groups	164
Use arrays	168
Multiples of 2	172
Multiples of 5 and 10	176
Share and group	180
End of unit check	184

Unit 5 – Multiplication and division (2) — 186

Multiply by 3	188
Divide by 3	192
The 3 times-table	196
Multiply by 4	200
Divide by 4	204
The 4 times-table	208
Multiply by 8	212
Divide by 8	216
The 8 times-table	220
Problem solving – multiplication and division (1)	224
Problem solving – multiplication and division (2)	228
Understand divisibility (1)	232
Understand divisibility (2)	236
End of unit check	240
What do we know now?	247

Let's get started!

How to use this book

These pages make sure we're ready for the unit ahead. Find out what we'll be learning and brush up on your skills!

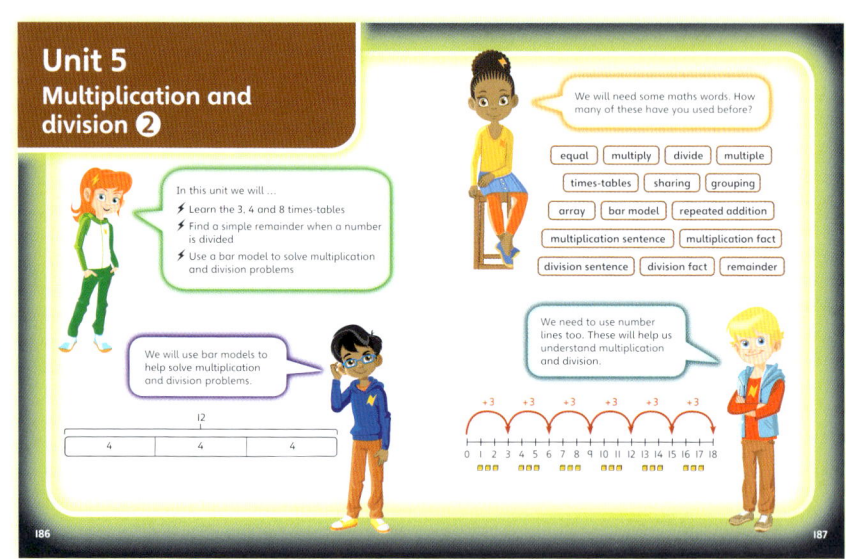

Discover

Lessons start with **Discover**.

Here, we explore new maths problems.

Can you work out how to find the answer?

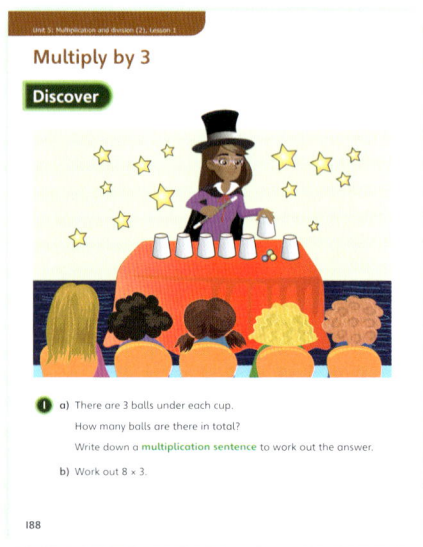

Don't be afraid to make mistakes. Learn from them and try again!

4

Share

Next, we share our ideas with the class.

Did we all solve the problems the same way? What ideas can you try?

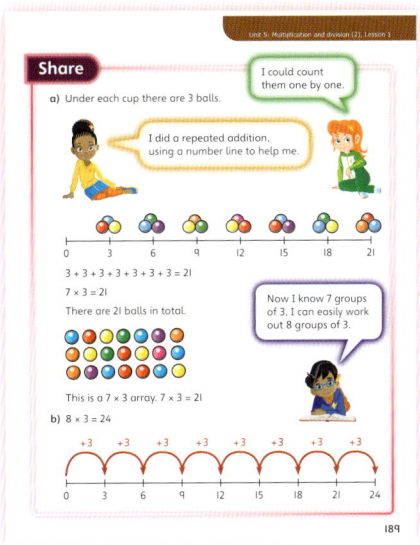

Think together

Then we have a go at some more problems together. Use what you have just learnt to help you.

We'll try a challenge too!

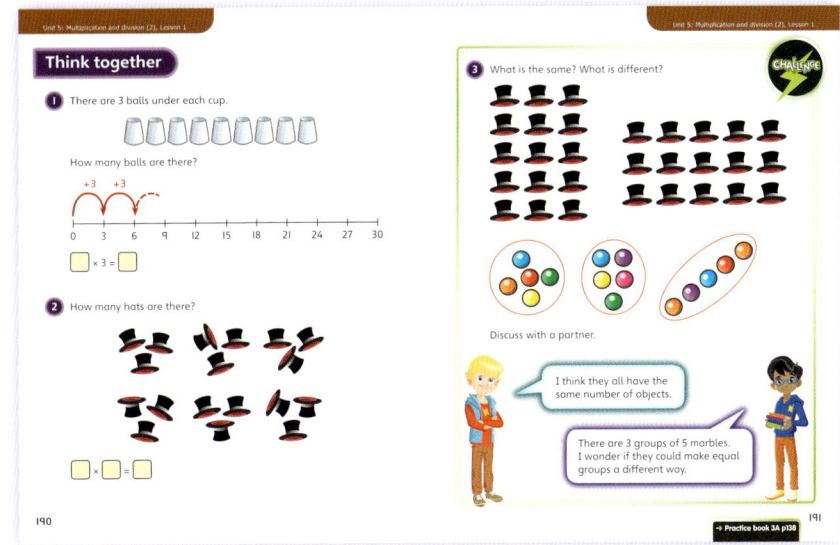

This tells you which page to go to in your **Practice Book**.

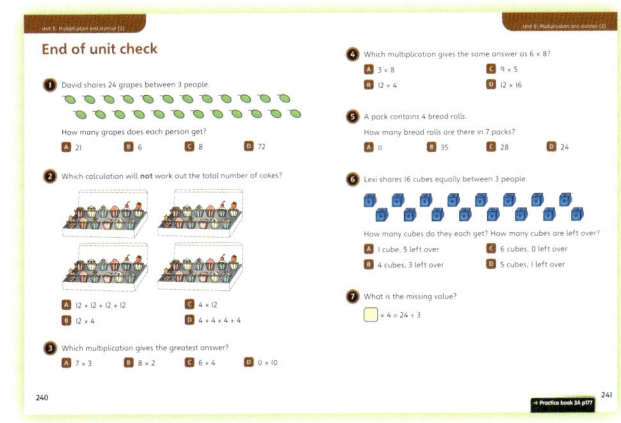

At the end of each unit there's an **End of unit check**. This is our chance to show how much we have learnt.

Unit 1
Place value within 1,000

In this unit we will ...
- Count in 100s
- Partition a number in 100s, 10s and 1s
- Find 100, 10 and 1 more or less
- Compare and order numbers up to 1,000
- Count in 50s

In Year 2 we used place value grids to organise our work. What number does this show?

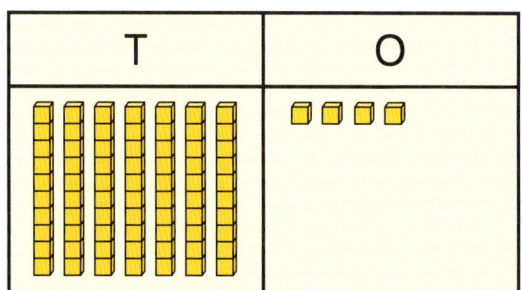

We will need some maths words. How many of these can you remember?

hundreds (100s)   tens (10s)   ones (1s)

place value   more   less

greater than (>)   less than (<)   equal to

order   compare   estimate

exchange   ascending   descending

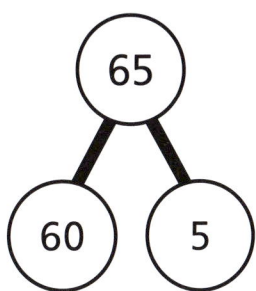

We will also use part-whole models and number lines.

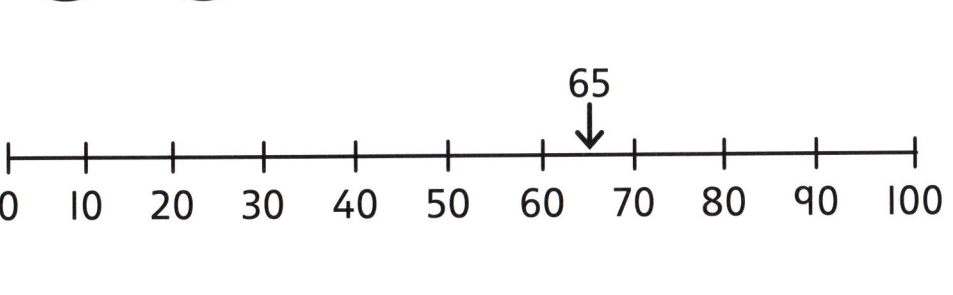

Unit 1: Place value within 1,000, Lesson 1

Represent and partition numbers to 100

Discover

1) a) Draw or make Emma's number from base 10 equipment. What number has Emma made?

b) What number has Andy made?

Share

a)

I counted the 10s then the 1s.

10 20 30 31 32 33 34 35 36

Emma has made the number 36.

b)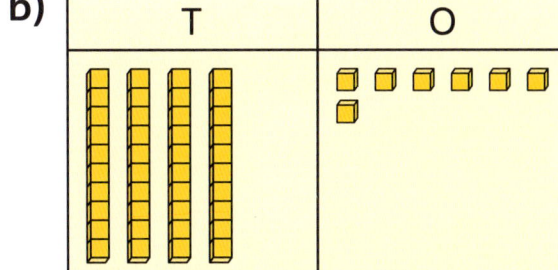

T	O
4	6

46
40 6

Andy has made the number 46.

I put the base 10 equipment into a place value grid. Then I drew a part-whole model.

Unit 1: Place value within 1,000, Lesson 1

Think together

1 How many colour pencils are there?

2 What numbers are shown here?

a)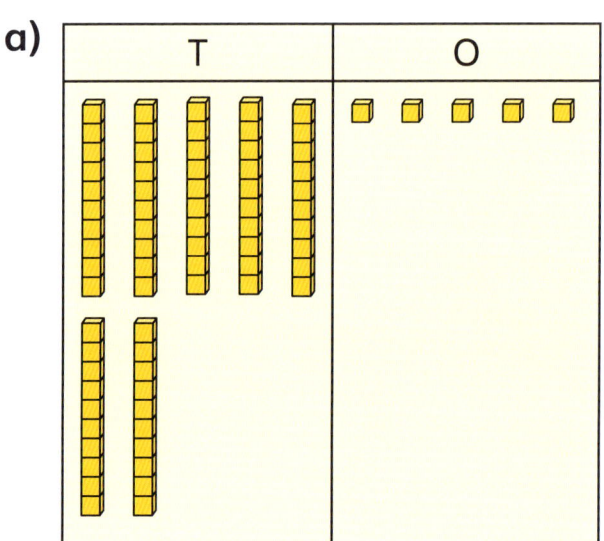

b)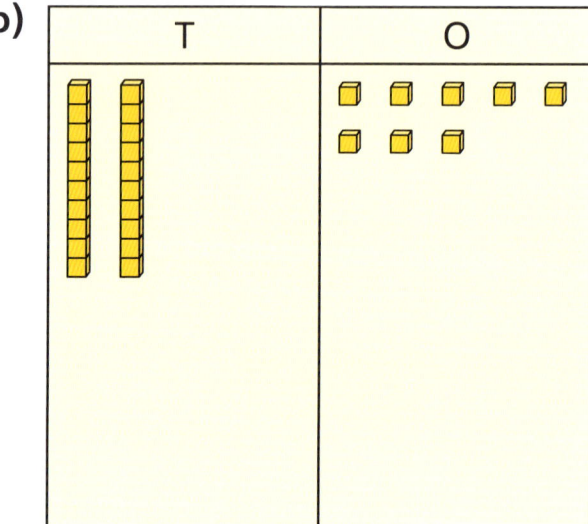

10

Unit 1: Place value within 1,000, Lesson 1

3 a) Complete the part-whole model. Use base 10 equipment to help you.

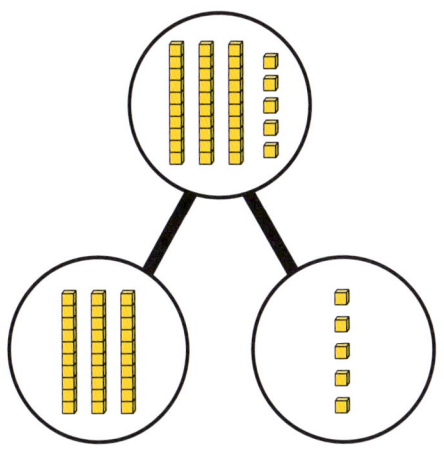
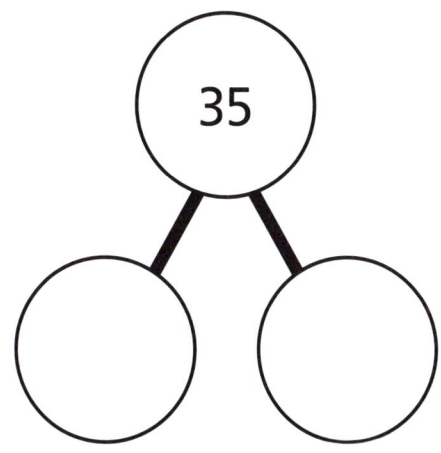

b) What is the mistake in this part-whole model?

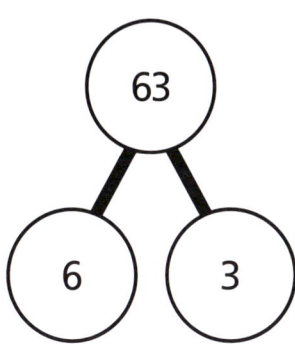

I wonder if I can use the base 10 equipment to help me see what is wrong.

→ Practice book 3A p6

Unit 1: Place value within 1,000, Lesson 2

Number line to 100

Discover

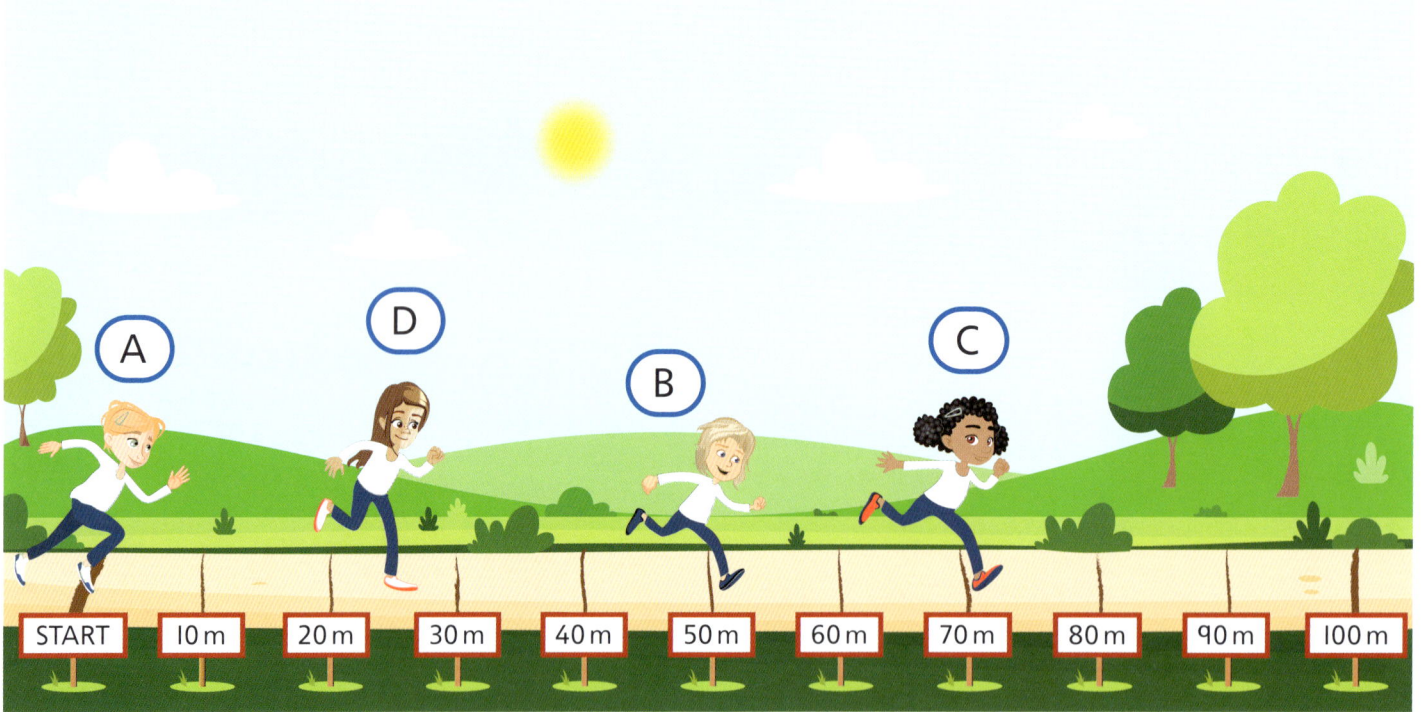

1 a) How far has runner B run?

How far has runner C run?

b) How far has runner D run?

Share

a)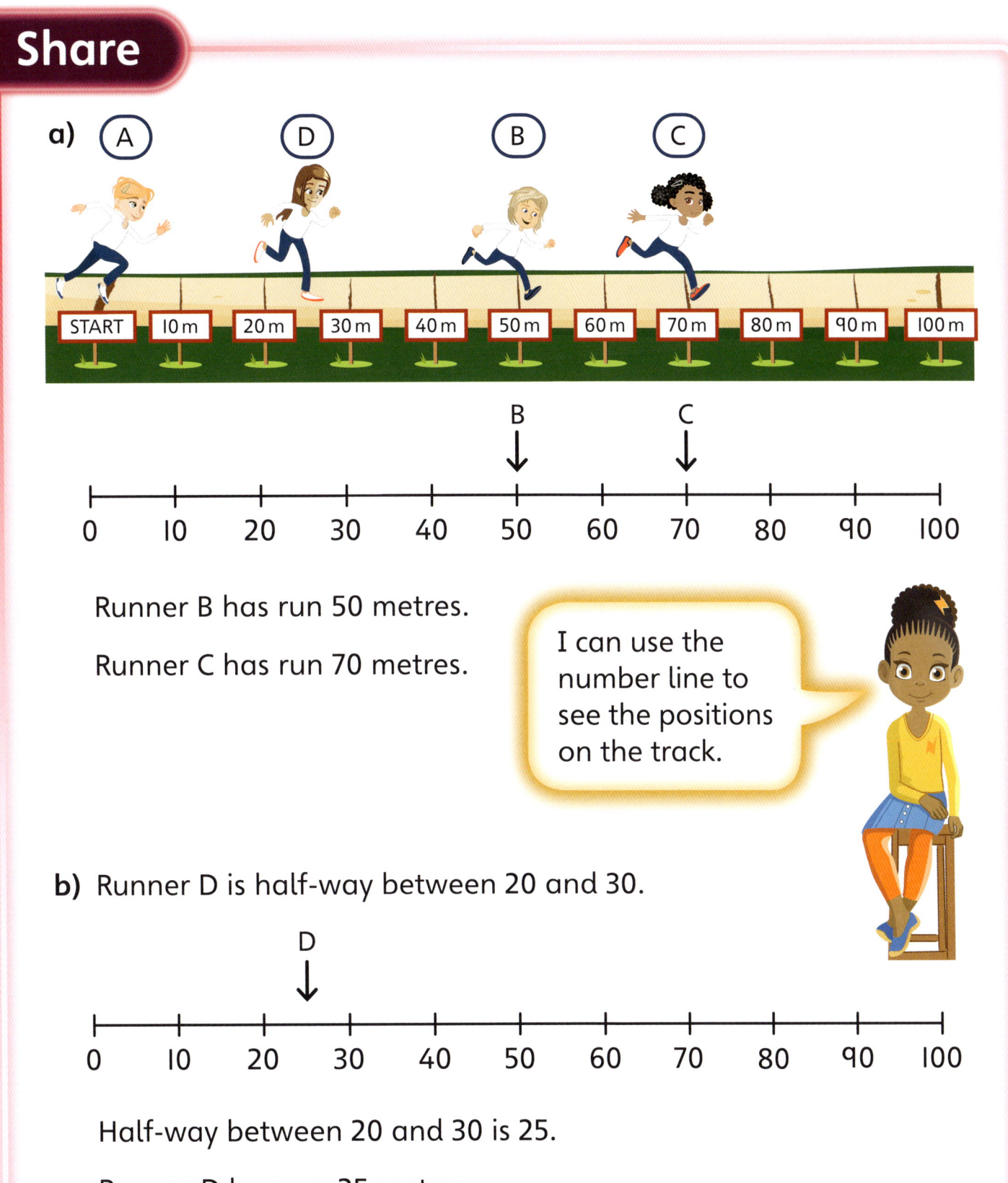

Runner B has run 50 metres.

Runner C has run 70 metres.

I can use the number line to see the positions on the track.

b) Runner D is half-way between 20 and 30.

Half-way between 20 and 30 is 25.

Runner D has run 25 metres.

Unit 1: Place value within 1,000, Lesson 2

Think together

1) What numbers are the arrows pointing to?

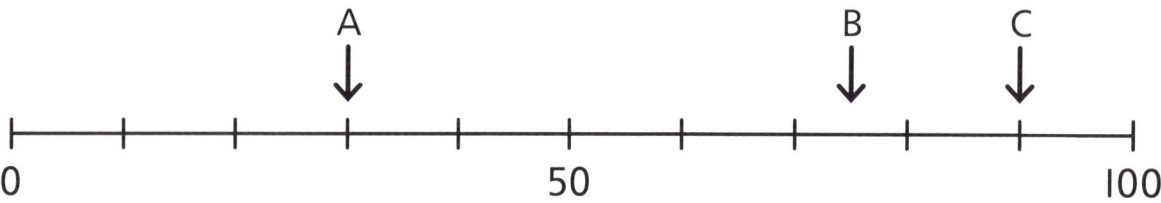

2) What numbers are the arrows pointing to?

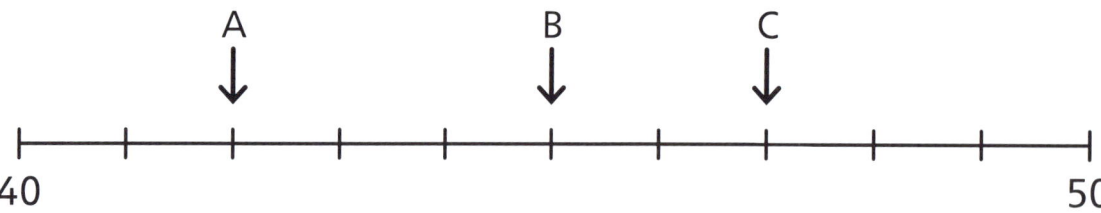

I don't think this number line is going up in 10s. I will check.

Unit 1: Place value within 1,000, Lesson 2

3

This number line is marked in 10s and 1s.

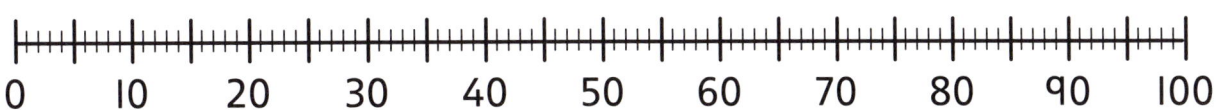

a) Point to the 10s markings.

Point to the 1s markings.

b) Point to the following numbers.

| 25 | 57 | 92 |

I know that 57 lies between 50 and 60.

→ Practice book 3A p9

Unit 1: Place value within 1,000, Lesson 3

100s

Discover

1 a) How many dice?

b) How many counters?

16

Share

a) We can count the dice.

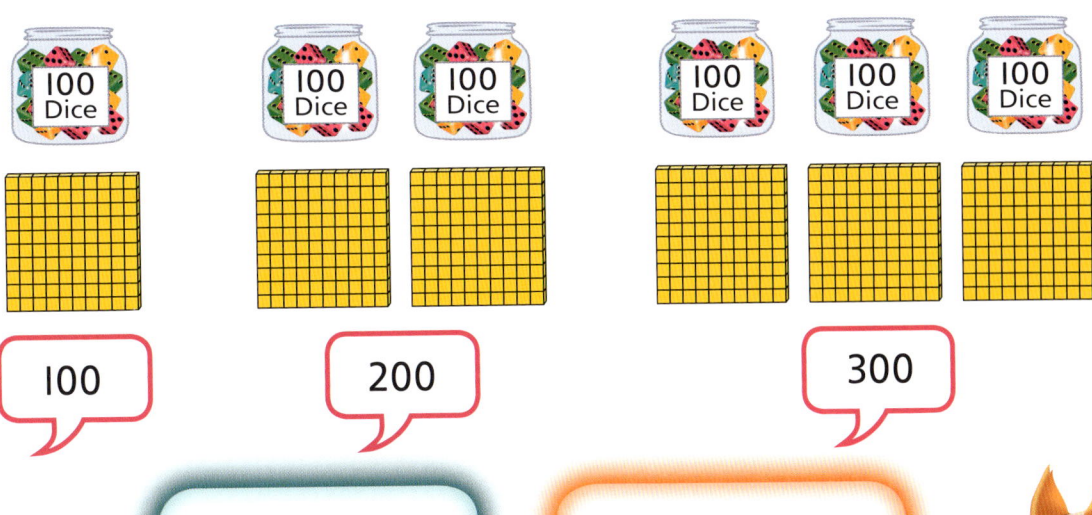

"I counted up in 100s."

"Each flat represents 100."

There are 100 dice in each jar.

There are 300 dice in total.

b)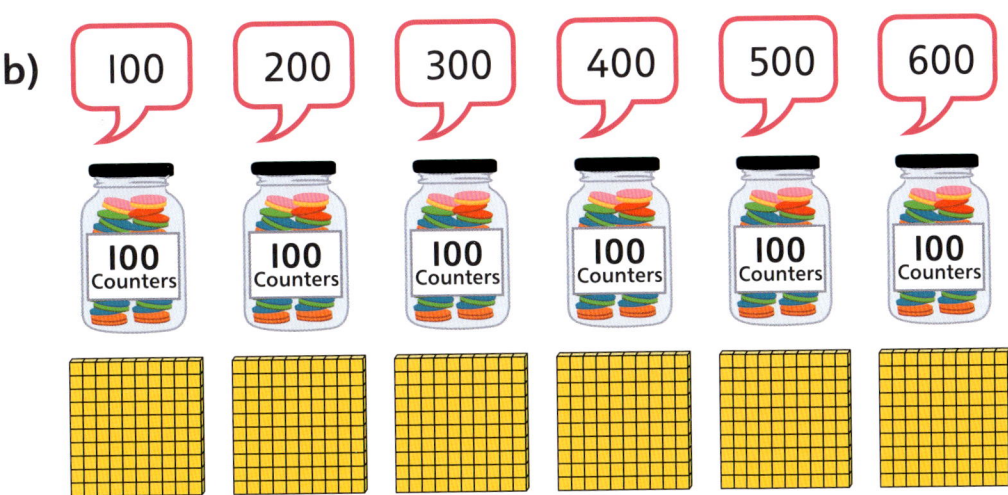

There are 6 jars of 100 counters.

There are 600 counters in total.

Unit 1: Place value within 1,000, Lesson 3

Think together

1) Each jar contains 100 counters.

How many counters are there in each row?

		0	zero
(1 jar)	(1 hundred square)	100	one hundred
(2 jars)	(2 hundred squares)	200	two hundred
(3 jars)	(3 hundred squares)	300	three hundred
(4 jars)	(4 hundred squares)		
(5 jars)	(5 hundred squares)		
(6 jars)	(6 hundred squares)		
(7 jars)	(7 hundred squares)		
(8 jars)	(8 hundred squares)		

Unit 1: Place value within 1,000, Lesson 3

2 What are the missing numbers?

a) | 0 | 100 | 200 | 300 | ☐ | ☐ | 600 | 700 |

b) | 500 | 400 | ☐ | 200 | ☐ | 0 |

c) ☐, 600, ☐, 800, ☐

3 How many marbles are there?

Write the number in numerals and words.

There are ☐ marbles.

There are _____ marbles.

CHALLENGE

I think there is another name for this. I wonder what it is.

When I count in 100s, I know what comes after 9 **hundreds**. It must be 10 hundreds.

→ Practice book 3A p12

Unit 1: Place value within 1,000, Lesson 4

Represent numbers to 1,000

Discover

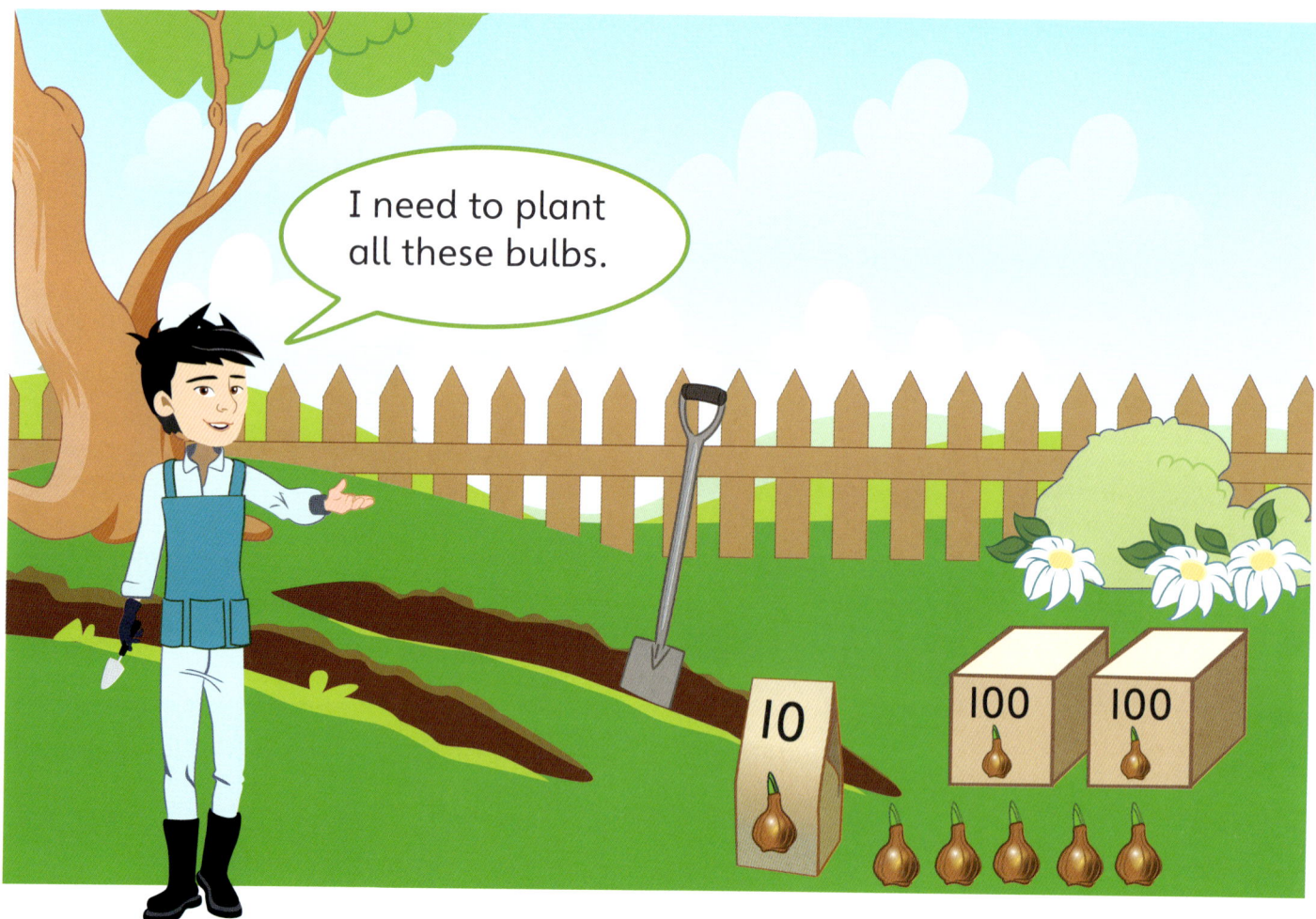

1) a) How many bulbs need to be planted?

b) Make this number with base 10 equipment.
How many 100s, 10s and 1s did you use?

Share

a)

I will start by counting the boxes of 100.

100   200   210   211   212   213   214   215

There are 215 bulbs to be planted.

b)

  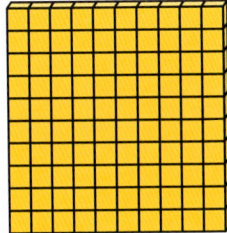

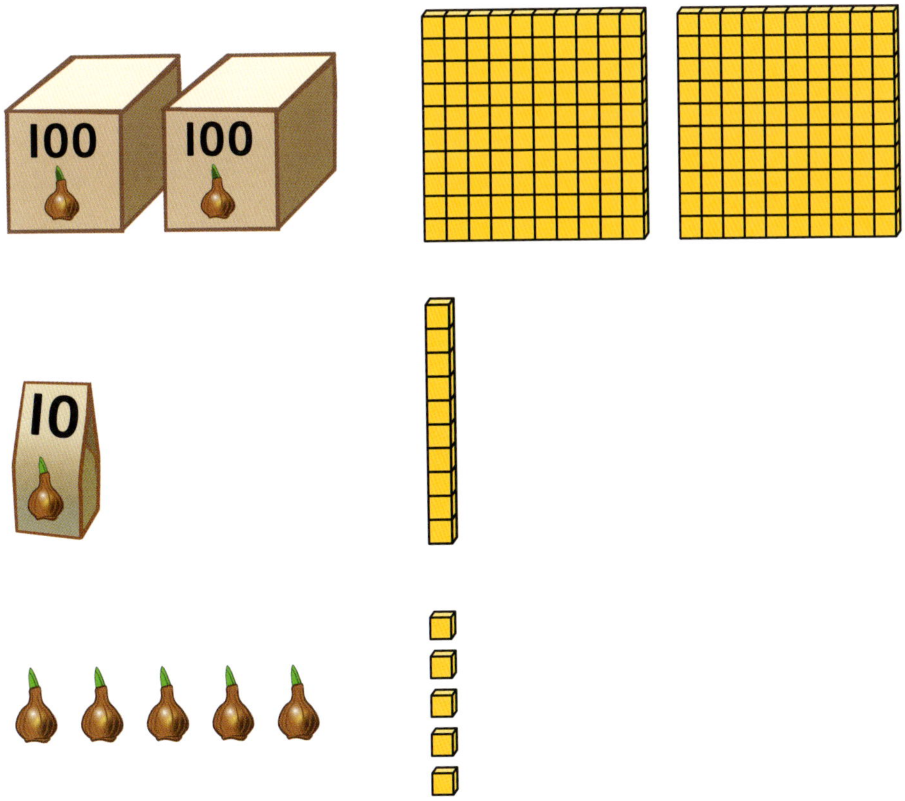

215 has 2 hundreds, 1 ten and 5 ones.

21

Unit 1: Place value within 1,000, Lesson 4

Think together

1 How many sunflower seeds are there?

2 What numbers are represented by this base 10 equipment?

a)

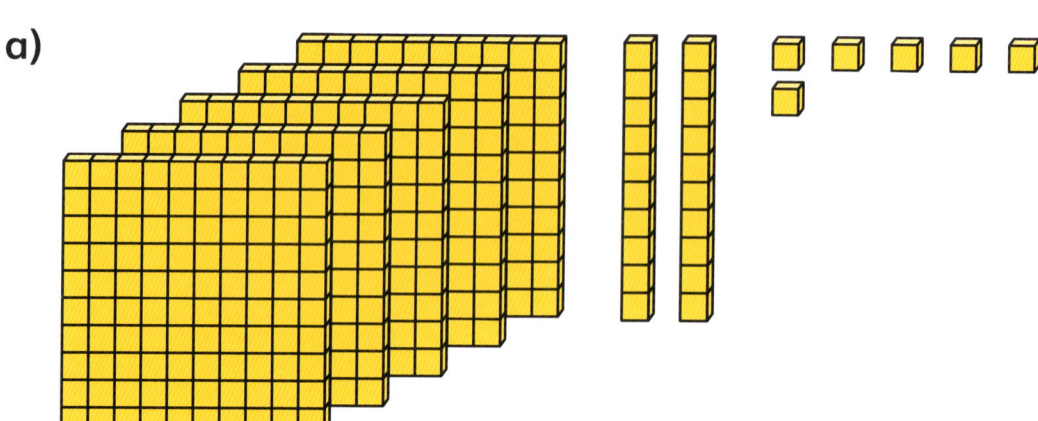

b)

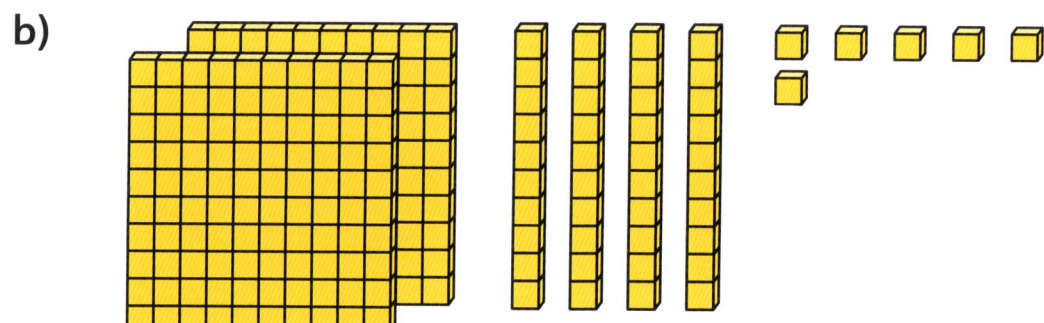

22

③ Here are three digit cards:

| 3 | 4 | 7 |

Use the cards to make some 3-digit numbers.

a) Use base 10 equipment to make your numbers.

b) How many 100s does each number have?

c) How many 10s does each number have?

d) How many 1s does each number have?

I wonder how many numbers I can make with these cards.

Unit 1: Place value within 1,000, Lesson 5

Partition numbers to 1,000

Discover

1 a) Use base 10 equipment to represent 235.

b) Complete the part-whole model.

24

Unit 1: Place value within 1,000, Lesson 5

Share

a) There are 235 children in the school.

100   200   210   220   230   231   232   233   234   235

I counted the 100s first, then the 10s and then the 1s.

I put the base 10 equipment in a part-whole model to work out the parts.

b)

235 = 200, 30, 5

25

Unit 1: Place value within 1,000, Lesson 5

Think together

1 a) Represent the number using base 10 equipment.

 I have 251 swap cards at home.

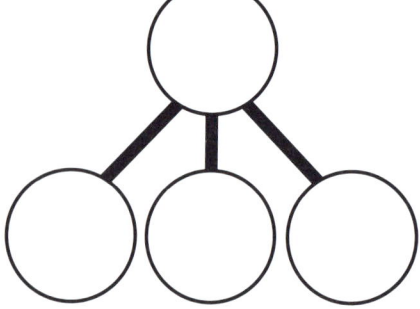

b) Show the number on a part-whole model.

 2 Draw a part-whole model for each of these representations.

a)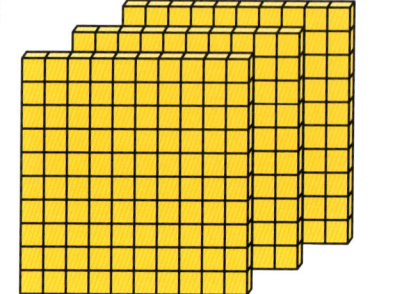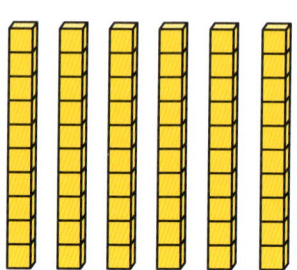

b)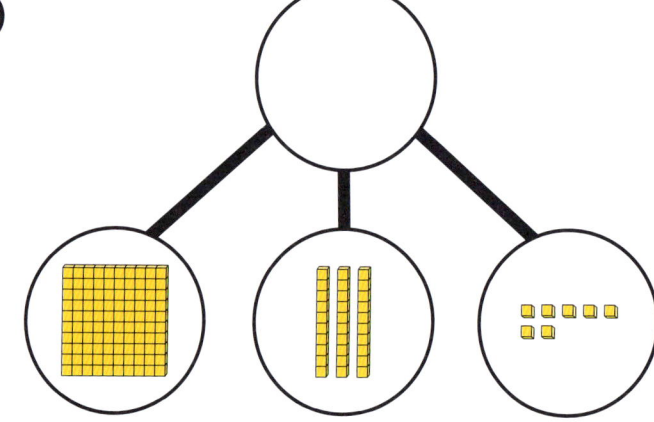

26

Unit 1: Place value within 1,000, Lesson 5

3 Here is a part-whole model for the number 528.

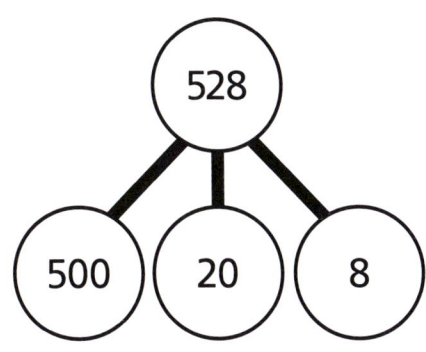

You can write 528 in expanded form, like this:

528 = 500 + 20 + 8

Draw a part-whole model for each number. Write each number in expanded form.

| 615 | 293 | 304 | 340 |

I will make each number out of base 10 equipment to help me.

Some of the part-whole models might not have three parts.

27

→ Practice book 3A p18

Unit 1: Place value within 1,000, Lesson 6

Partition numbers to 1,000 flexibly

Discover

1) a) What number has Lexi made?

   Represent this number in a part-whole model.

   b) Find a different way to partition Lexi's number into three parts.

   Show your answer in a part-whole model.

Unit 1: Place value within 1,000, Lesson 6

Share

a)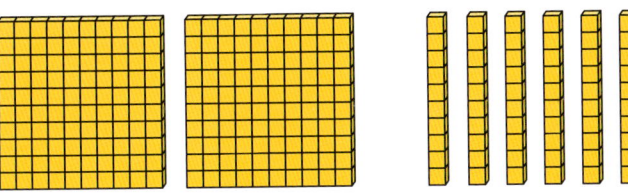

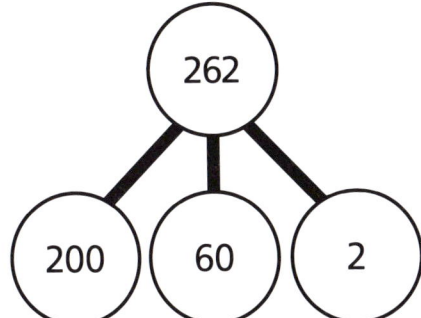

b) Here are two ways to partition 262.

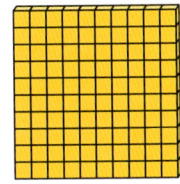 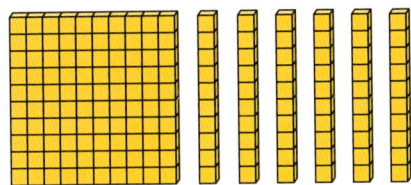 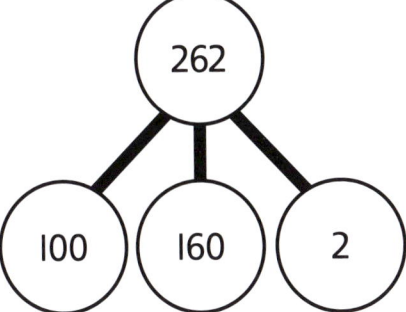

  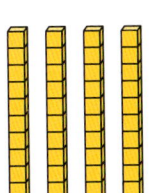 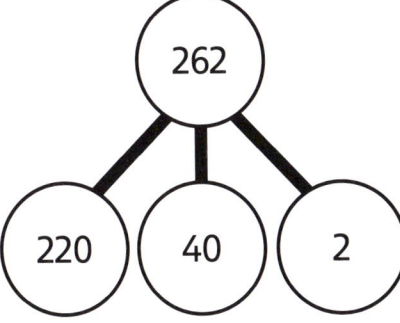

I could write a number sentence. 262 = 100 + 160 + 2.

29

Unit 1: Place value within 1,000, Lesson 6

Think together

1 Here is the number 354.

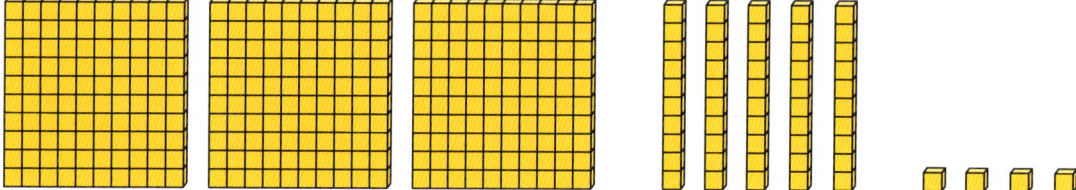

Here are three ways you can partition 354.

Draw a part-whole model for each partition.

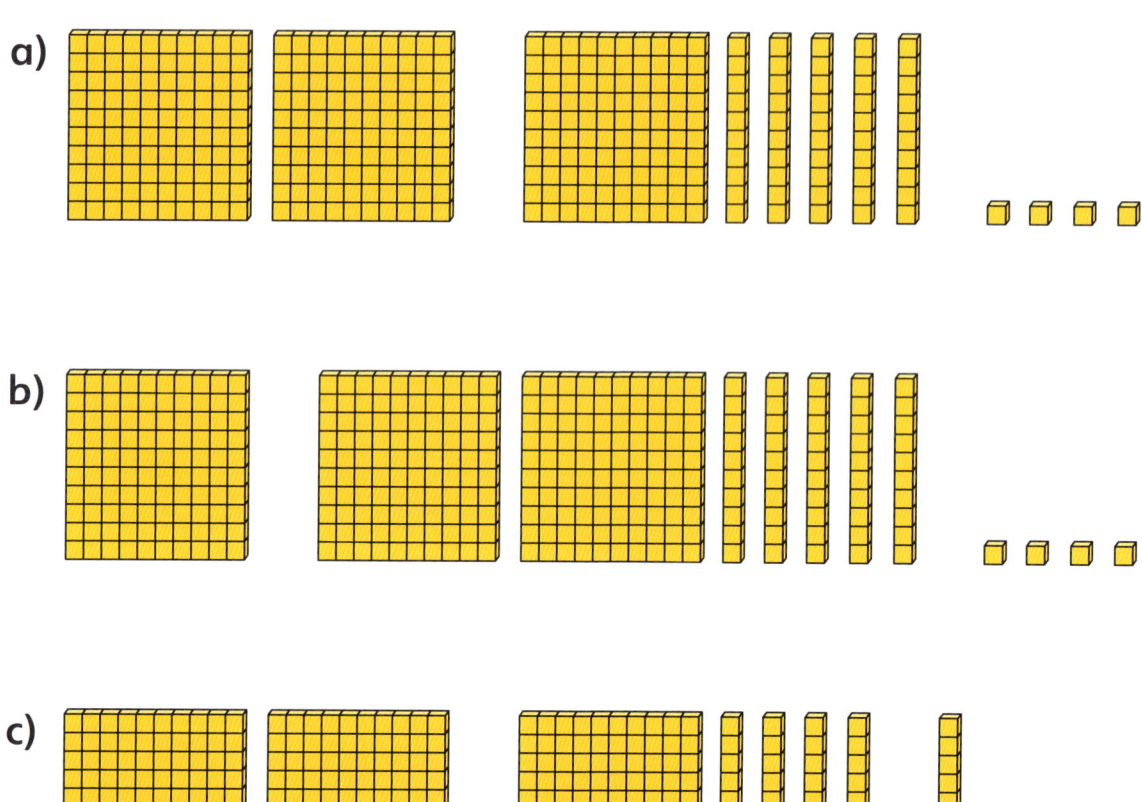

a)

b)

c)

Unit 1: Place value within 1,000, Lesson 6

② What numbers are missing?

a)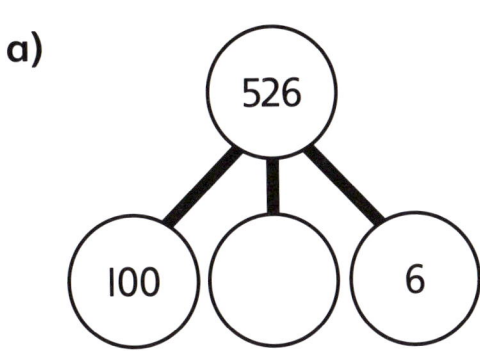

b)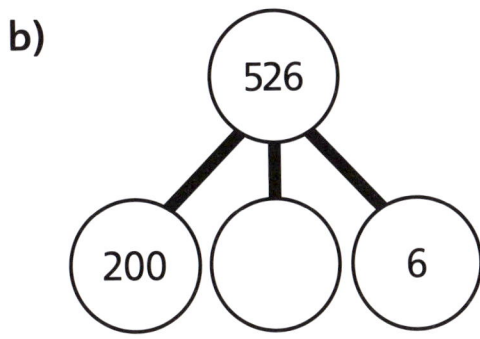

c)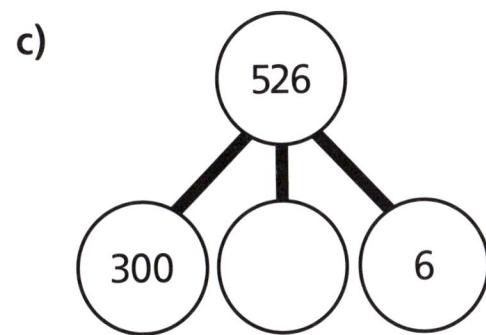

d) 526 = 400 + ☐ + 6

e) 526 = 500 + 10 + ☐

f) ☐ + 210 + 6 = 526

CHALLENGE

③ What number is represented here?

☐ = 200 + 150 + 7

I will use base 10 equipment to help me.

→ Practice book 3A p21

31

Unit 1: Place value within 1,000, Lesson 7

100s, 10s and 1s

Discover

1 a) Make 425 using base 10 equipment.

b) Make 425 using place value counters.

How many of each counter did you use?

Share

a)

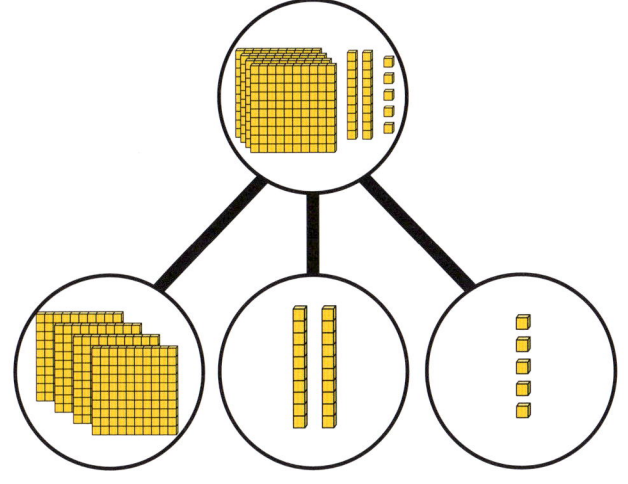 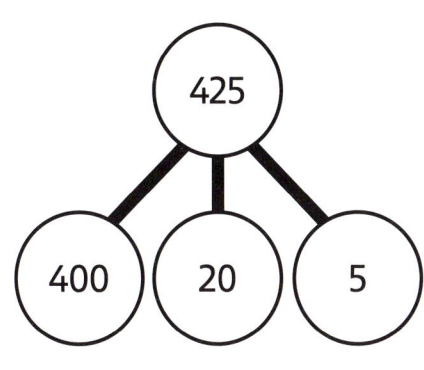

425 = 400 + 20 + 5

b)

You can use place value counters to represent numbers. There are counters for 100s, 10s and 1s.

4 hundreds, 2 tens and 5 ones.

Unit 1: Place value within 1,000, Lesson 7

Think together

1 a) Make the number 236 with place value counters.

H	T	O

b) How many of each counter did you use?

2 What numbers are represented in the place value grids?

a)

H	T	O
100	10 10 10	1 1 1 1 1 1

b)

H	T	O
100 100 100		1 1 1 1 1 / 1 1 1

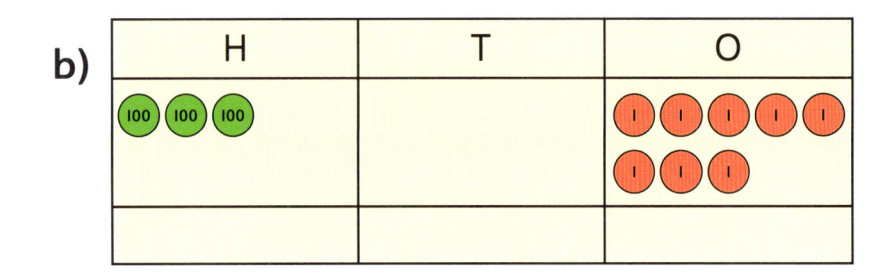

34

Unit 1: Place value within 1,000, Lesson 7

  a) Use counters to represent each number on a place value grid.

600 + 20 + 7

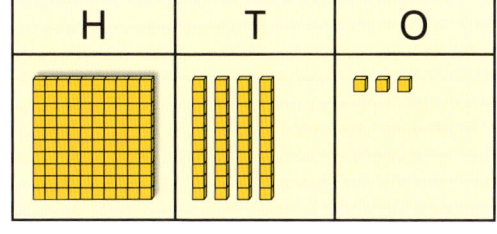

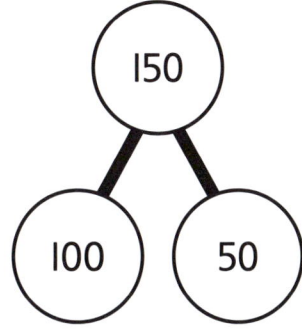

85

b) Meg made one of the above numbers. Which number did she make?

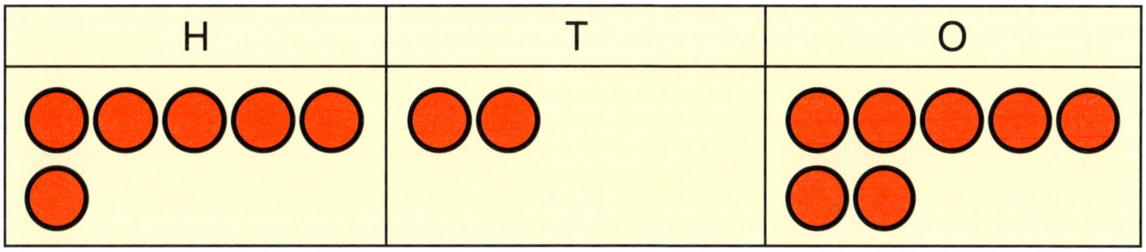

H	T	O
●●●●● ●	●●	●●●●● ●●●

I don't think this is a number. There are no numbers on the counters.

I think the column the counter is in tells us its value.

→ Practice book 3A p24

35

Unit 1: Place value within 1,000, Lesson 8

Use a number line to 1,000

Discover

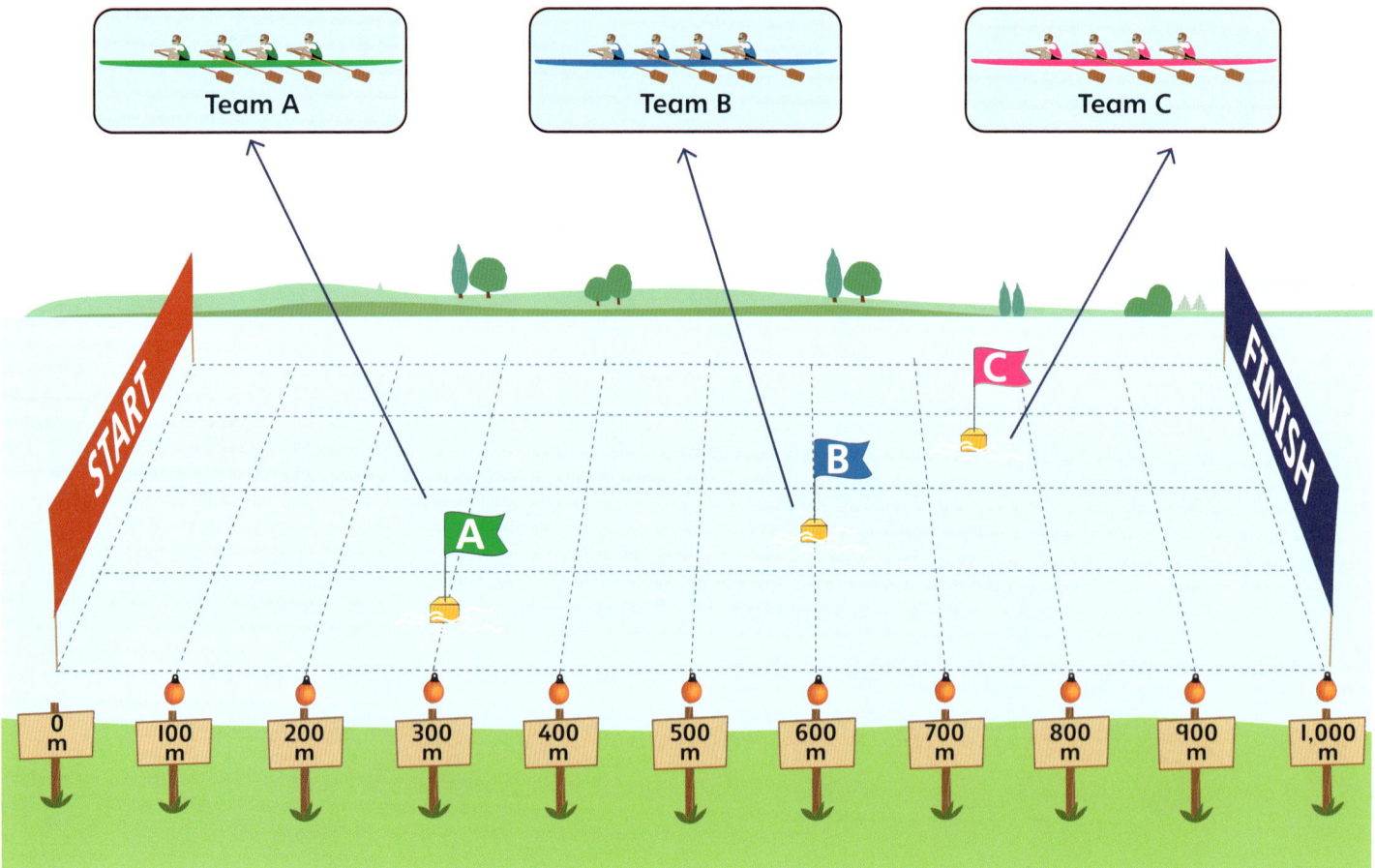

1 a) How far has boat A travelled?

How far has boat B travelled?

Estimate how far boat C has travelled.

b) Boat D has travelled 900 metres.

Where will it be?

36

Unit 1: Place value within 1,000, Lesson 8

Share

a)

I used a number line to help me. The number line goes up in 100s, from 0 to 1,000.

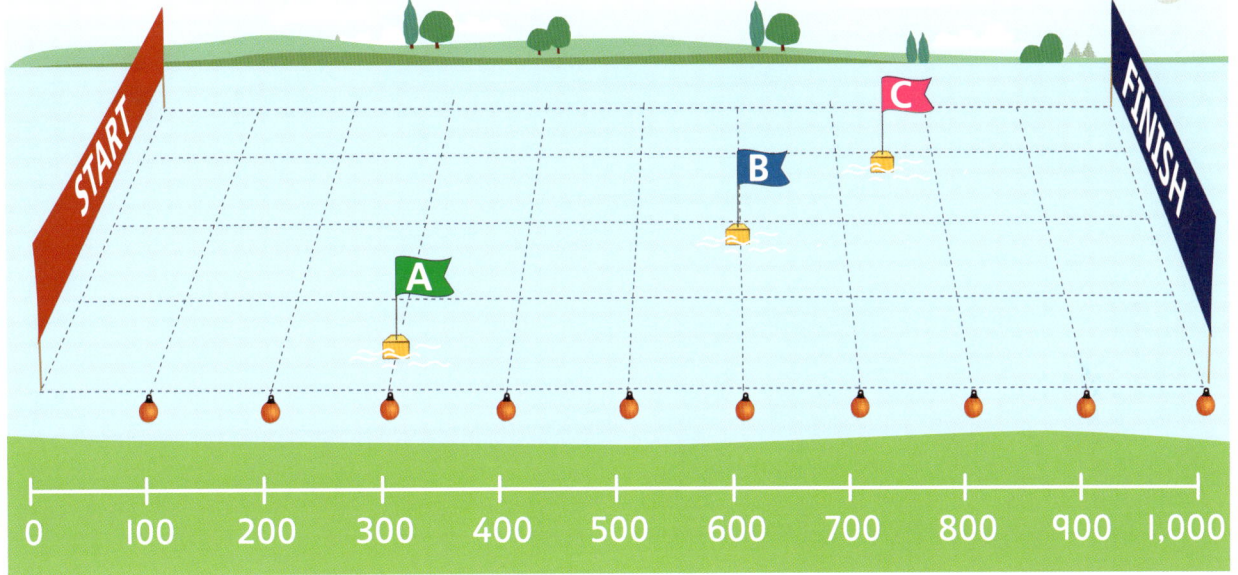

Boat A has travelled 300 metres.

Boat B has travelled 600 metres.

Boat C has travelled about 750 metres.

750 lies half-way between 700 and 800.

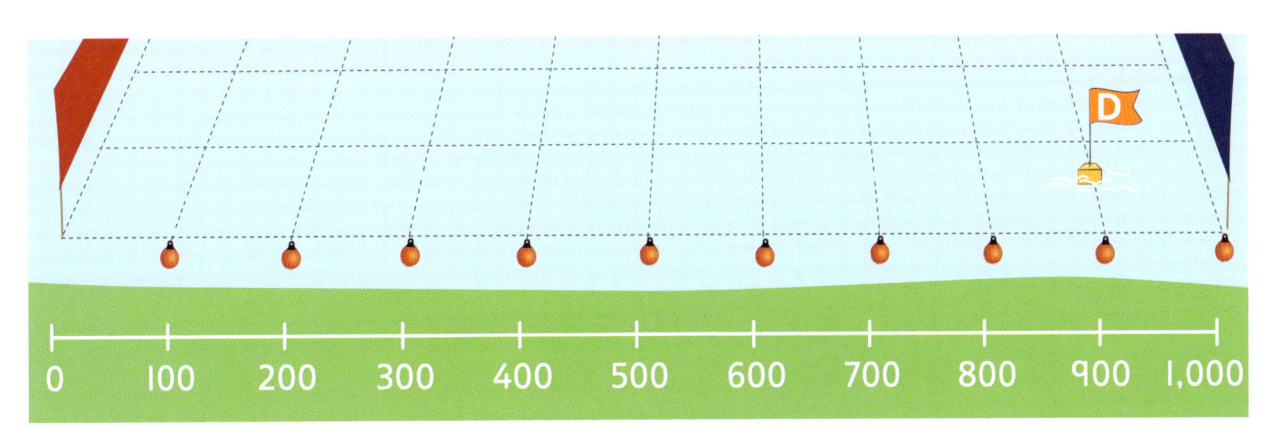

b) Boat D will be here.

Unit 1: Place value within 1,000, Lesson 8

Think together

1 This is another boat race.

Team A   Team B   Team C

0   ☐   ☐   300   400   ☐   600   ☐   800   ☐   1,000

a) What are the missing numbers?

b) How far has boat A travelled?

c) How far has boat C travelled?

d) Estimate how far boat B has travelled.

2 a) What numbers are shown by the arrows?

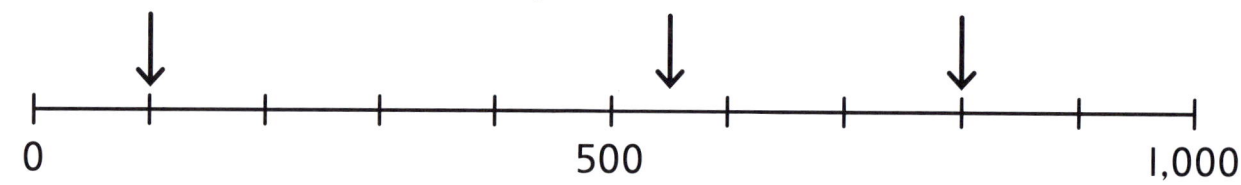

0 ──────── 500 ──────── 1,000

b) Point to the numbers 300, 500 and 990.

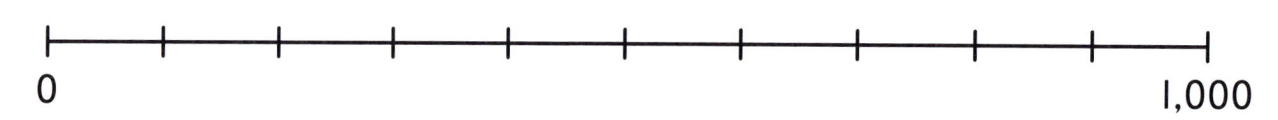

0 ──────────────────── 1,000

38

Unit 1: Place value within 1,000, Lesson 8

3 **a)** Work out all the missing numbers.

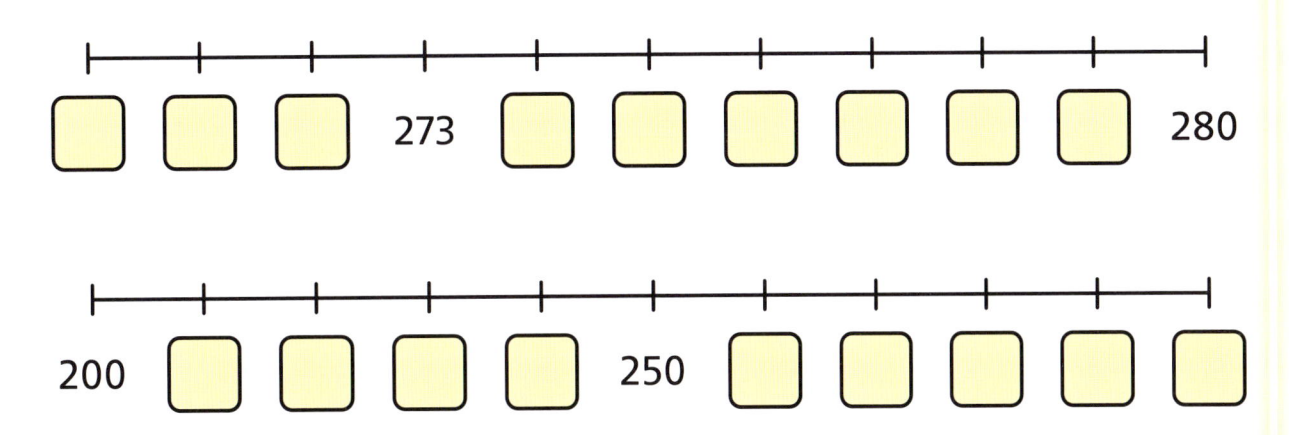

| | | | 273 | | | | | | | 280 |

| 200 | | | | | 250 | | | | | |

b) Point to 275 on each number line.

> I don't think these number lines go up in 100s this time. I will try a number in the first blank box and see if it works as I count up to 250.

> Last year we saw number lines that went up in 10s and 1s. I wonder if any of these do that.

→ Practice book 3A p27

Unit 1: Place value within 1,000, Lesson 9

Estimate on a number line to 1,000

Discover

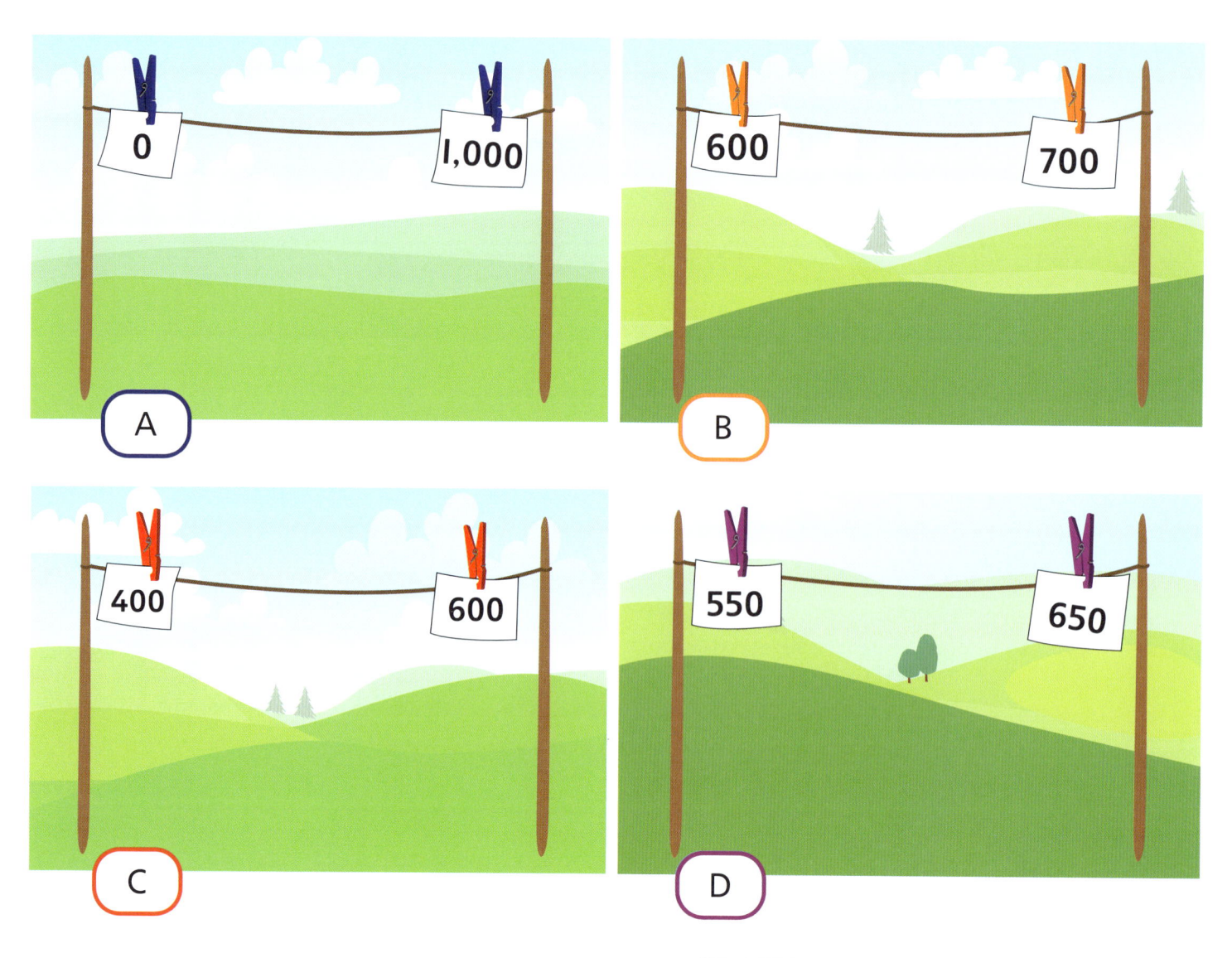

A: 0 — 1,000

B: 600 — 700

C: 400 — 600

D: 550 — 650

1 a) Which number lines can you peg **500** to?

b) Where should the number 395 go on this number line?

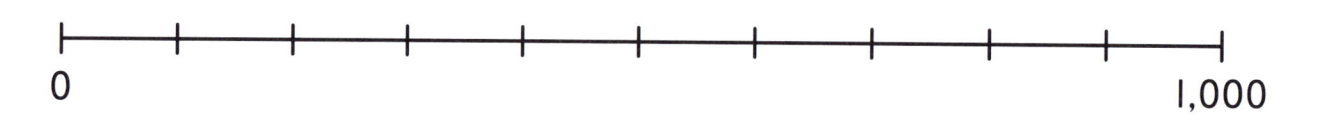

0 — 1,000

40

Share

Unit 1: Place value within 1,000, Lesson 9

a)

"I know that 500 is half-way between 0 and 1,000. It is also half-way between 400 and 600."

"500 comes before 600 and 550, so it does not fit on B or D."

You can peg 500 on lines A and C.

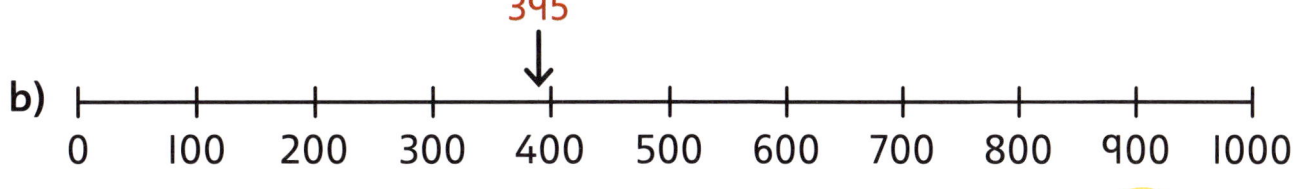

b) 395

"I labelled the intervals on my line. I know that 395 is close to 400."

41

Unit 1: Place value within 1,000, Lesson 9

Think together

1) Which of the numbers can go on this line?

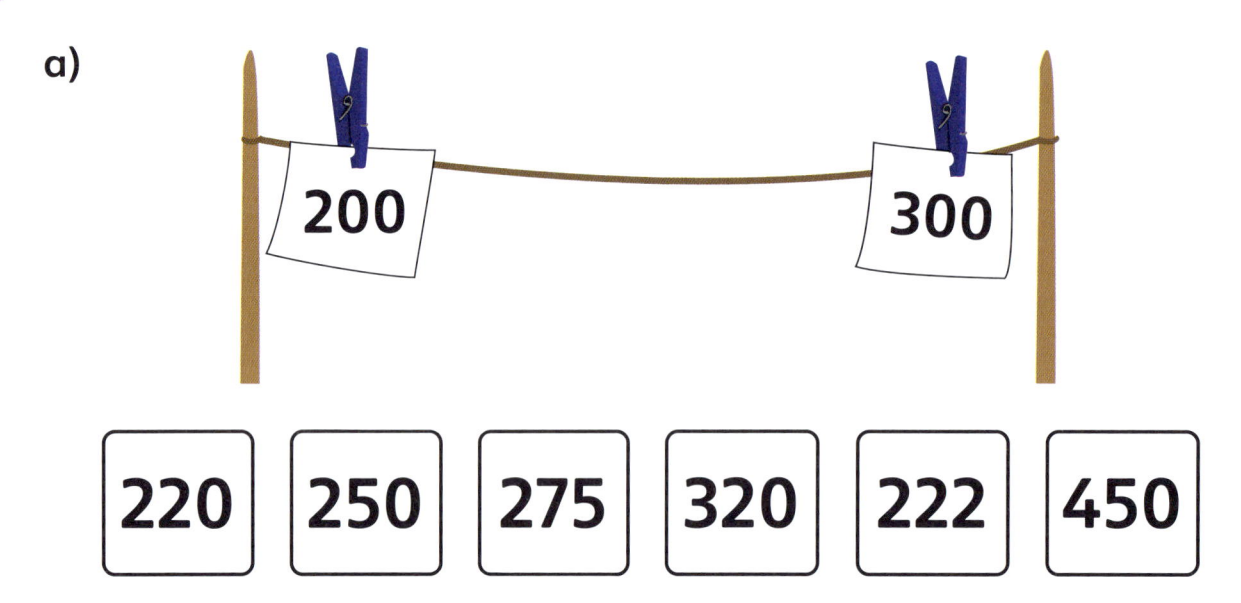

a)

[200] ———————————— [300]

| 220 | 250 | 275 | 320 | 222 | 450 |

2) Estimate which numbers the arrows are pointing to.

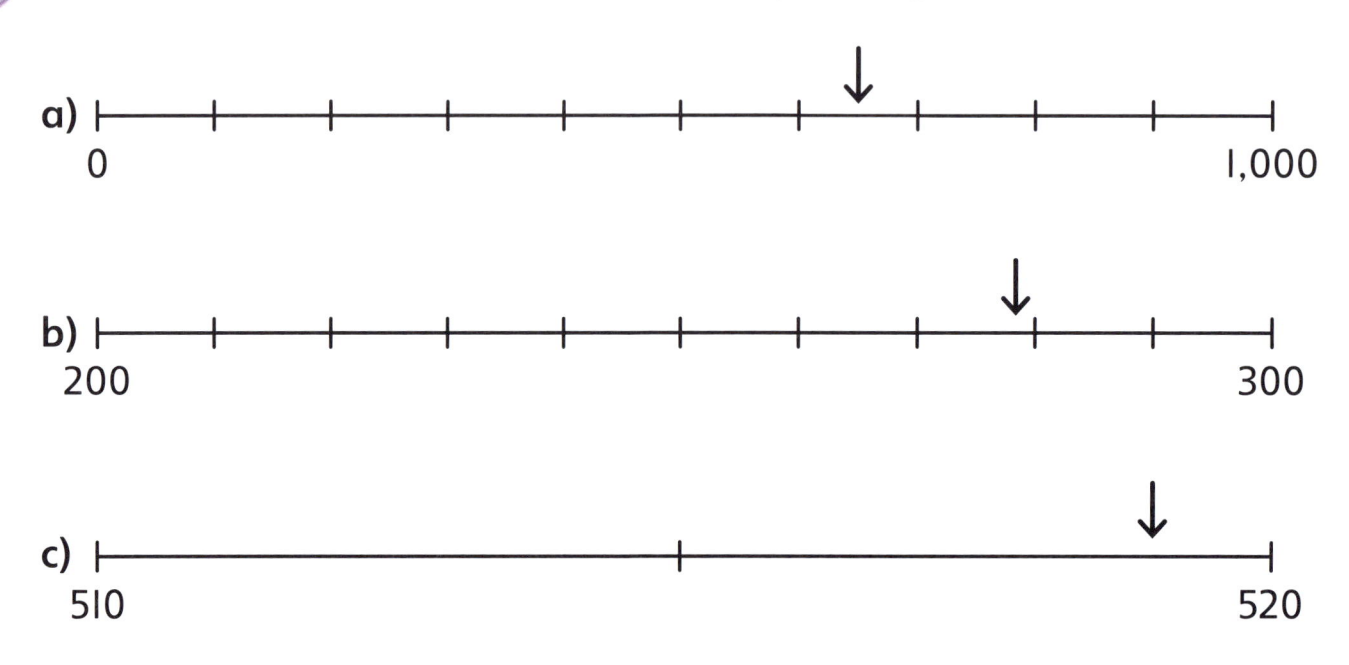

a) 0 —————↓———————— 1,000

b) 200 ————————↓———— 300

c) 510 ————————————↓— 520

42

Unit 1: Place value within 1,000, Lesson 9

CHALLENGE

3 **a)** Where do these numbers go on the number line?

| 200 | 580 | 995 |

0 ———————————————————— 1,000

b) Where do these numbers go on the number line?

| 325 | 349 | 385 |

300 ———————————————————— 400

I'm going to draw the number line in my book.

That's a good idea. I will try to divide the line into 10 equal parts. I think that will help me.

→ Practice book 3A p30

Unit 1: Place value within 1,000, Lesson 10

Find 1, 10 and 100 more or less

Discover

1) a) How many points does Amal have?

Amal receives 100 more.

How many points does he have now?

b) Holly has 204 points.

She loses 1 point.

How many points does she have now?

44

Share

I can represent the points using place value counters.

a)

H	T	O
100 100	10 10 10 10 10	1 1 1
2	5	3

Amal has 253 points.

H	T	O
100 100 (100)	10 10 10 10 10	1 1 1
3	5	3

Amal receives 100 more.

100 more than 253 is 353.

Amal now has 353 points.

b) Holly has 204 points and loses 1 point.

1 less than 204 is 203.

Holly now has 203 points.

H	T	O
100 100		1 1 1 ⌀
2	0	3

Unit 1: Place value within 1,000, Lesson 10

Think together

1 Work out these amounts.

a) 10 more than

H	T	O
100 100 100	10 10 10 10 10 10	1 1 1 1 1

b) 100 less than

H	T	O
6	4	8

c) 1 more than 248.

2 Complete the missing numbers.

a) 563 —100 more→ ☐

☐ ←100 less— 563

b) 228 —10 more→ ☐

☐ ←10 less— 228

c) 718 —1 more→ ☐

☐ ←1 less— 718

46

Unit 1: Place value within 1,000, Lesson 10

CHALLENGE

3 a) Kate is working out 10 more than 195.

Help her work out the correct answer.

H	T	O
100	10 10 10 10 10 / 10 10 10 10	1 1 1 1 1
1	9	5

Kate: I think the answer is 1,105.

I think Kate needs to **exchange** some 10s for 100.

b) Ebo is solving the problem in the box.

What mistake has he made?

457 is 100 more than _____

Ebo: The answer is 557.

I can check Ebo's answer and see if the sentence is true.

→ Practice book 3A p33

Unit 1: Place value within 1,000, Lesson 11

Compare numbers to 1,000

Discover

1) a) Which is the greater number?

240   395

b) Which is the smaller number?

542   589

Share

a)

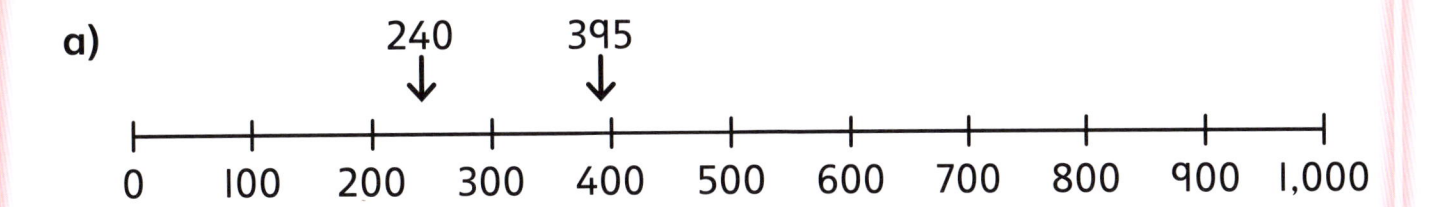

```
        240       395
         ↓         ↓
  ├───┼───┼───┼───┼───┼───┼───┼───┼───┼───┤
  0  100 200 300 400 500 600 700 800 900 1,000
```

I know that 395 is greater than 240 because 395 has more 100s.

b)

H	T	O
⑤	4	2

H	T	O
⑤	8	9

542 and 589 have the same number of 100s

H	T	O
5	④	2

H	T	O
5	⑧	9

542 has 4 tens. 589 has 8 tens.

4 tens is less than 8 tens.

So 542 is less than 589, or 542 < 589.

542 is the smaller number.

I compared the 100s first. They were the same, so I compared the 10s.

Unit 1: Place value within 1,000, Lesson 11

Think together

1 In each pair, which is the smaller number?

a) 542   589

b) 183   92

2 Complete the sentences using <, > or =.

a)
H	T	O
9	4	8

◯

H	T	O
8	2	0

b)
H	T	O
3	8	5

◯

H	T	O
3	6	8

c) 600 ◯ 950

d) 392 ◯ 300 + 90 + 2

I remember that
< means less than.
> means greater than.
= means equal to.

50

Unit 1: Place value within 1,000, Lesson 11

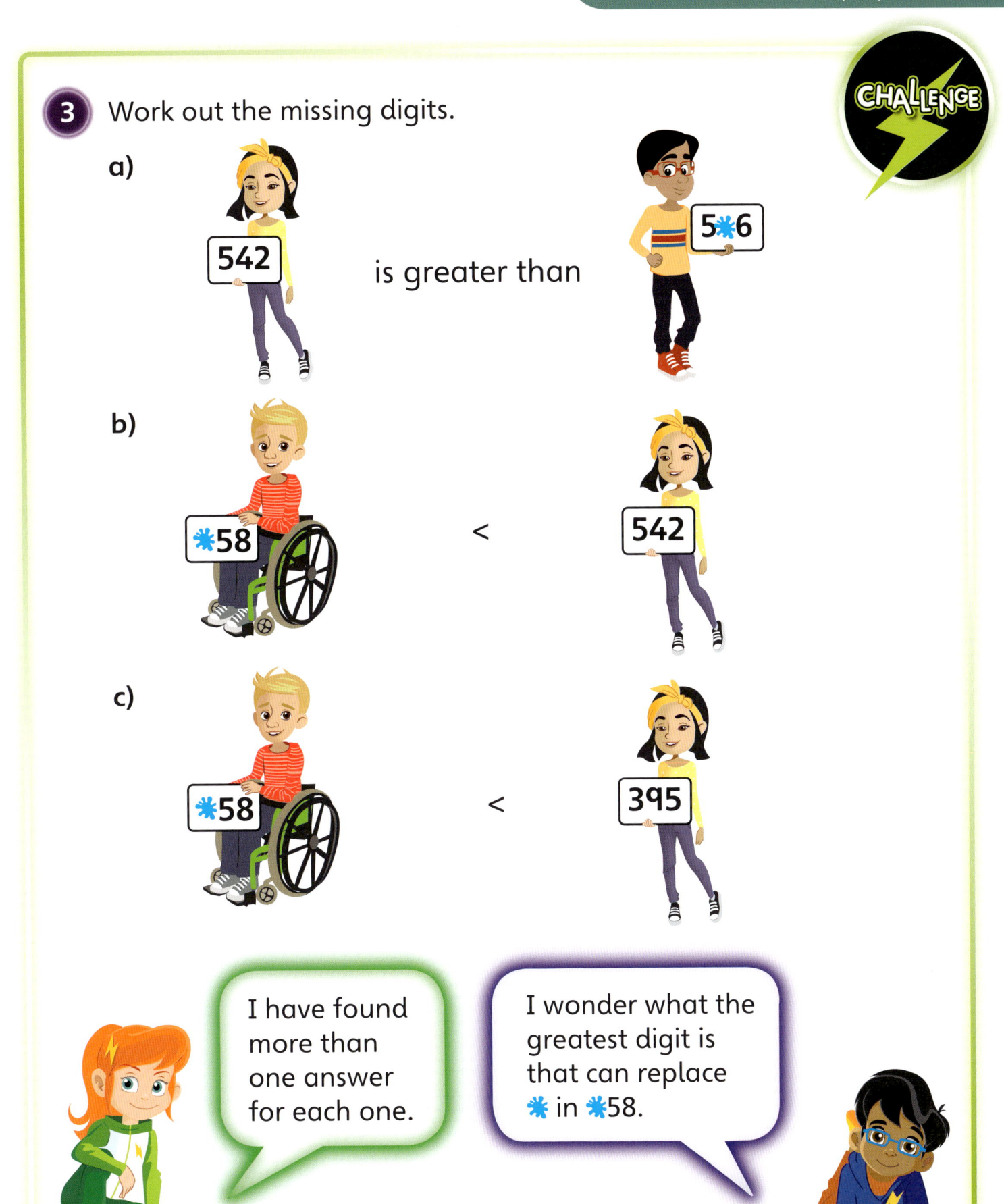

CHALLENGE

3 Work out the missing digits.

a) 542 is greater than 5✶6

b) ✶58 < 542

c) ✶58 < 395

I have found more than one answer for each one.

I wonder what the greatest digit is that can replace ✶ in ✶58.

51

→ Practice book 3A p36

Unit 1: Place value within 1,000, Lesson 12

Order numbers to 1,000

Discover

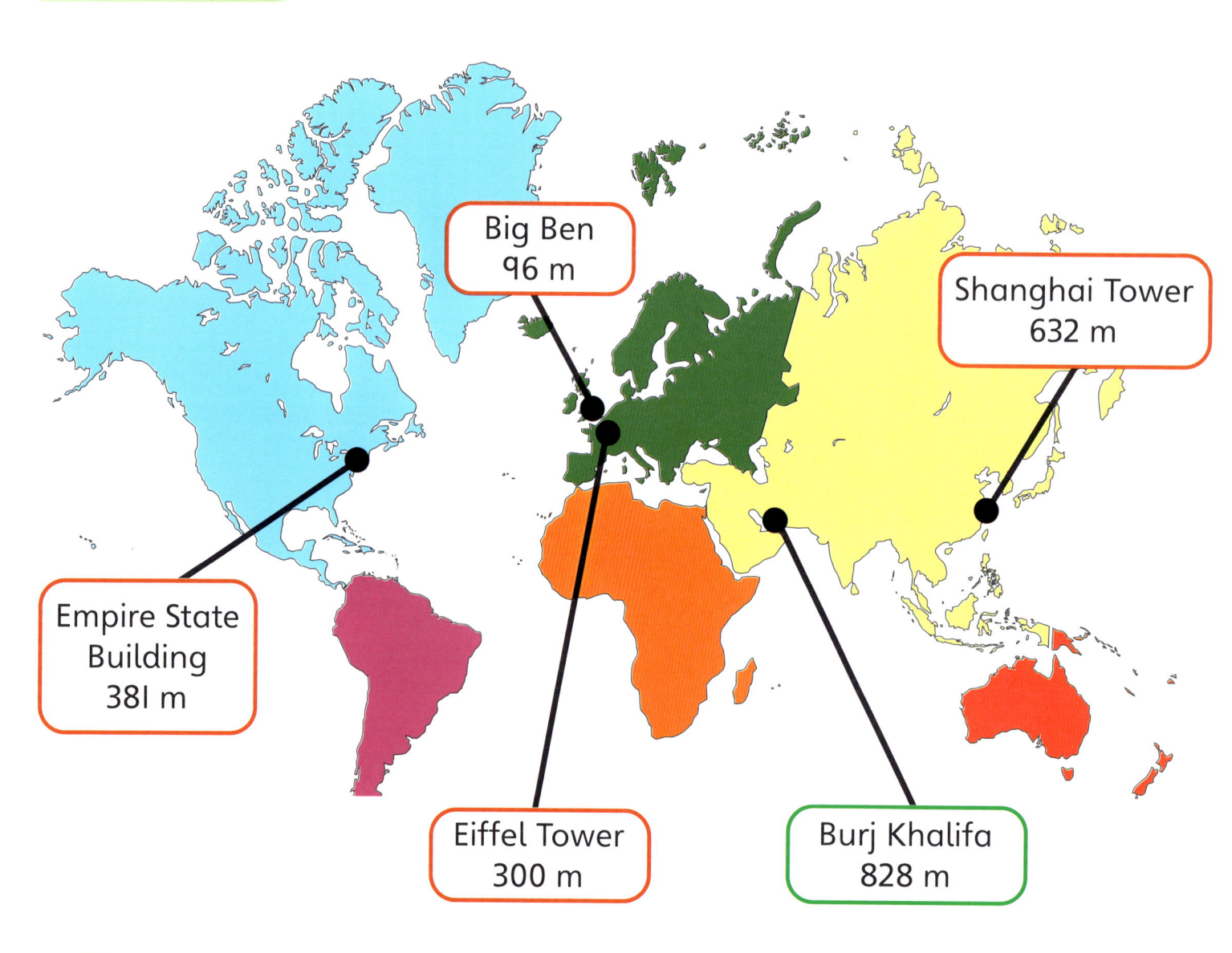

Big Ben
96 m

Shanghai Tower
632 m

Empire State Building
381 m

Eiffel Tower
300 m

Burj Khalifa
828 m

1 a) Which is taller, the Empire State Building or Big Ben?

b) Put the buildings in order of height.

Start with the shortest.

52

Share

a) Empire State Building

H	T	O
3	8	1

Big Ben

H	T	O
	9	6

There are 3 hundreds for the Empire State Building. This is greater than 0 hundreds for Big Ben.

So 381 > 96

The Empire State Building is taller than Big Ben.

I put the numbers onto a number line to compare them.

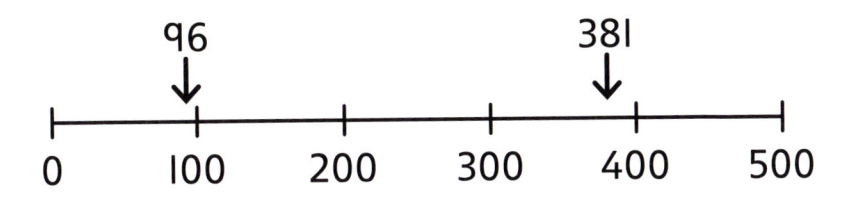

b)

	H	T	O
Big Ben		9	6
Eiffel Tower	3	0	0
Empire State Building	3	8	1
Shanghai Tower	6	3	2
Burj Khalifa	8	2	8

I compared the 100s, then the 10s, then the 1s.

Unit 1: Place value within 1,000, Lesson 12

Think together

1 Put these ships in order of length. Start with the shortest.

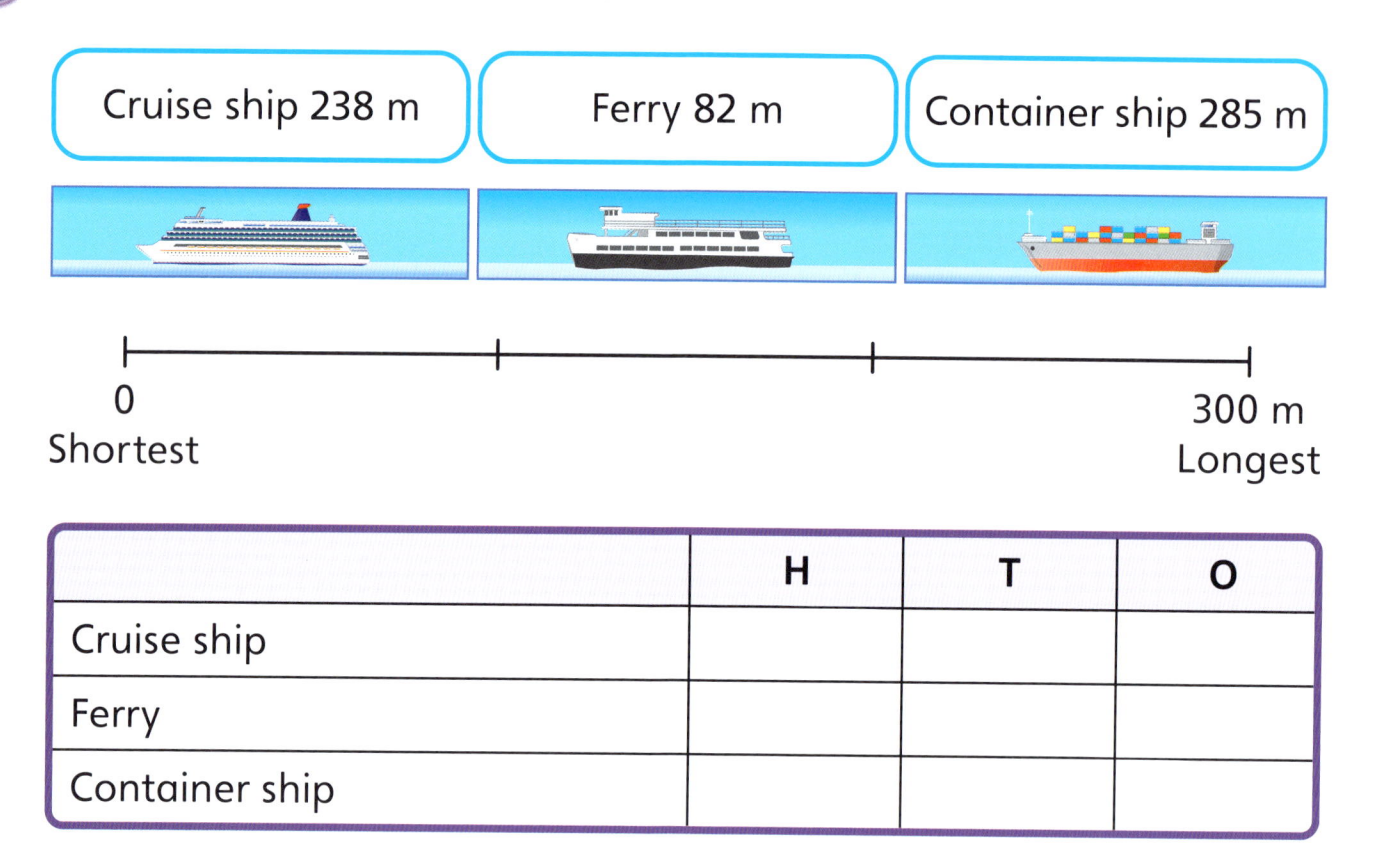

Cruise ship 238 m   Ferry 82 m   Container ship 285 m

0 Shortest — 300 m Longest

	H	T	O
Cruise ship			
Ferry			
Container ship			

2 Four boxes contain some counters.

Order the number of counters from fewest to most.

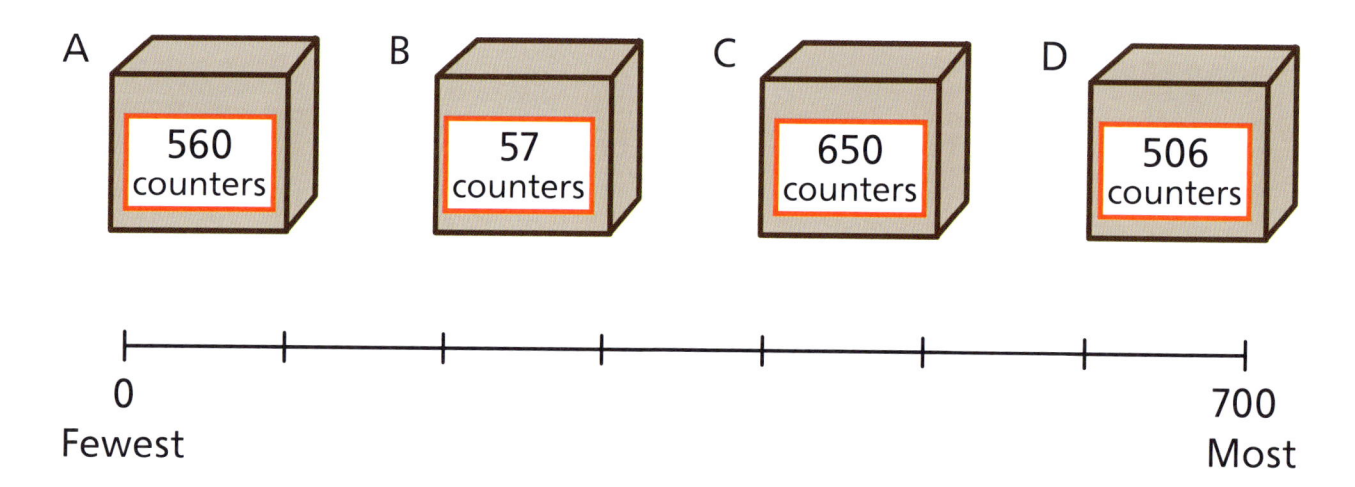

A 560 counters   B 57 counters   C 650 counters   D 506 counters

0 Fewest — 700 Most

54

Unit 1: Place value within 1,000, Lesson 12

CHALLENGE

3 **a)** Put these numbers in ascending order.

276   300   188   712

> **Ascending** means from smallest to greatest.
> **Descending** means from greatest to smallest.

b) These numbers are in ascending order.

18_   1_5   _74   32_

Find a possible value for each of the missing digits.

I think there is more than one answer.

I wonder what the smallest and largest digits that can go in each number are.

55

→ Practice book 3A p39

Unit 1: Place value within 1,000, Lesson 13

Count in 50s

Discover

1 a) How many stars are on each flag?

How many stars are on 4 flags?

b) Sylvie counts 350 stars.

How many flags has she counted?

Share

a)

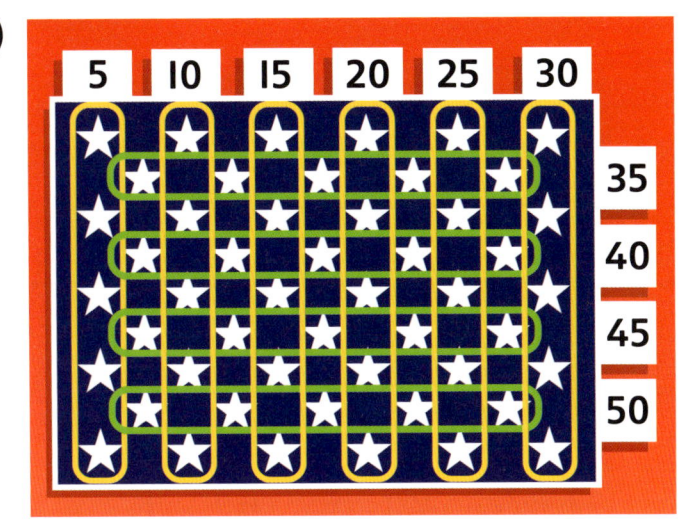

I counted the stars in 5s. I saw that they were in columns and rows.

5, 10, 15, 20, 25, 30, 35, 40, 45, 50

There are 50 stars on each flag.

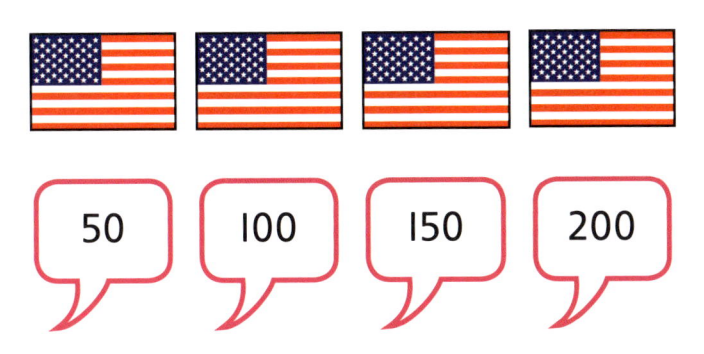

50   100   150   200

I counted up in 50s.

There are 200 stars on 4 flags.

b)

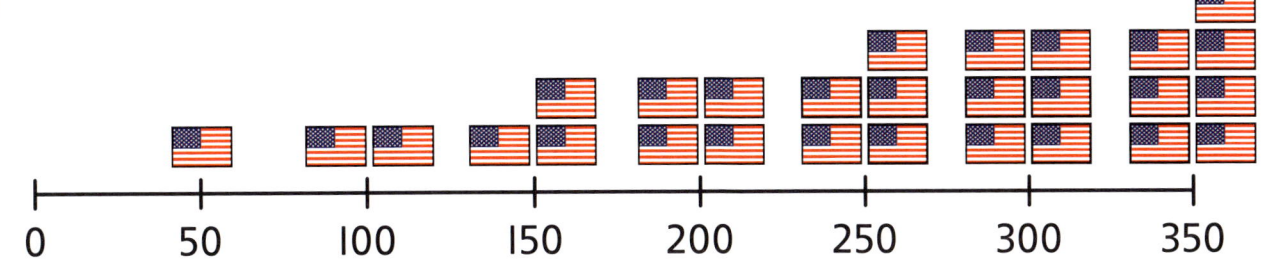

0   50   100   150   200   250   300   350

Sylvie counted 350 stars on 7 flags.

Unit 1: Place value within 1,000, Lesson 13

Think together

1 Work out the missing numbers.

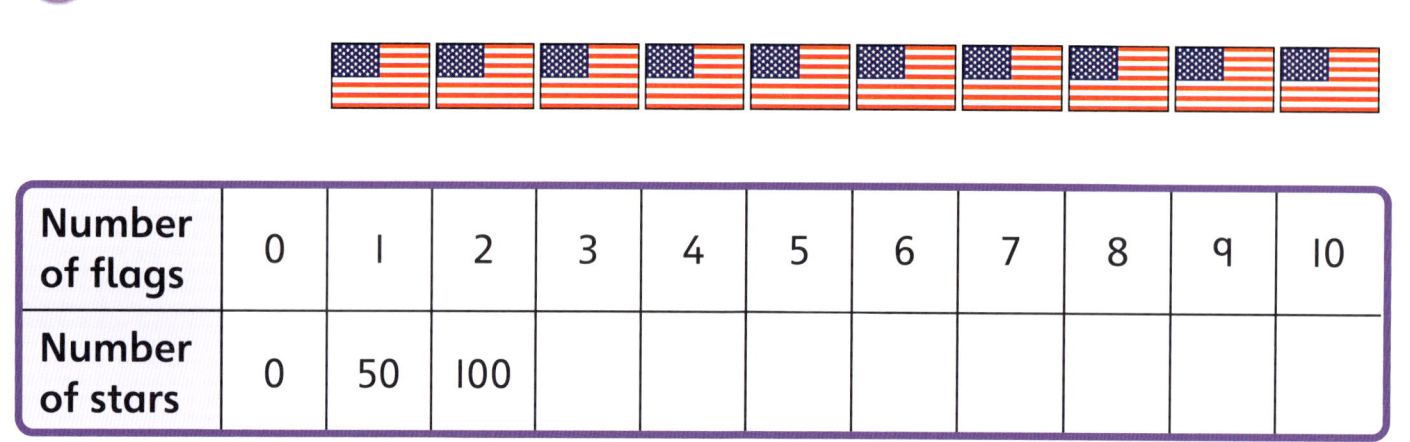

Number of flags	0	1	2	3	4	5	6	7	8	9	10
Number of stars	0	50	100								

2 a) How many stars on 15 flags?

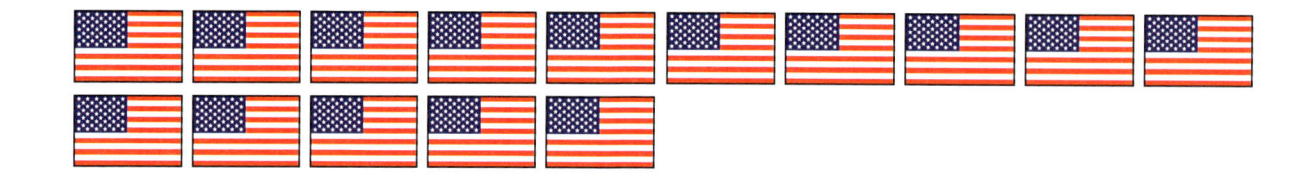

b) How many stars on 16 flags?

c) How many stars on 17 flags?

I wonder if I have to start at 0 each time.

Unit 1: Place value within 1,000, Lesson 13

CHALLENGE

③ Here is a 0 to 1,000 number line.

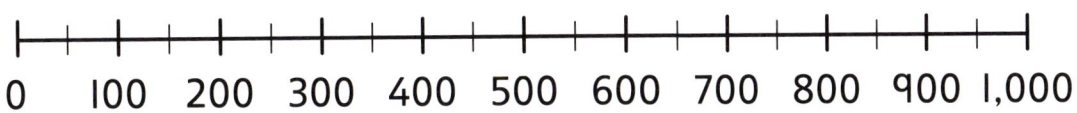

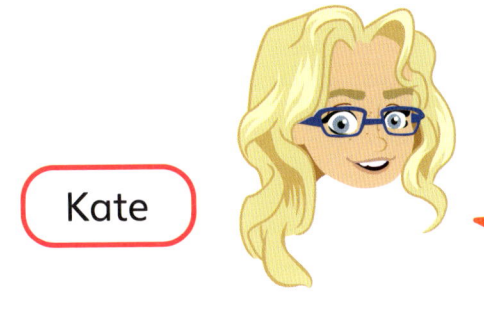

```
0  100  200  300  400  500  600  700  800  900  1,000
```

Kate: I can use the number line to count in 50s from 0 to 1,000 and back again.

Which of these numbers will Kate say?

| 95 | 750 | 650 | 400 | 50 | 505 | 355 | 250 |

What did you notice about all the numbers Kate says?

Think of a rule about the numbers Kate will say.

The number line goes up in 100s. I am not sure how Kate can use it to count in 50s.

I have noticed something interesting about the last two digits of the numbers Kate says.

→ Practice book 3A p42

59

Unit 1: Place value within 1,000

End of unit check

1 What number is shown?

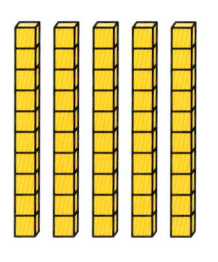

A 325   B 352   C 523   D 532

2 Which number line shows the arrow pointing to 350?

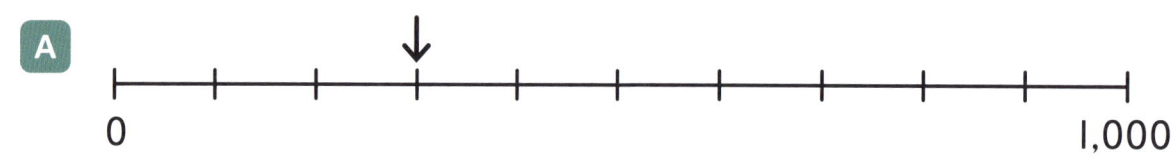

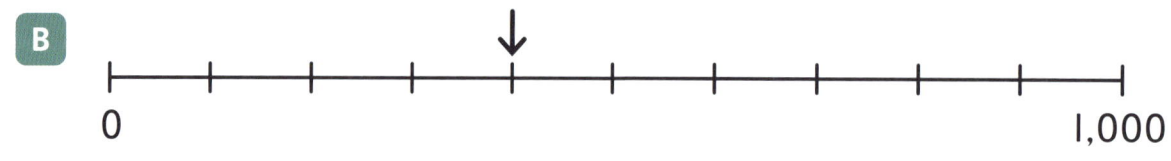

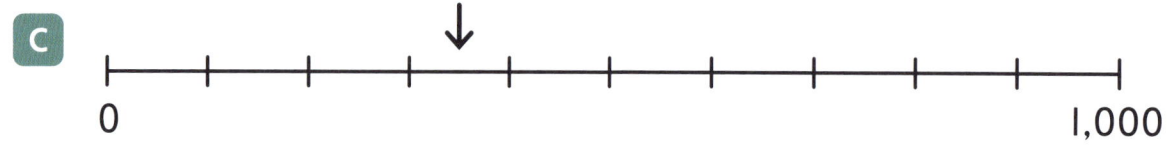

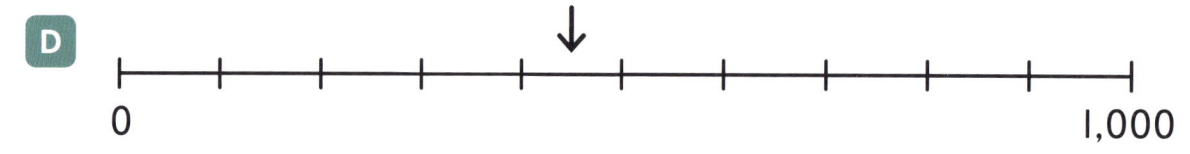

A

B

C

D

3 10 more than ☐ is 385.

A 485   B 285   C 395   D 375

60

Unit 1: Place value within 1,000

4) Which statement is correct?

H	T	O
4	2	9

H	T	O
3	8	1

A) 429 < 381

B) 429 = 381

C) 429 > 381

D) None of them

5) The number track goes up in 50s.

| 200 | 250 | 300 | | | | 500 |

What number should be in the shaded box?

A) 350   B) 303   C) 450   D) 499

6) Which set of numbers is in order from smallest to greatest?

A) 54, 540, 504, 450

B) 450, 504, 54, 540

C) 540, 504, 450, 54

D) 54, 450, 504, 540

7) There are three boxes of counters.

Box X contains 160 counters. Box Y contains 84 counters. Box Z contains 100 more counters than Box Y.

Put the boxes in order. Start with the one with the fewest counters.

→ Practice book 3A p45

61

Unit 2
Addition and subtraction ①

In this unit we will …
- ⚡ Apply number bonds within 10
- ⚡ Add and subtract 1s, 10s and 100s
- ⚡ Add and subtract 1s and 10s across 100
- ⚡ Learn when to exchange 1s, 10s and 100s
- ⚡ Add and subtract using mental and written methods

Do you remember how to use base 10 equipment? What numbers do these represent?

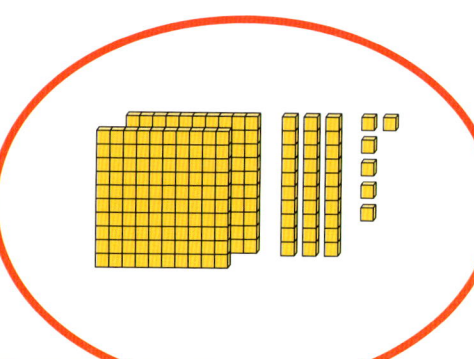

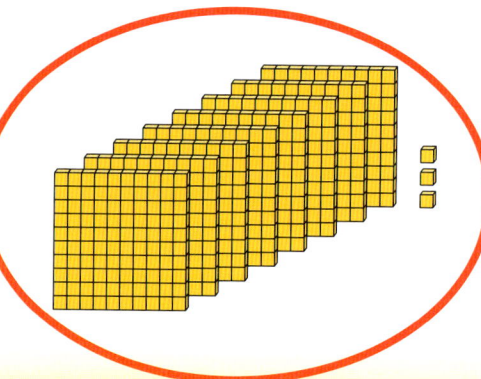

We will need some maths words. Are any of these new?

- addition
- subtraction
- mental method
- exchange
- bonds

We need this too! Use it to write the number two hundred and thirty-four using digits.

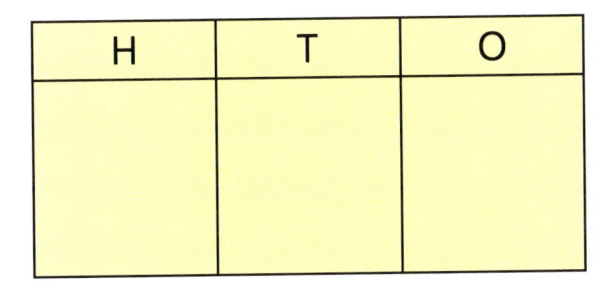

H	T	O

Unit 2: Addition and subtraction (1), Lesson 1

Use known number bonds

Discover

1 a) How many bricks are on the ground?

How many bricks are on the lorry?

b) How many bricks are there in total?

Unit 2: Addition and subtraction (1), Lesson 1

Share

a) There are 100 bricks in each pack.

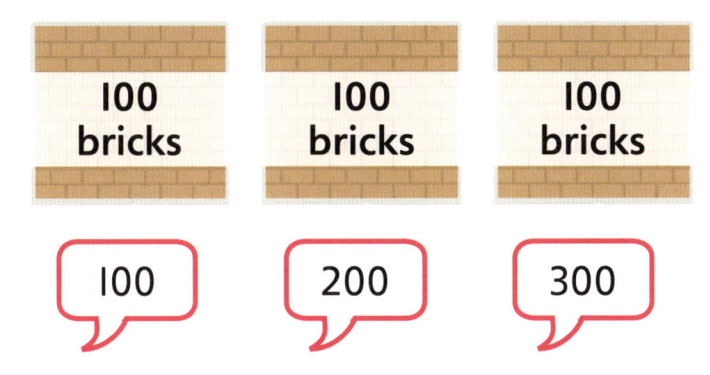

| 100 bricks | 100 bricks | 100 bricks |

100   200   300

There are 300 bricks on the ground.

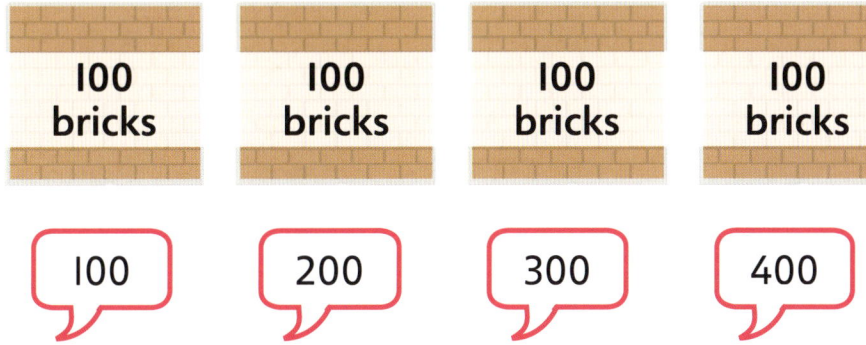

| 100 bricks | 100 bricks | 100 bricks | 100 bricks |

100   200   300   400

There are 400 bricks on the lorry.

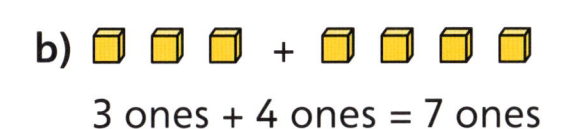

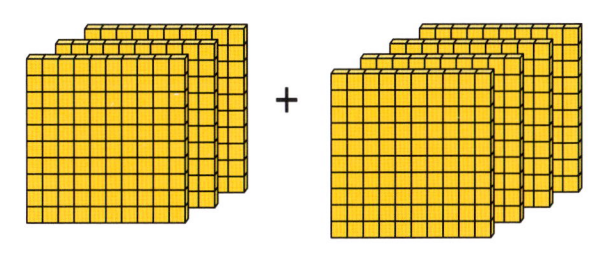

I will count in 100s.

b) ▫ ▫ ▫ + ▫ ▫ ▫ ▫

3 ones + 4 ones = 7 ones

3 hundreds + 4 hundreds = 7 hundreds

There are 700 bricks in total.

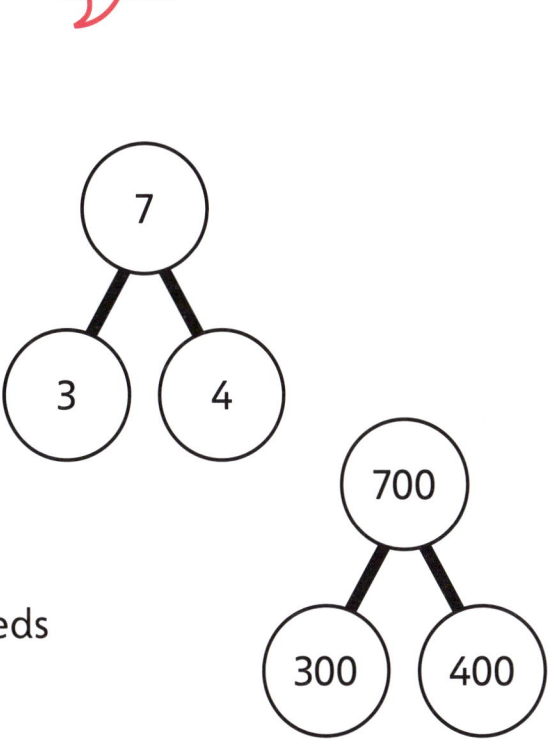

7
3 4

700
300 400

65

Unit 2: Addition and subtraction (1), Lesson 1

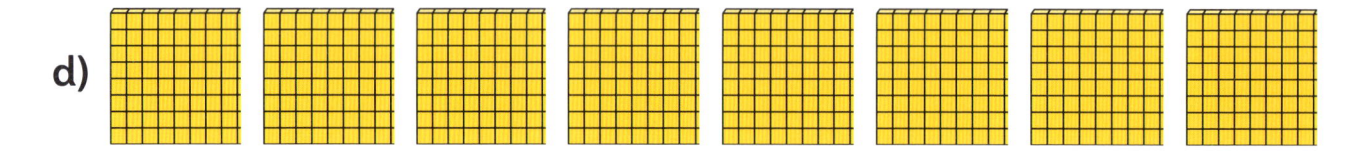

Think together

1) Use base 10 equipment to help you work out the answers.

a) 3 ones + 2 ones = ☐ ones

b) 3 hundreds + 2 hundreds = ☐ hundreds

c) 8 ones – 2 ones = ☐ ones

d) 8 hundreds – 2 hundreds = ☐ hundreds

I can see some patterns.

2 a) 2 + 6 = ☐

200 + 600 = ☐

b) 5 + 1 = ☐

500 + 100 = ☐

c) 7 − 5 = ☐

700 − 500 = ☐

d) 8 − 3 = ☐

800 − 300 = ☐

3 Emma uses this part-whole model to write a fact family of related 100s facts.

Write the rest of the fact family for Emma's part-whole model.

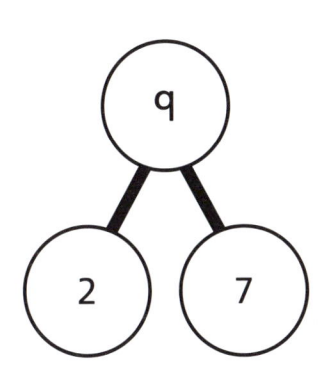

CHALLENGE

Part-whole model: whole = 9, parts = 2 and 7

200 + 700 = 900

900 − 200 = 700

I think there are 8 possible answers.

I will find all the additions first.

→ Practice book 3A p48

Unit 2: Addition and subtraction (1), Lesson 2

Add/subtract 1s

Discover

1 **a)** These people are outside the museum. Once they go in, how many visitors will be in the museum in total?

b) One person then leaves.

How many people are left in the museum?

Share

a) There are 245 people in the museum. 4 more go in.

We need to work out 245 + 4 = ☐

245 → 246 → 247 → 248 → 249 250
(+1, +1, +1, +1)

Counting on in 1s works, but it is easy to make a mistake.

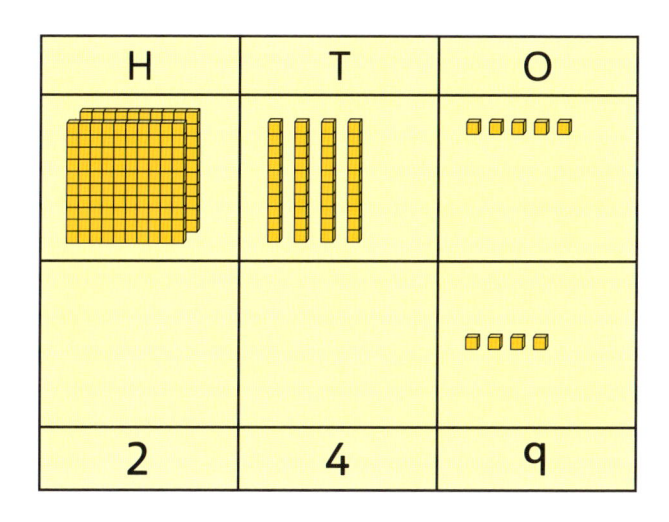

H	T	O
(1 hundred block)	(4 tens)	ooooo
		oooo
2	4	9

I arranged my work in a place value grid. It helped me to see that I am just adding the 1s.

5 ones + 4 ones = 9 ones.

245 + 4 = 249

There will be 249 visitors in the museum in total.

b) One less than 249 is 248.

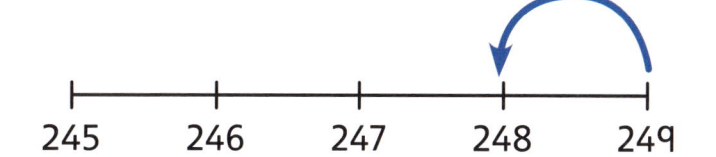

245 246 247 248 249
(−1 from 249 to 248)

248 people are left in the museum.

Unit 2: Addition and subtraction (1), Lesson 2

69

Unit 2: Addition and subtraction (1), Lesson 2

Think together

1 **a)** At 12 o'clock there were 319 people in the museum. Then 7 left.

How many people were left in the museum?

H	T	O
3	1	9

*I will work out the number **bonds** within 10 to solve this.*

b) Work out 291 + 6 = ☐.

I have noticed some patterns.

2 Work out

a) 352 + 3 = ☐

352 + 4 = ☐

352 + 5 = ☐

352 + 6 = ☐

352 + 7 = ☐

b) 718 − 3 = ☐

248 − 3 = ☐

178 − 3 = ☐

438 − 3 = ☐

908 − 3 = ☐

Unit 2: Addition and subtraction (1), Lesson 2

3 How many solutions can you find for each calculation?

| 0 | 1 | 2 | 3 | 4 | 5 | 6 | 7 | 8 | 9 |

a) 4 3 ☐ + ☐ = 4 3 5

b) 4 3 ☐ − ☐ = 4 3 5

I think I found all the solutions.

I wonder how I can tell if I have found them all.

→ Practice book 3A p51

Unit 2: Addition and subtraction (1), Lesson 3

Add/subtract 10s

Discover

Aki

1) a) What number has Aki made?

b) Aki adds 3 beads to the 10s.

Write this as an addition and find the new total.

Unit 2: Addition and subtraction (1), Lesson 3

Share

a) Aki's number has 3 hundreds, 5 tens and 1 one.

Aki has made the number 351.

b) Aki adds 3 beads to the 10s.

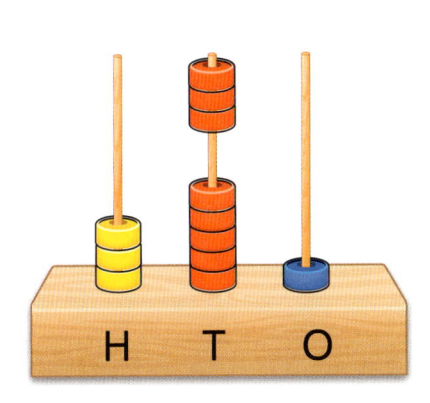

5 tens + 3 tens = 8 tens

50 + 30 = 80

351 + 30 = 381

Aki has made the number 381.

> I know 5 + 3 = 8, and I can use this to work out the 10s.
> Now there are 8 tens.

Unit 2: Addition and subtraction (1), Lesson 3

Think together

1) **a)** Work out 325 + 60.

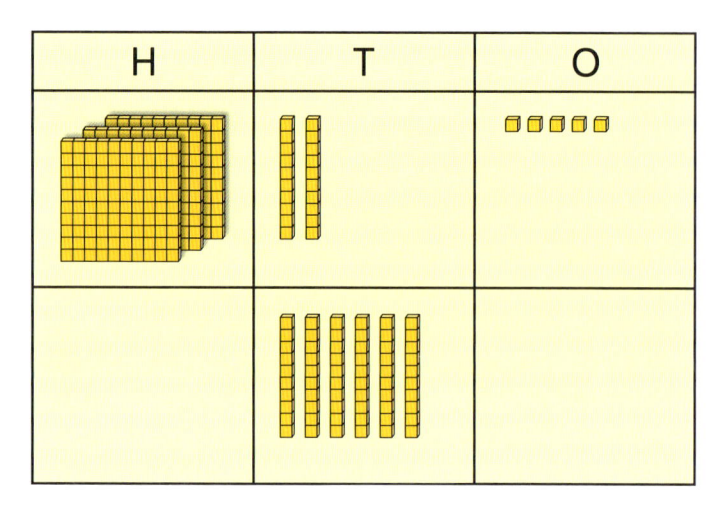

b) Work out 513 + 40.

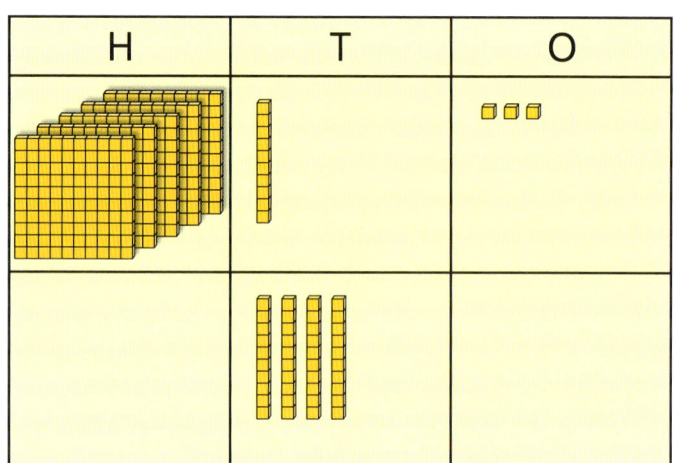

2) Ana takes 5 beads from the 10s.
Show this as a **subtraction**.

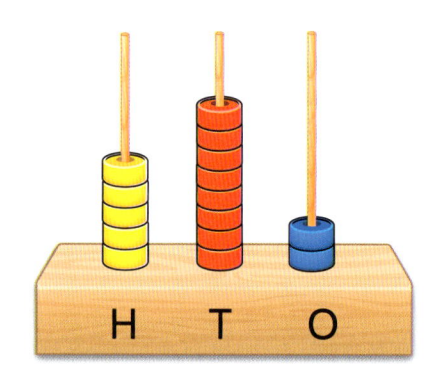

8 tens − ☐ tens = ☐ tens

582 − ☐ = ☐

Unit 2: Addition and subtraction (1), Lesson 3

3 a) Shawn makes the same number on each abacus.

A   H T O

B   H T O

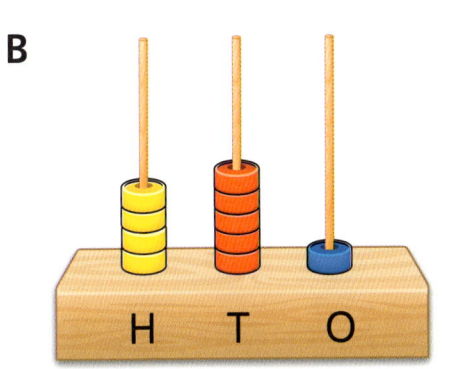

He takes 4 beads from the 10s of abacus **A**.

Then he places them on the 10s of abacus **B**.

What number does each abacus show now?

I can work out one answer by doing a subtraction and the other answer by doing an addition.

b) Work out

| 414 + 70 | 124 + 60 | 280 – 10 |

| 575 – 60 | 382 + 10 | 990 – 80 |

I'm going to make each number using base 10 equipment.

75

→ Practice book 3A p54

Unit 2: Addition and subtraction (1), Lesson 4

Add/subtract 100s

Discover

1 **a)** Jamilla is playing a computer game.

She shoots the spaceship and scores 300 points.

What will her score be now?

b) Jamilla shoots another spaceship. Her score is now 420.

Which spaceship did she shoot?

Unit 2: Addition and subtraction (1), Lesson 4

Share

a) Jamilla is on 520 points.

H	T	O

She scores 300 more points.

Jamilla's score will be 820 points.

5 hundreds + 3 hundreds is 8 hundreds.

b) Jamilla has 820 points.

H	T	O

She shoots a spaceship and now has 420 points.

H	T	O

Jamilla shot the −400 spaceship.

I crossed out 100s until I had 420. I crossed out 4 hundreds.

77

Unit 2: Addition and subtraction (1), Lesson 4

Think together

1 **a)** What is 268 + 300?

b) What is 317 + 400?

H	T	O

H	T	O

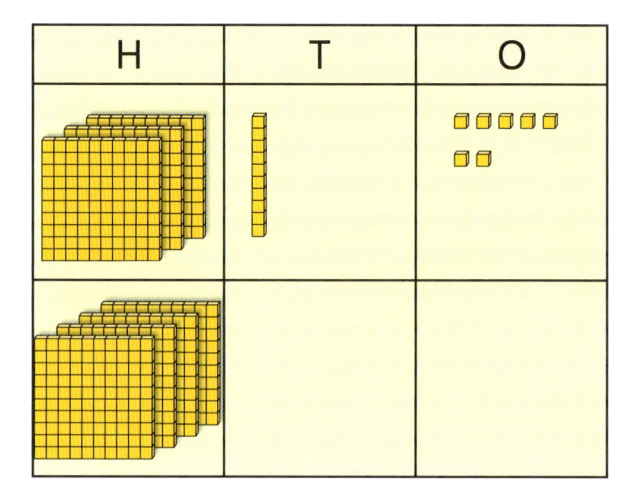

2 Mo has 629 raisins.

He gives 200 raisins away.

How many raisins does he have now?

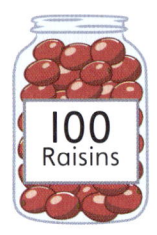

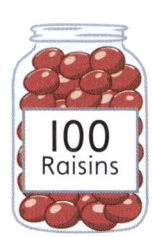

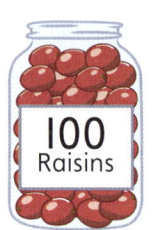

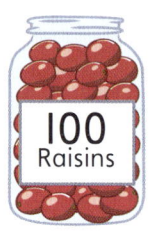

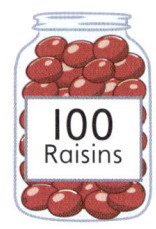

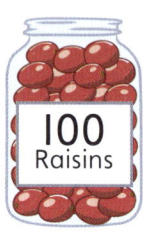

78

Unit 2: Addition and subtraction (1), Lesson 4

CHALLENGE

3 **a)** What number is represented here?

H	T	O

b) What is 200 more than this number?

c) What is 300 more than this number?

d) What is 200 less than this number?

e) What is 500 less than this number?

What patterns did you notice? Which digit changed each time? Why?

I used place value equipment to help me.

I tried to answer them in my head.

79

→ Practice book 3A p57

Unit 2: Addition and subtraction (1), Lesson 5

Spot the pattern

Discover

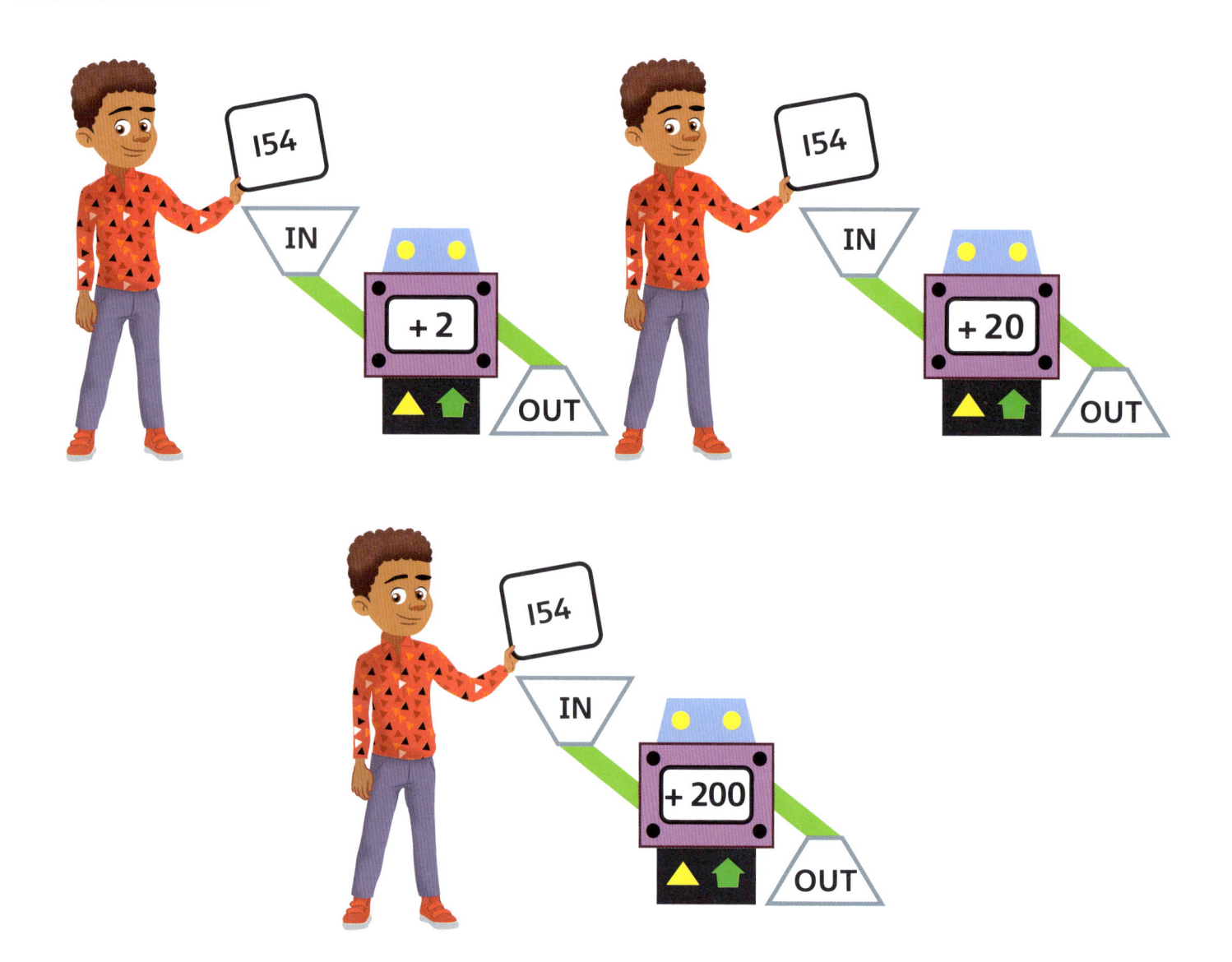

1. a) Lee inputs 154 into each function machine.

What will the outputs be? Try to work them out in your head.

b) Jamie inputs a number into the + 200 machine. The output is 797.

What number did she put in?

Share

a) The first machine adds 1s. The second adds 10s. The third adds 100s.

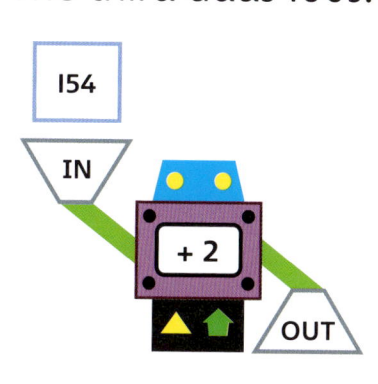

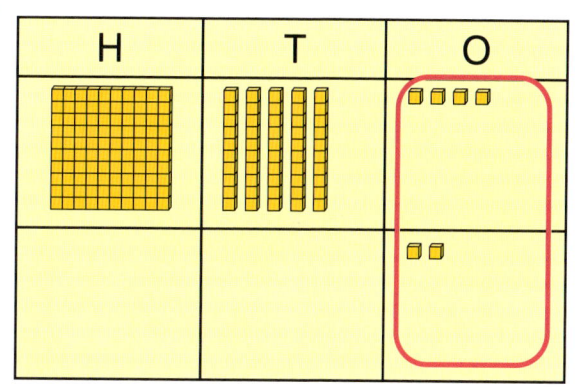

154 + 2 = 156

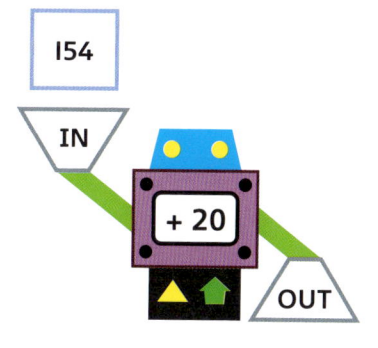

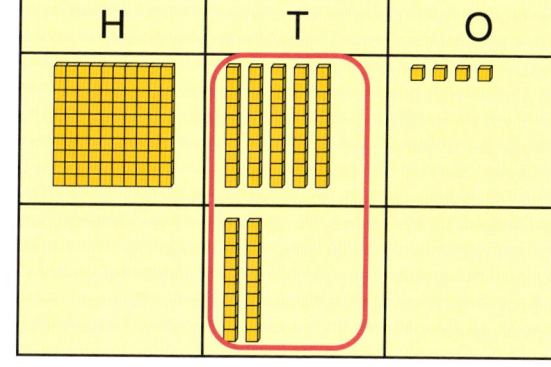

154 + 20 = 174

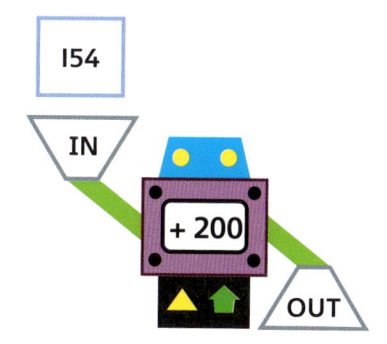

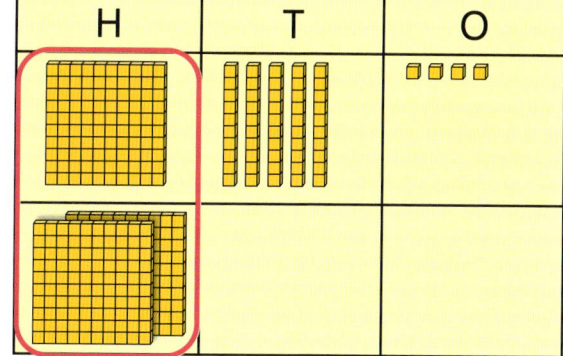

154 + 200 = 354

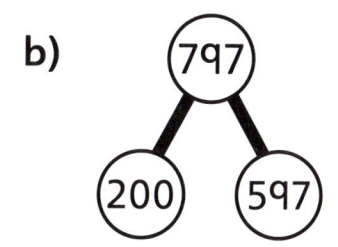

b)

Part-whole model: 797 (whole), 200 and 597 (parts).

This is a missing number problem. I used a part-whole model to help.

797 − 200 = 597

Jamie put in 597.

Unit 2: Addition and subtraction (1), Lesson 5

81

Unit 2: Addition and subtraction (1), Lesson 5

Think together

1) Find the outputs for these machines.

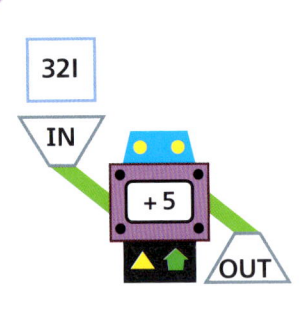

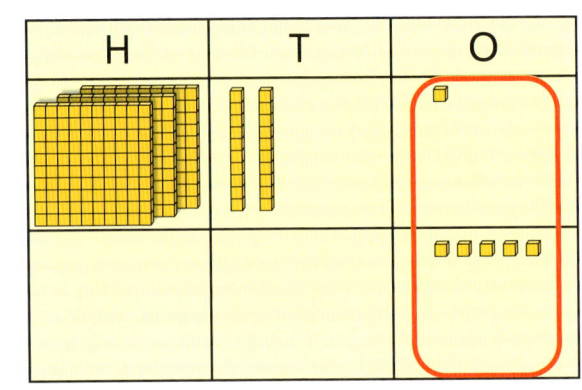

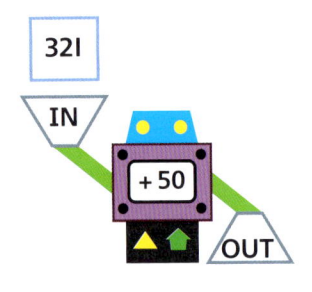

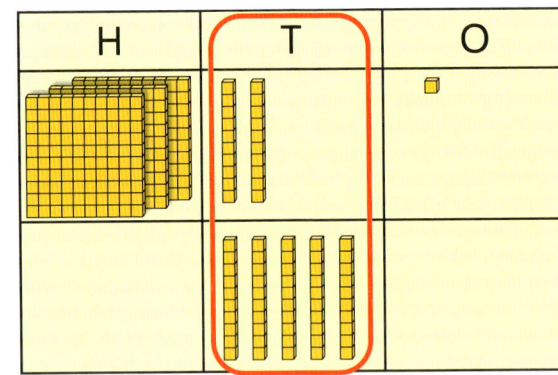

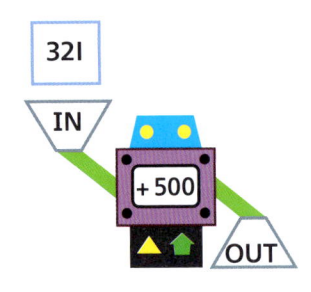

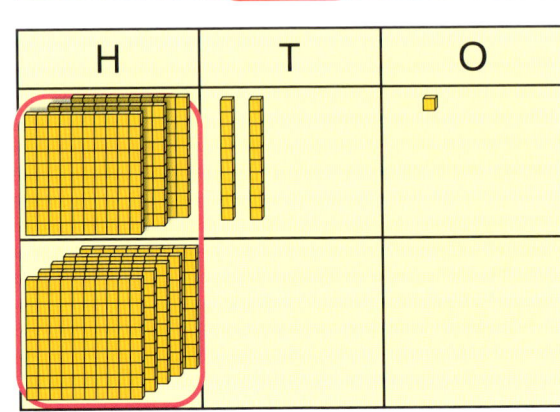

321 IN → +5 → OUT

321 + 5 = ☐

321 IN → +50 → OUT

321 + 50 = ☐

321 IN → +500 → OUT

321 + 500 = ☐

2) 546 is input into each machine. Find the missing outputs.

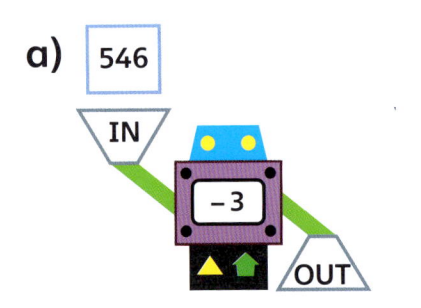

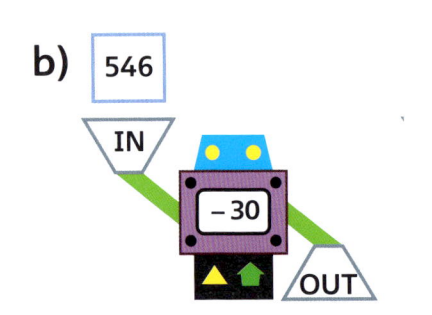

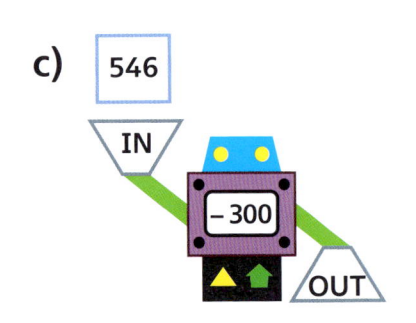

a) 546 IN → −3 → OUT

b) 546 IN → −30 → OUT

c) 546 IN → −300 → OUT

Unit 2: Addition and subtraction (1), Lesson 5

3 **a)** The functions are missing from these machines.

Write the calculations to work out the missing functions.

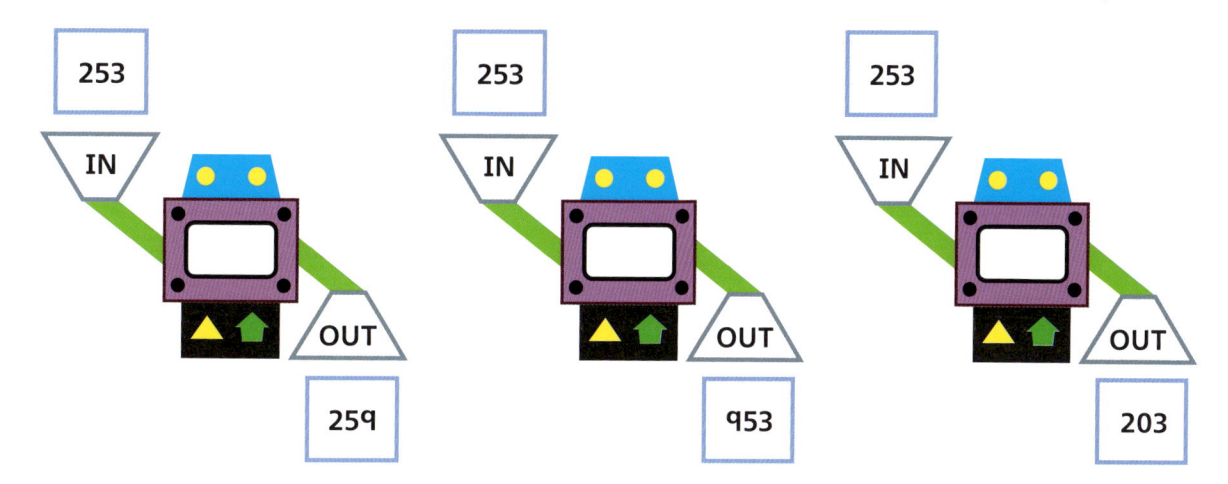

IN: 253 → OUT: 259

IN: 253 → OUT: 953

IN: 253 → OUT: 203

CHALLENGE

I will guess the function and test my ideas by doing additions.

Let's try to work it out by looking at which digits change.

b) Work out the missing parts of these calculations.

113 = 111 + ☐

131 = 111 + ☐

311 = 111 + ☐

555 = 755 ◯ ☐

555 = 557 ◯ ☐

555 = 575 ◯ ☐

83

→ Practice book 3A p60

Unit 2: Addition and subtraction (1), Lesson 6

Add 1s across 10

Discover

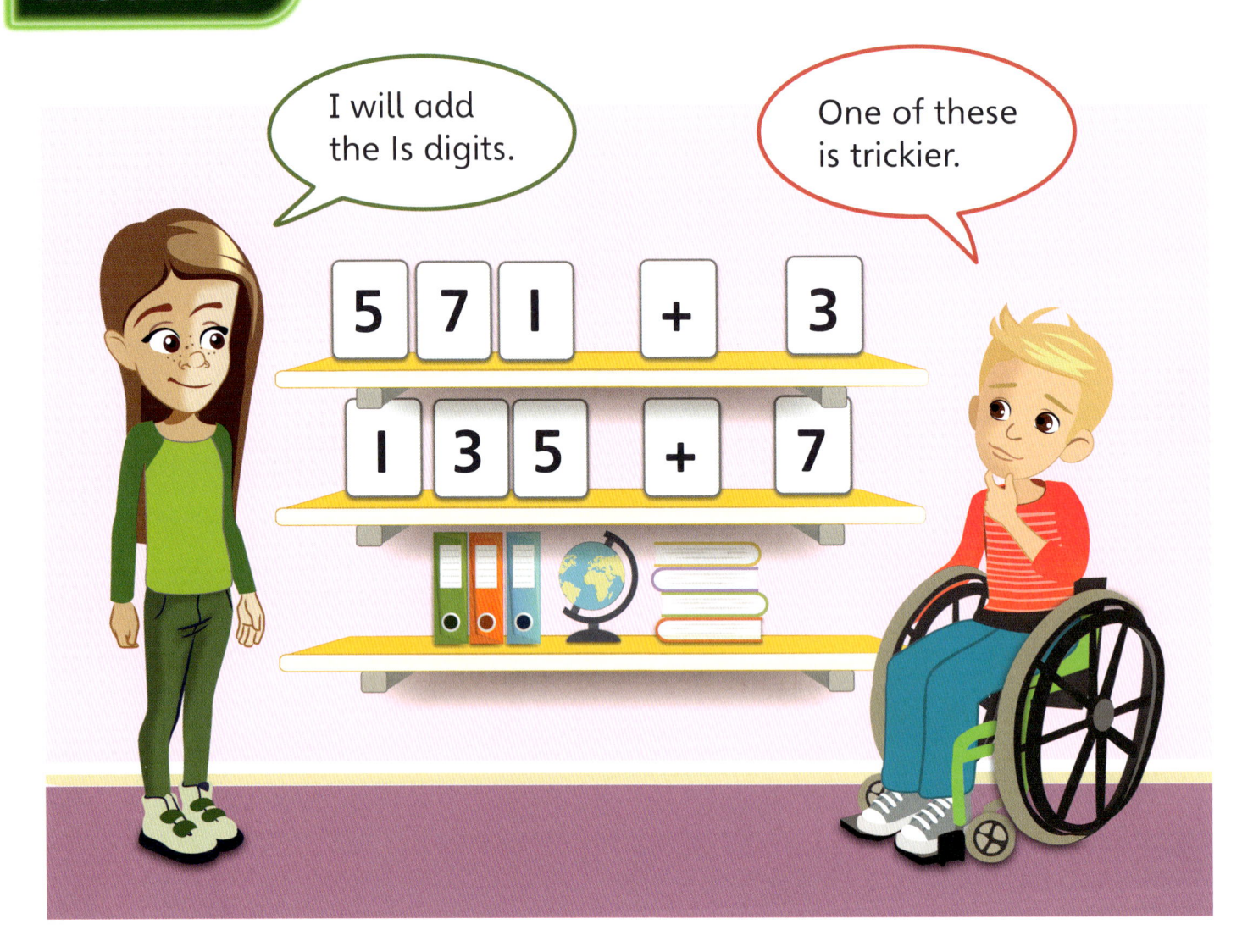

"I will add the 1s digits."

"One of these is trickier."

571 + 3

135 + 7

1. a) Work out 571 + 3.

   b) Work out 135 + 7.

84

Share

a) 571 + 3 = 574

I added the 1s.
1 + 3 = 4

b)

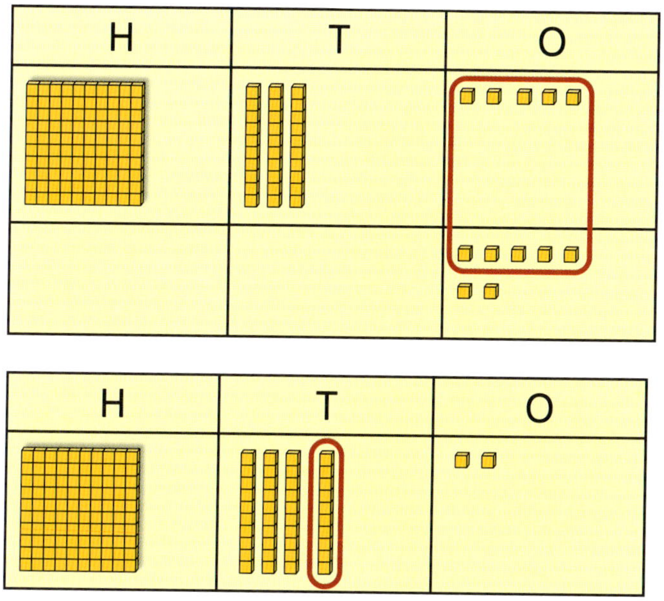

135 + 7 = 142

I added 5 more to make the next 10.
Then I added on the 2.

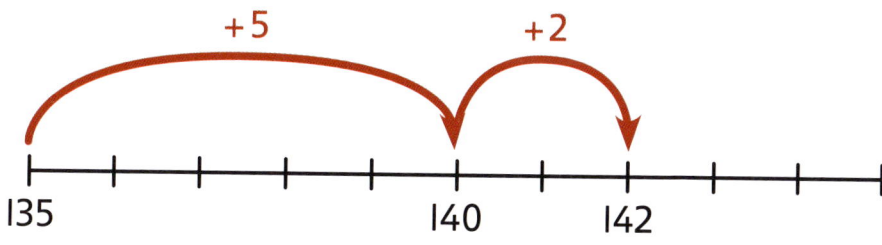

The 5 ones and 5 more make 1 ten. I exchanged 10 ones for 1 ten.

+5   +2
135   140   142

Unit 2: Addition and subtraction (1), Lesson 6

Think together

1 Solve these additions.

a) ☐ 3 ☐ 1 ☐ 6 ☐ + ☐ 5 ☐

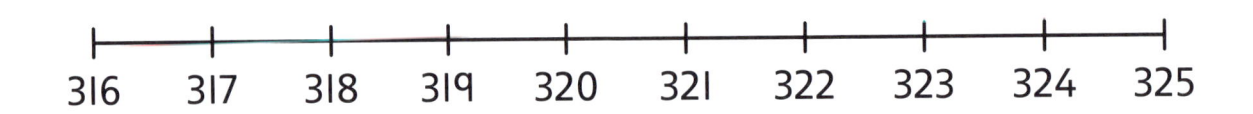

```
├──┼──┼──┼──┼──┼──┼──┼──┼──┤
316 317 318 319 320 321 322 323 324 325
```

b) ☐ 1 ☐ 4 ☐ 8 ☐ + ☐ 5 ☐

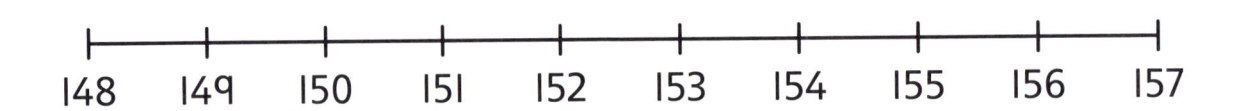

```
├──┼──┼──┼──┼──┼──┼──┼──┼──┤
148 149 150 151 152 153 154 155 156 157
```

2 Which of these additions change the 10s digit?

a) 248 + 6

b) 842 + 6

c) 217 + 9

d) 324 + 6

I'm going to try to work out the additions in my head.

86

Unit 2: Addition and subtraction (1), Lesson 6

3 **a)** What are the missing numbers?

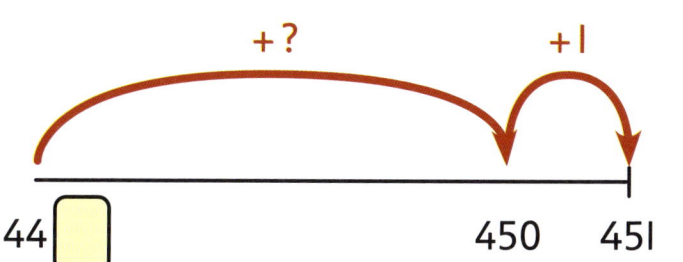

4 4 ☐ + ☐ = 4 5 ☐

44☐ ——+?——→ 450 —+1→ 451

"I want to find all the solutions."

b) Think of an example to support Astrid's idea.

"When I add a 3-digit number and 1s, the 100s digit increases by 1."

Discuss with a partner and share your reasons with the class.

→ Practice book 3A p63

Unit 2: Addition and subtraction (1), Lesson 7

Add 10s across 100

Discover

Beech: 184 years old

Birch

Horse chestnut

Oak

1 a) The birch tree is 10 years older than the beech tree.
How old is the birch tree?

b) The horse chestnut tree is 20 years older than the beech tree.
How old is the horse chestnut tree?

Share

Unit 2: Addition and subtraction (1), Lesson 7

a) 8 tens + 1 ten = 9 tens

H	T	O

184 + 10 = ?
I can add the 10s.

184 + 10 = 194

The birch tree is 194 years old.

b)

H	T	O

184 + 20 = ?
I added the 10s.
8 tens + 2 tens = 10 tens
There are 10 tens. I know that is not 1,104.

H	T	O

Exchange 10 tens for 1 hundred.

184 + 20 = 204

The horse chestnut tree is 204 years old.

89

Unit 2: Addition and subtraction (1), Lesson 7

Think together

1 The oak tree is 50 years older than the beech tree.

How old is the oak tree?

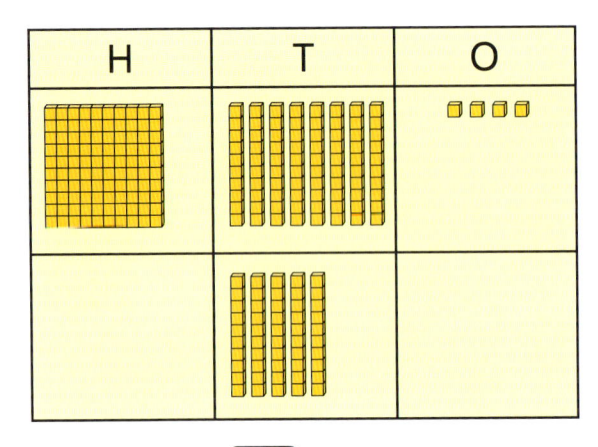

H	T	O

184 + 50 = ☐

2 Work out 263 + 70.

H	T	O

263 + 70 = ☐

I'm going to try and work this out in my head.

Unit 2: Addition and subtraction (1), Lesson 7

3 Mia has made the number 458.

H	T	O
100 100 100 100	10 10 10 10 10	1 1 1 1 1 1 1 1 1

For which of the following calculations will Mia need to do an exchange?

a) 458 + 20

b) 458 + 30

c) 458 + 60

d) 458 + 80

CHALLENGE

I can tell if it's possible to do an exchange just by looking and thinking about the calculation.

I wonder if the 1s digit will ever change.

→ Practice book 3A p66

91

Unit 2: Addition and subtraction (1), Lesson 8

Subtract 1s across 10

Discover

We had 151 parcels to deliver.

We have already delivered 7.

1 **a)** Make 151 using base 10 equipment.

Show how you can subtract 7 from 151.

How many parcels do they have left?

b) Show the subtraction on a number line.

Share

a) There were 151 parcels. Then 7 were delivered.

Can I subtract the 1s? I could do 7 − 1 = 6. So is the answer 156?

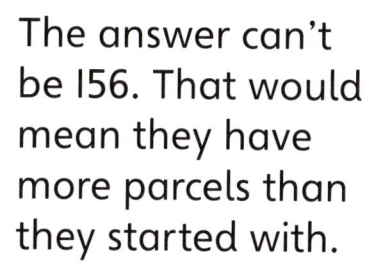

The answer can't be 156. That would mean they have more parcels than they started with.

Exchange 1 ten for 10 ones.

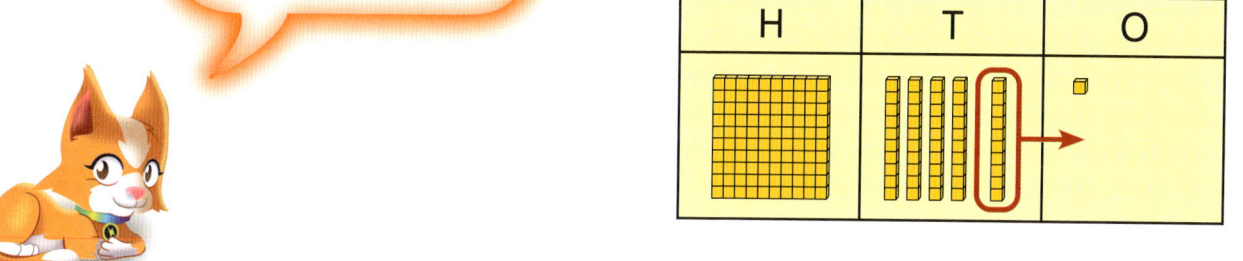

They still have 144 parcels to deliver.

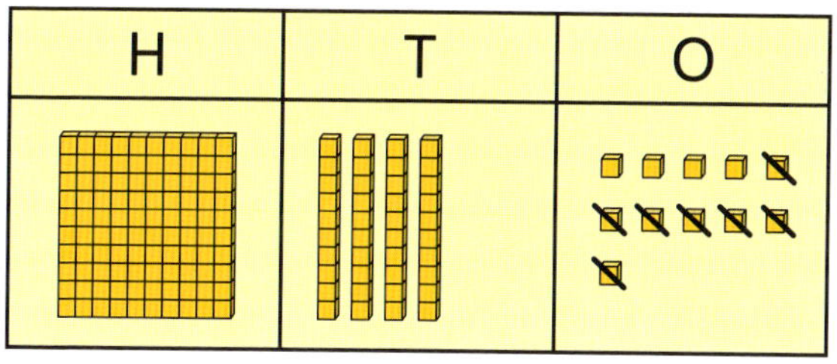

b) First jump back 1 to 150 and then another 6 to 144.

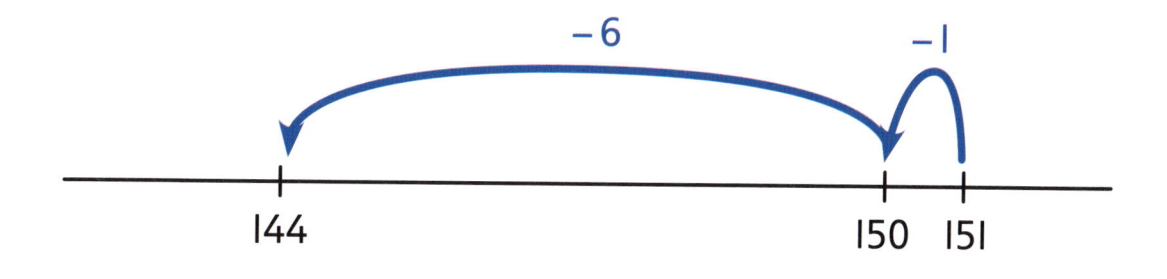

Unit 2: Addition and subtraction (1), Lesson 8

Unit 2: Addition and subtraction (1), Lesson 8

Think together

1 They have 144 parcels, then deliver 8. How many are left?

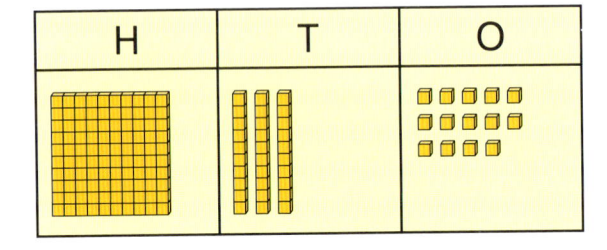

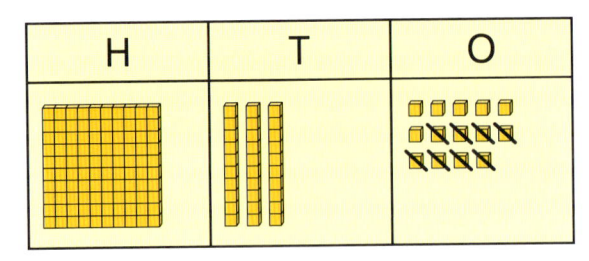

H	T	O
(100)	(30)	(4)

H	T	O
(100)	(20)	(14)

H	T	O
(100)	(20)	(9)

I wonder if I can do some of these in my head.

2 Work out the subtractions. Use the number line to help.

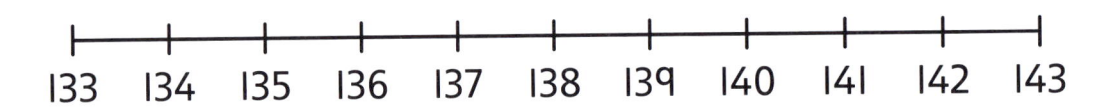

133 134 135 136 137 138 139 140 141 142 143

a) 143 − 2 = ☐

b) 143 − 5 = ☐

c) 143 − 7 = ☐

d) 143 − 8 = ☐

94

Unit 2: Addition and subtraction (1), Lesson 8

CHALLENGE

3 a)

> I started with the number 236. I subtracted a number. I now have 229.

What number did Olivia subtract?

b) Max has these two subtractions:

250 − 7 = ☐

205 − 7 = ☐

How can he solve them?

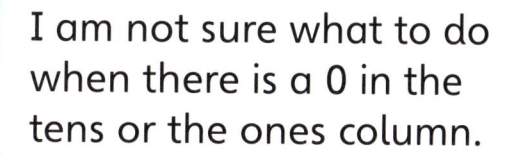

> I am not sure what to do when there is a 0 in the tens or the ones column.

> I think sometimes it is better to use a number line to jump back.

→ Practice book 3A p69

95

Unit 2: Addition and subtraction (1), Lesson 9

Subtract 10s across 100

Discover

1) a) Jen has 210 m of dinosaur fabric to sell.

   How much is left after she sells 20 m?

   b) Jen sells some more dinosaur fabric. Now she has 140 m left.

   How much did she sell?

Share

a) 210 − 20 = ☐

I tried subtracting the 10s.
20 − 10 = 10
That gave me the answer: 210 m left.

That can't be correct. That's what I started with.

You have to exchange 1 hundred for 10 tens.

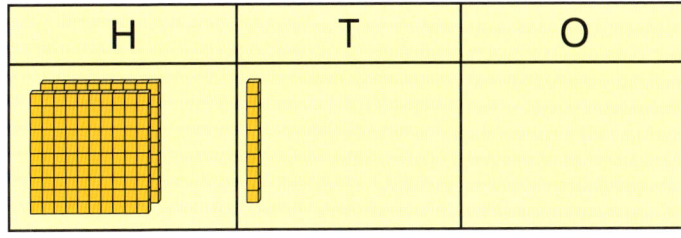

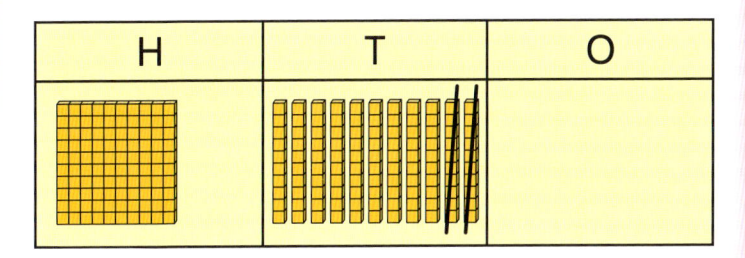

11 tens − 2 tens = 9 tens

210 − 20 = 190

Jen has 190 m of dinosaur fabric left.

b) 190 − 50 = 140

Jen has sold 50 m more dinosaur fabric.

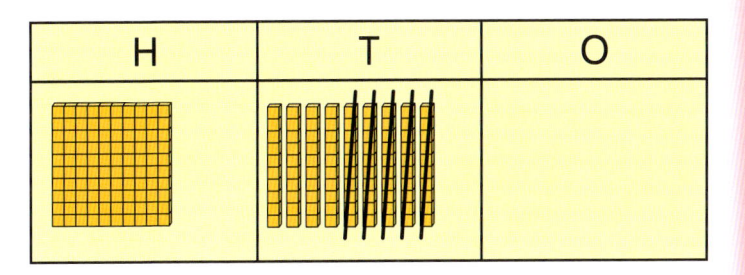

Think together

1) Jen has 335 m of space fabric and sells 50 m.

How much is left?

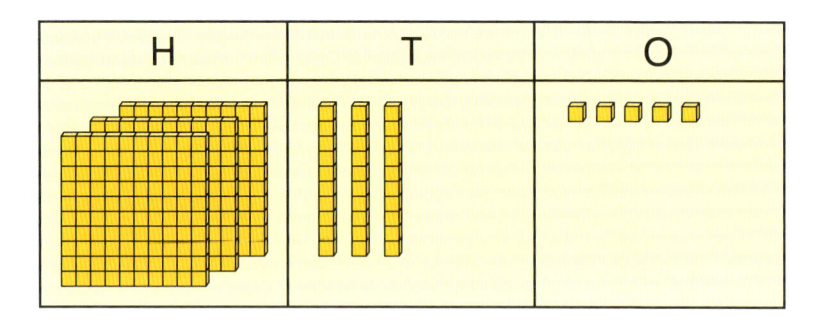

H	T	O

335 − 50 = ☐

2) Toshi has 80 m of bee fabric to sell.

Jen has 213 m of bee fabric to sell.

How much more bee fabric does Jen have than Toshi?

H	T	O

213 ◯ 80 = ☐ m

Jen has ☐ m more bee fabric than Toshi.

I think I need to find the difference. I can use subtraction.

Unit 2: Addition and subtraction (1), Lesson 9

CHALLENGE

3 **a)** Rani is trying to solve 235 − 60.

She has drawn a part-whole model to help her.

Explain what Rani has done.

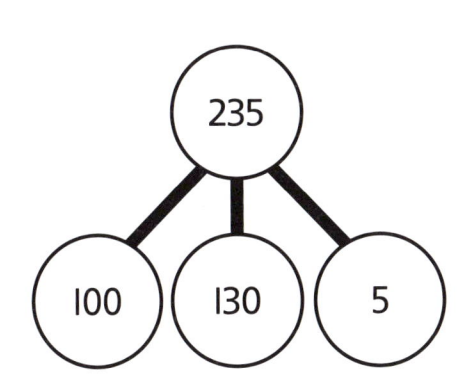

235
100   130   5

"The part-whole model is a different way of showing 235."

b) Use a method like Rani's to work out:

328 − 40 = ☐

328 − 50 = ☐

328 − 70 = ☐

"I will partition 328 flexibly."

→ Practice book 3A p72

Unit 2: Addition and subtraction (1), Lesson 10

Make connections

Discover

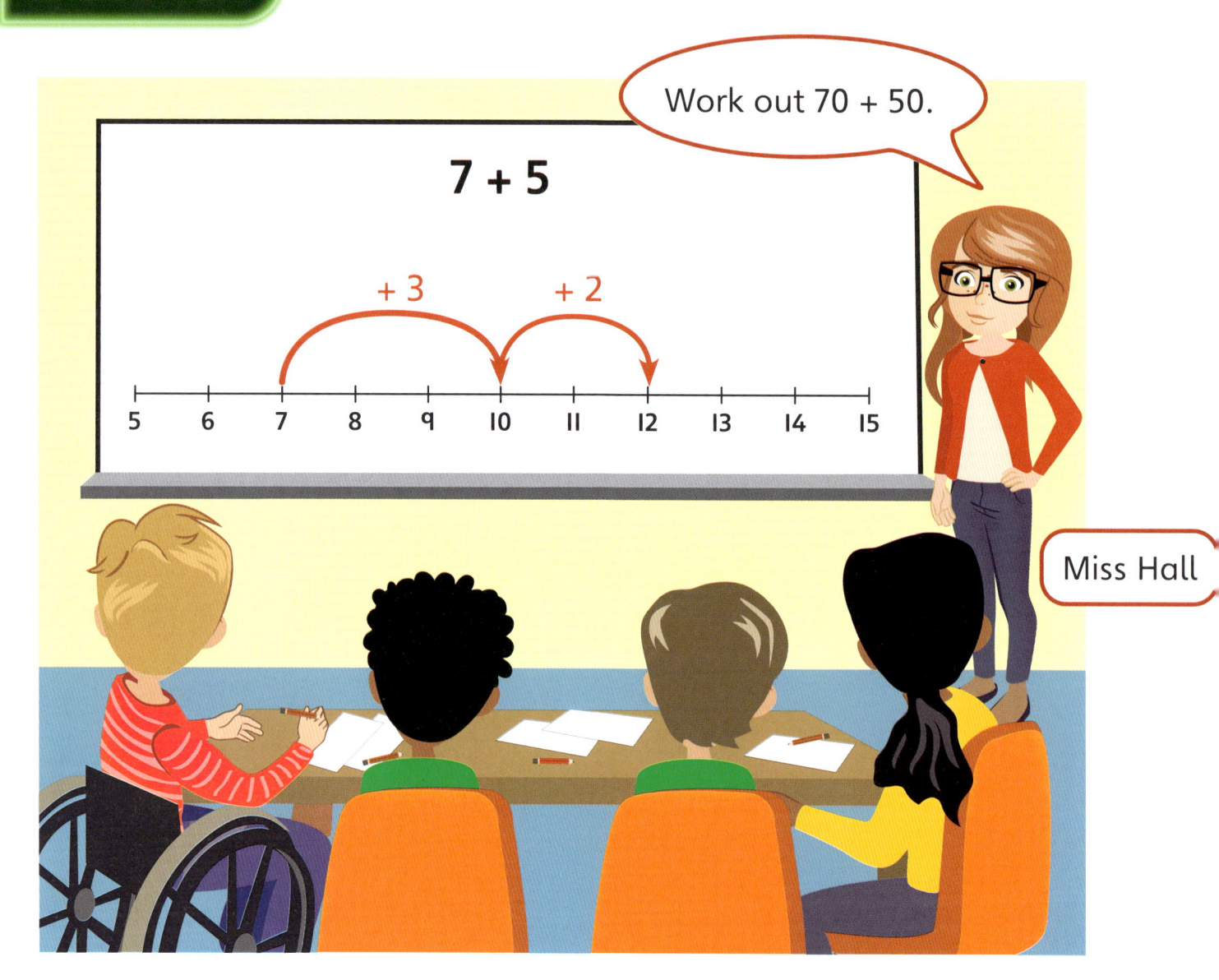

Miss Hall: Work out 70 + 50.

On the board: 7 + 5, with a number line from 5 to 15 showing +3 jump from 7 to 10 and +2 jump from 10 to 12.

1 a) What calculation is shown on the number line?

b) How can you use the calculation to work out the answer to Miss Hall's question?

Share

a) Starting at 7, we add 3 to make 10 and then add 2 more.

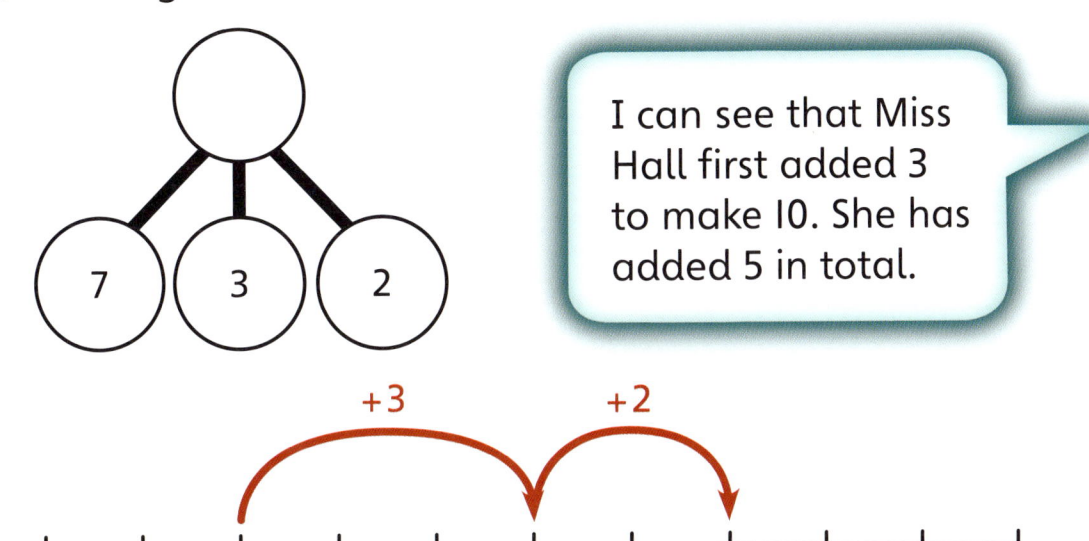

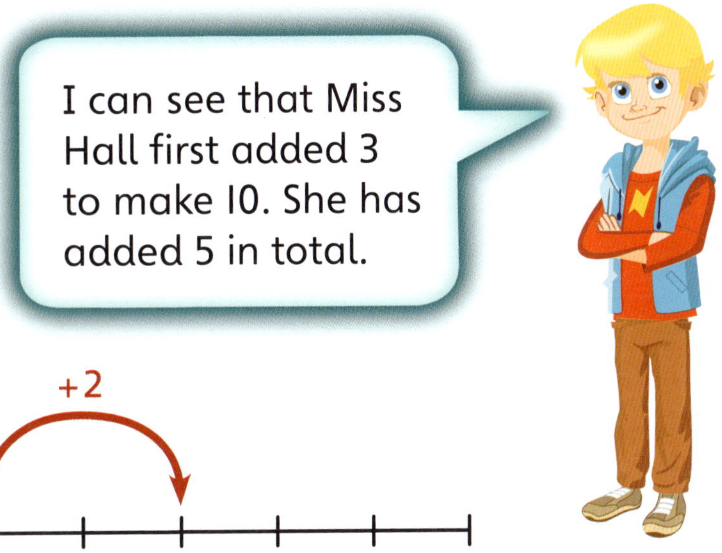

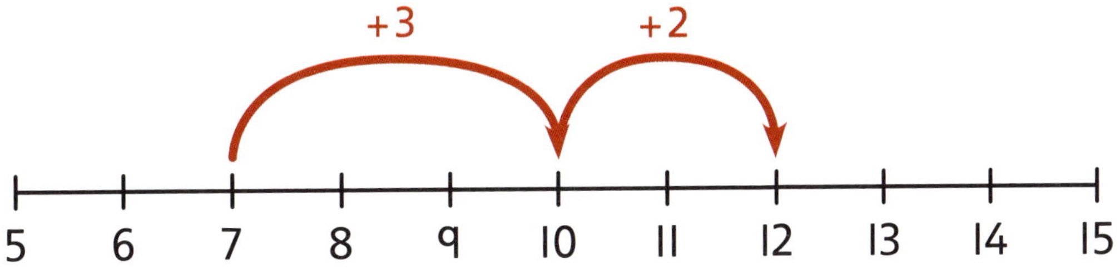

I can see that Miss Hall first added 3 to make 10. She has added 5 in total.

+3   +2

The addition shown is 7 + 5 = 12

b) Use the calculation in a) to work out 70 + 50.

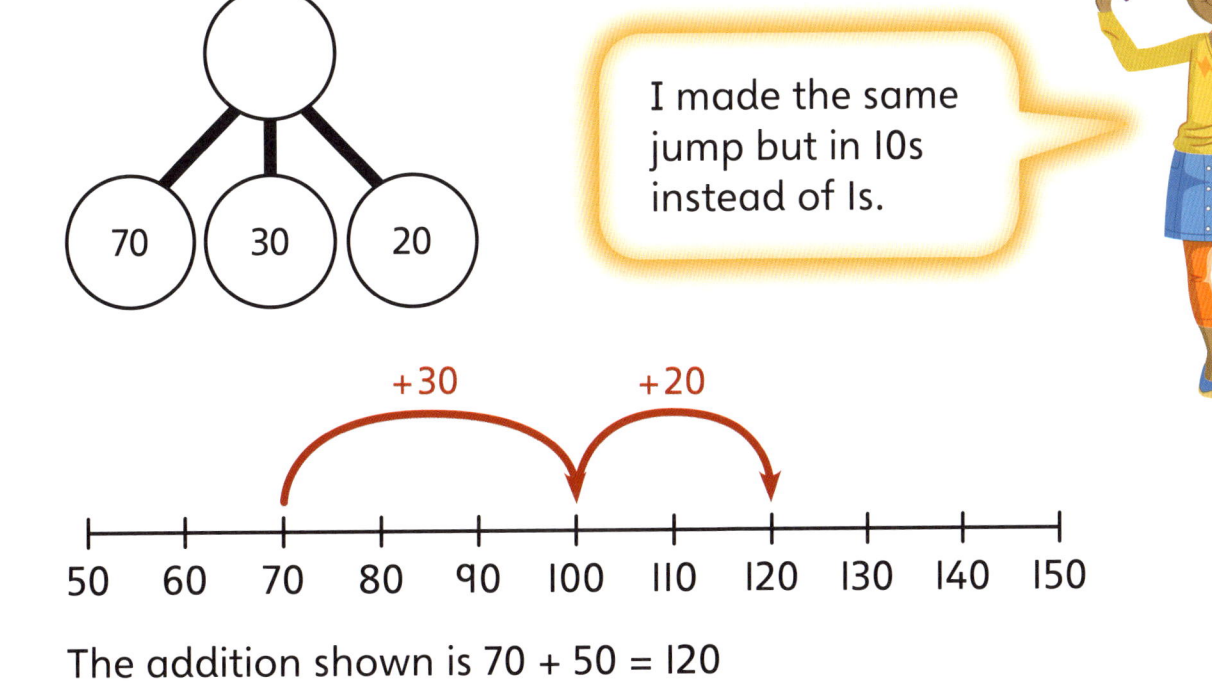

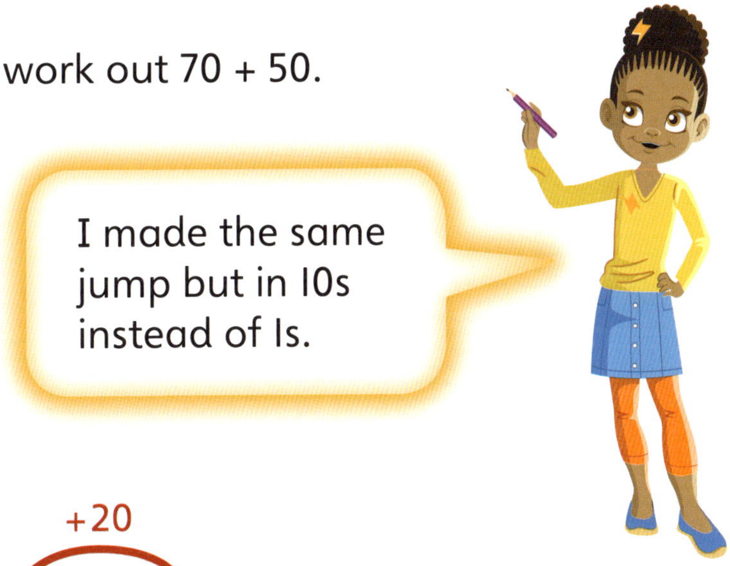

I made the same jump but in 10s instead of 1s.

+30   +20

The addition shown is 70 + 50 = 120

101

Unit 2: Addition and subtraction (1), Lesson 10

Think together

1 **a)** Work out 8 + 6.

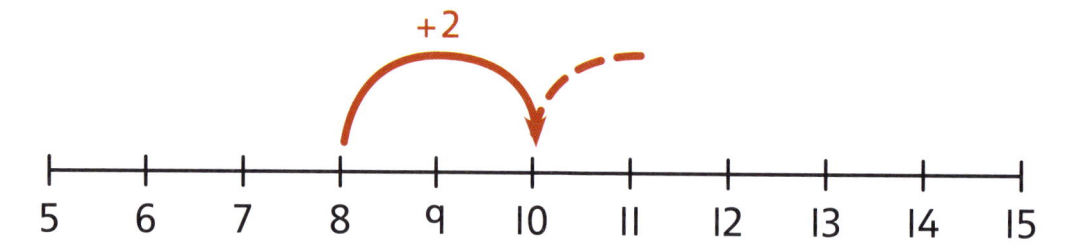

```
        +2
     ⌢
  ┼──┼──┼──┼──┼──┼──┼──┼──┼──┼──┼
  5  6  7  8  9  10 11 12 13 14 15
```

b) Work out 80 + 60.

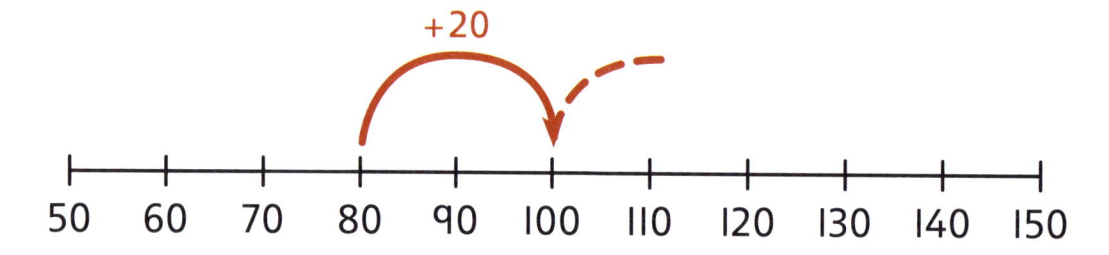

```
           +20
        ⌢
  ┼──┼──┼──┼──┼──┼──┼──┼──┼──┼──┼
  50 60 70 80 90 100 110 120 130 140 150
```

c) What is the same and what is different about your additions in **a)** and **b)**?

2 **a)** Work out 11 − 6.

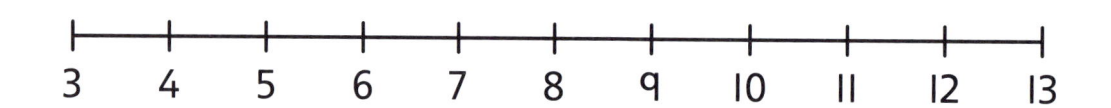

```
  ┼──┼──┼──┼──┼──┼──┼──┼──┼──┼──┼
  3  4  5  6  7  8  9  10 11 12 13
```

b) Work out 110 − 60.

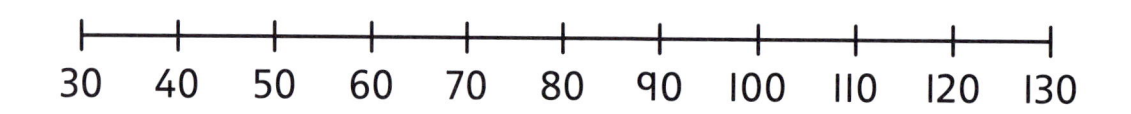

```
  ┼──┼──┼──┼──┼──┼──┼──┼──┼──┼──┼
  30 40 50 60 70 80 90 100 110 120 130
```

102

Unit 2: Addition and subtraction (1), Lesson 10

CHALLENGE

3

I know that 8 + 5 = 13

Work out the answers to these questions.

5 + 8 = ☐

50 + 80 = ☐

80 + 50 = ☐

130 − 80 = ☐

I know the answers to these straight away!

How do you know the answers?

Are there other ones you know straight away?

→ Practice book 3A p75

Unit 2: Addition and subtraction (1)

End of unit check

1 Amy scored 500 points. Ciara scored 200 points. How many more did Amy score?

A 700
B 300
C 500
D 200

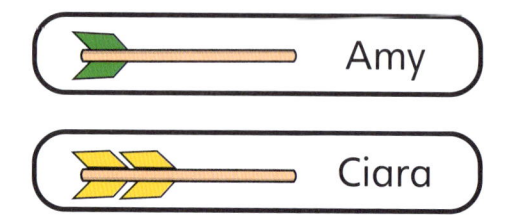

2 Which calculation needs you to exchange 10 ones for 1 ten?

A 321 + 7
B 327 − 1
C 1 + 327
D 321 − 7

3 What is 30 less than the number shown?

A 255
B 230
C 195
D 175

Unit 2: Addition and subtraction (1)

4) Which calculation has an answer with a 9 in the tens column?

A) 234 − 30   B) 234 − 60   C) 234 + 60   D) 234 + 50

5) Which calculation does this represent?

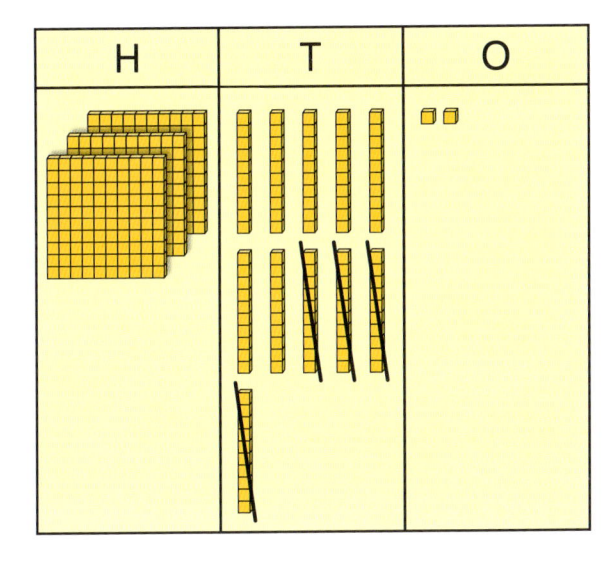

H	T	O

A) 312 − 4   B) 312 + 40   C) 412 − 40   D) 372 + 40

6) Work out the missing digits in this calculation.

2 ☐ 9 = 9 0 + ☐ 5 ☐

105

→ Practice book 3A p78

Unit 3
Addition and subtraction (2)

In this unit we will …
- Add and subtract 3-digit numbers
- Decide if we need to exchange
- Exchange across more than one column
- Learn how to check our answers in different ways
- Use bar models to solve 1- and 2-step problems

Do you remember how to find the missing information on comparison bar models?

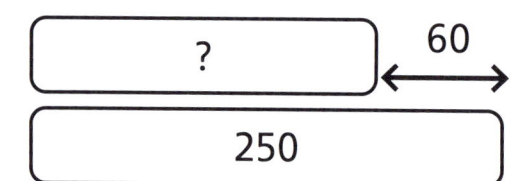

| ? | ↔ 60 |
| 250 | |

106

We will need some maths words. Which words have you come across before? Which word means to find a rough answer?

exchange   column method

estimate   mental method   multiple

sum   digit   approximate   add

subtract   difference   plus

minus   total   place value

We need to remember about parts and wholes. Use this part-whole model to find a family of 8 facts.

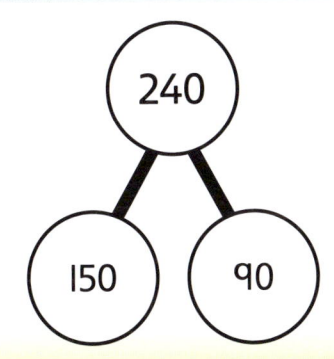

240
150   90

Unit 3: Addition and subtraction (2), Lesson 1

Add two numbers

Discover

1 a) Richard uses **digit** cards to make the numbers ⬚3⬚ ⬚2⬚ ⬚6⬚ and ⬚5⬚ ⬚4⬚ ⬚1⬚.

Make Richard's numbers using base 10 equipment.

b) Richard adds the numbers together.

What is his total?

108

Share

a)

H	T	O
(3 hundreds blocks)	(2 tens)	(6 ones)
(5 hundreds blocks)	(4 tens)	(1 one)

3 2 6

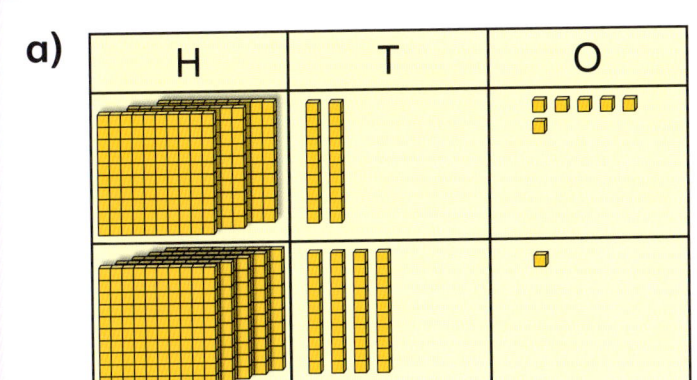

5 4 1

I can use a place value grid to organise my thinking.

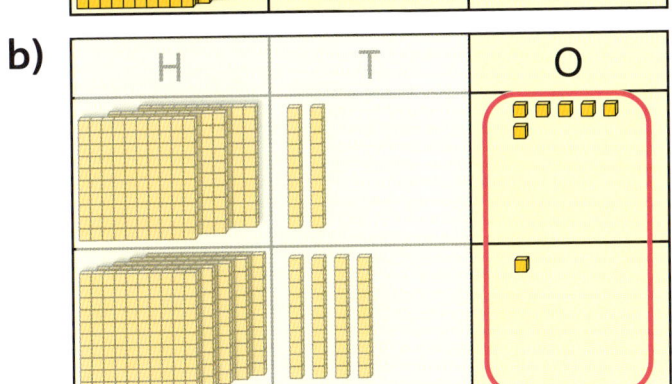

b)

	H	T	O
	3	2	6
+	5	4	1
			7

	H	T	O
	3	2	6
+	5	4	1
		6	7

	H	T	O
	3	2	6
+	5	4	1
	8	6	7

Richard's total is 867.

109

Unit 3: Addition and subtraction (2), Lesson 1

Think together

1 **a)** Richard makes two different numbers.

His numbers are ⎡1⎤⎡4⎤⎡2⎤ and ⎡3⎤⎡5⎤⎡6⎤.

What is his total?

H	T	O

	H	T	O
	1	4	2
+	3	5	6

b) Jamilla uses the digit cards to make two numbers.

Her numbers are ⎡4⎤⎡1⎤⎡3⎤ and ⎡5⎤⎡6⎤⎡2⎤.

What is her total?

H	T	O

	H	T	O
+			

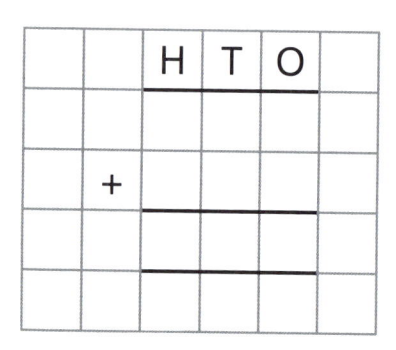

110

Unit 3: Addition and subtraction (2), Lesson 1

2 Work out

a) 112 + 215 = ☐

b) 345 + 612 = ☐

c) 308 + 481 = ☐

d) 630 + 253 = ☐

3 Lexi makes two numbers with these digit cards.

| 1 | 2 | 3 | 4 | 5 | 6 |

She gets a total of 993.

What numbers did she start with to get this total?

	H	T	O
+			

I wonder if the total will stay the same if I swap digit cards between the numbers.

I think there is more than one answer.

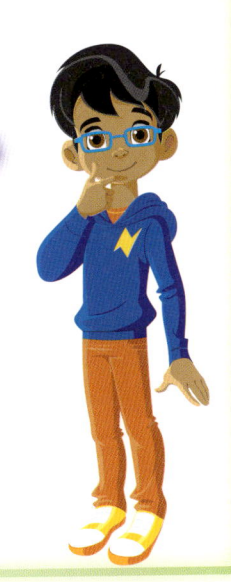

CHALLENGE

111

→ Practice book 3A p80

Unit 3: Addition and subtraction (2), Lesson 2

Subtract two numbers

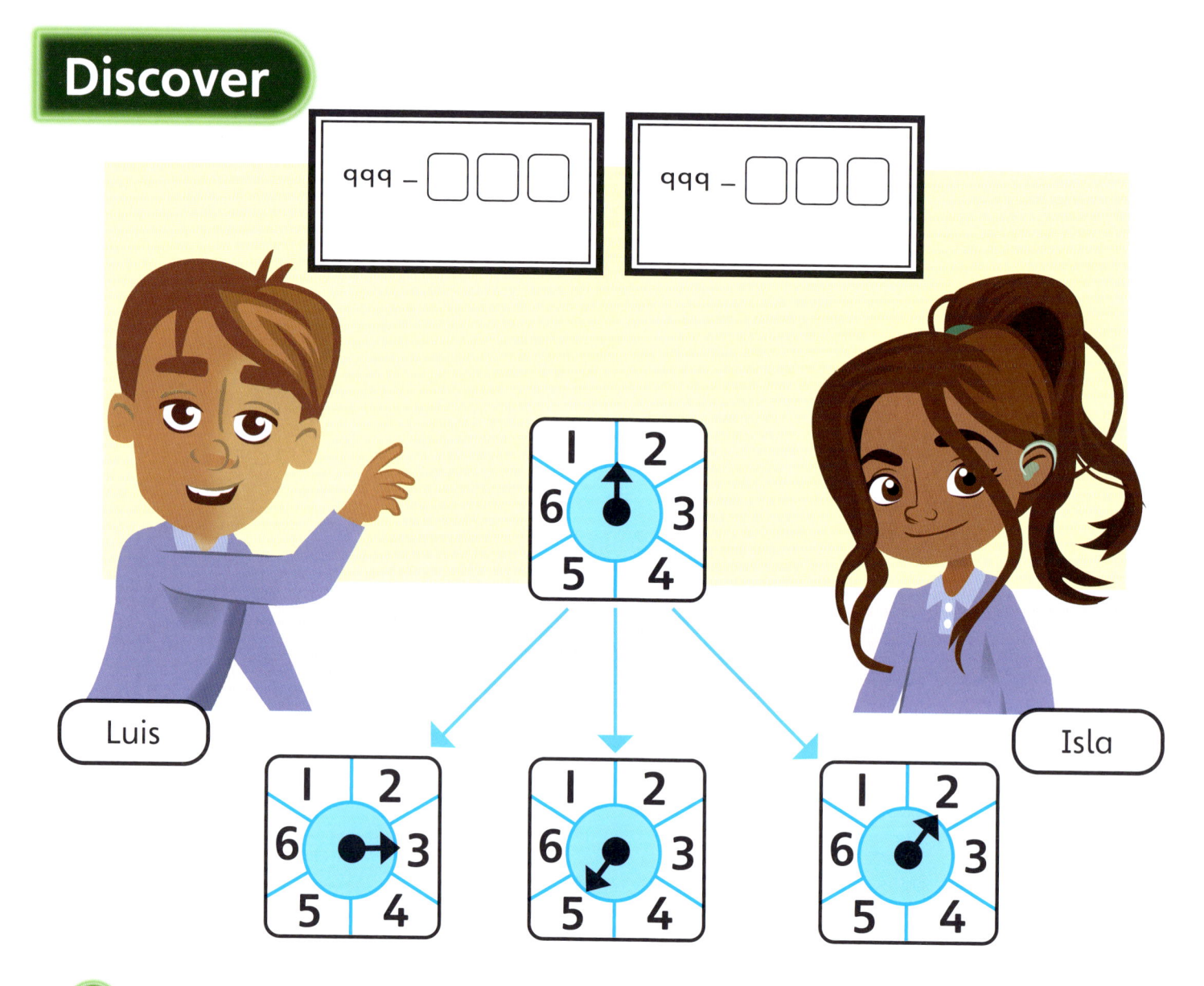

Discover

Luis

Isla

1. a) Luis spins 3, 5 and 2.

   He makes the subtraction 999 – 352.

   What is his score?

   b) Isla spins 1, 6 and 6.

   Use 1, 6 and 6 in different combinations.

   What could Isla's score be?

Share

a) This is a subtraction with two 3-digit numbers.

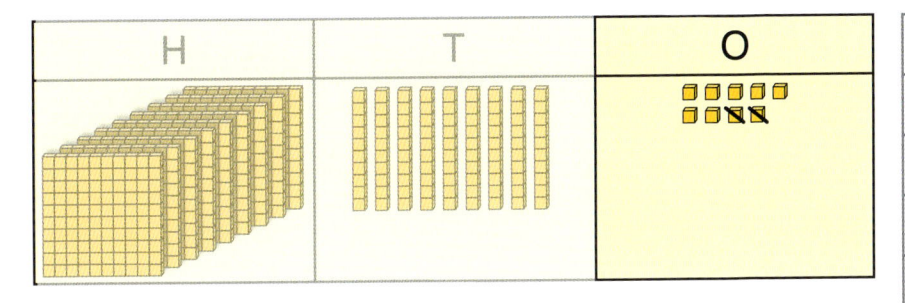

	H	T	O
	9	9	9
−	3	5	2
			7

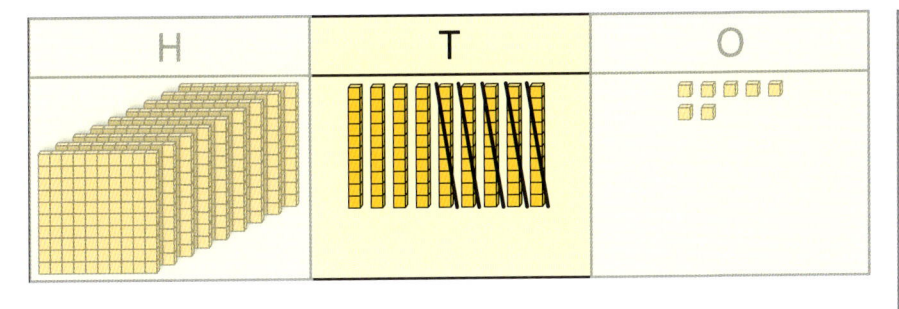

	H	T	O
	9	9	9
−	3	5	2
		4	7

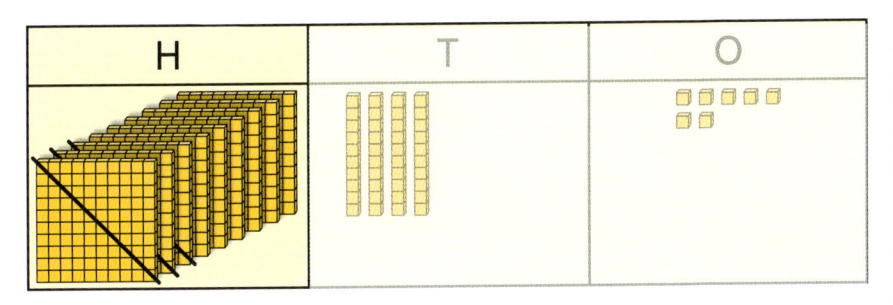

	H	T	O
	9	9	9
−	3	5	2
	6	4	7

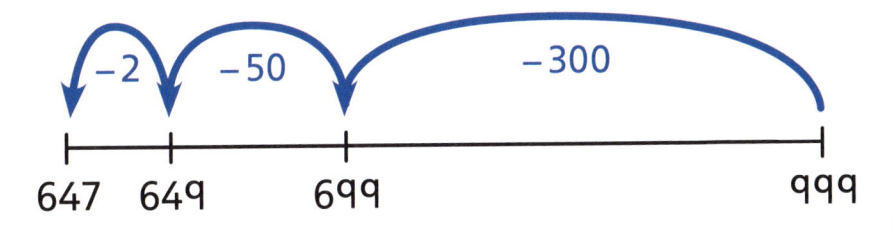

Number line: 647 —(−2)→ 649 —(−50)→ 699 —(−300)→ 999

Luis scored 647.

> I checked using a number line.

b) Isla could score 833, 383 or 338.

113

Unit 3: Addition and subtraction (2), Lesson 2

Think together

1) Jamilla spins 4, 3 and 5 and makes the number 435.

   What is her score?

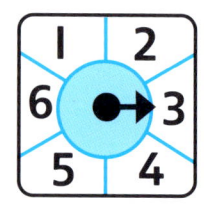

2) Ebo has the subtraction 678 − ☐☐☐.

   He spins 4, 4 and 6.

   Find three different scores Ebo can make.

114

Unit 3: Addition and subtraction (2), Lesson 2

3 Each child subtracts a 3-digit number from 999 using these digit cards.

What number does each child make?

| 9 | 6 | 4 |

Mo: My answer is an even number.

Ambika: My answer is a **multiple** of 10.

Andy: My answer is an odd number greater than 500.

Reena: My answer is less than 100.

I could just try some different examples.

I will think about the digits logically. Some of the subtractions I can do mentally.

115

→ Practice book 3A p83

Unit 3: Addition and subtraction (2), Lesson 3

Add two numbers (across 10)

Discover

Number of birds:
Morning: 126
Afternoon: 217

1 a) Make the numbers using base 10 equipment.

b) How many birds have Amal and Jen seen in total?

Share

a) and b) Amal and Jen saw 126 birds in the morning and 217 birds in the afternoon.

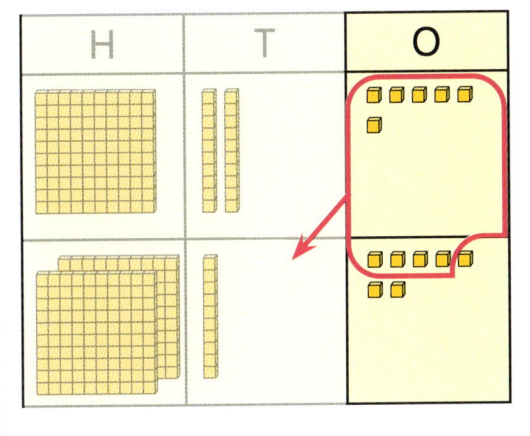

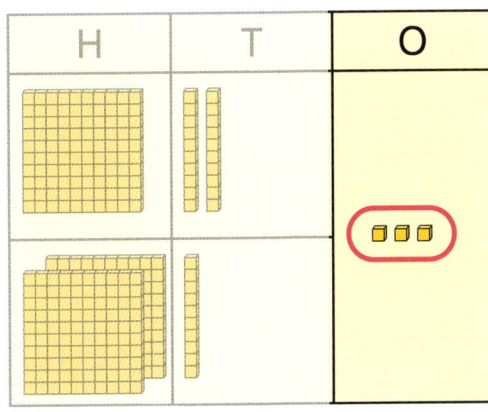

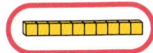

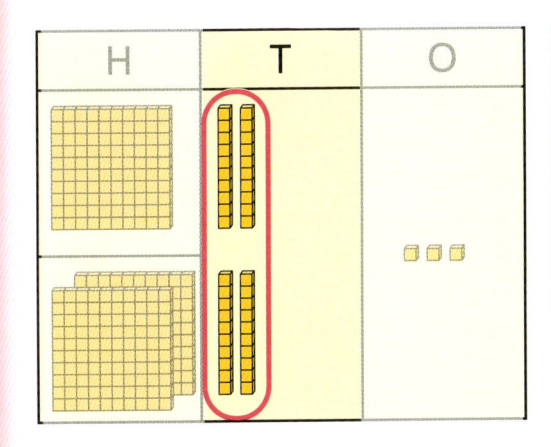

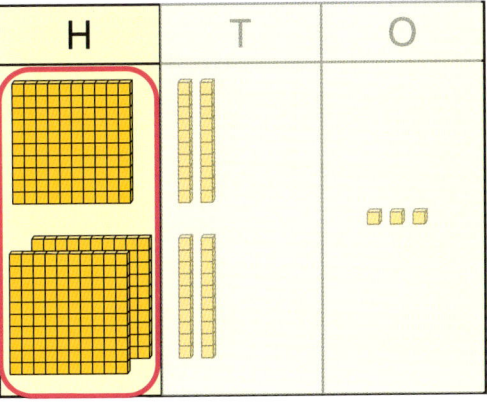

You need to add the 1s first.

Then add the 10s. Remember to add the exchanged 10 too.

Then add the 100s.

126 + 217 = 343

Amal and Jen saw 343 birds in total.

Unit 3: Addition and subtraction (2), Lesson 3

Think together

1) Amal and Jen spot more birds the next day.

They see 226 in the morning and 215 in the afternoon.

How many birds did they see altogether?

I wonder if I need to exchange any 1s or 10s. I will use base 10 equipment to check.

	H	T	O
		2	2	6
+		2	1	5

2) a) What is the sum of the two numbers shown in the place value grid?

	H	T	O
		3	7	8
+		2	1	7

b) Work out

126 + 239 = ☐

348 + 348 = ☐

The sum is the answer when you add two numbers together.

3 a) Aki is working out an addition.

	H	T	O
	4	2	7
+	1	3	✱
			2

I wonder how I can add a number to 7 to make 2.

What is the hidden digit?

Complete the calculation.

b) Work out

427 + 13✱ = ☐☐4

427 + 13✱ = ☐☐5

42✱ + 13✱ = ☐☐2

I'm going to make up my own missing digit problem for a partner.

119

→ Practice book 3A p86

Unit 3: Addition and subtraction (2), Lesson 3

Unit 3: Addition and subtraction (2), Lesson 4

Add two numbers (across 100)

Discover

Add together 185 and 341.

1 a) Help Mr Jones make the numbers in the place value grid.

b) Add the two numbers together to find the total.

Share

a)

b) Add the ones.

Add the tens.

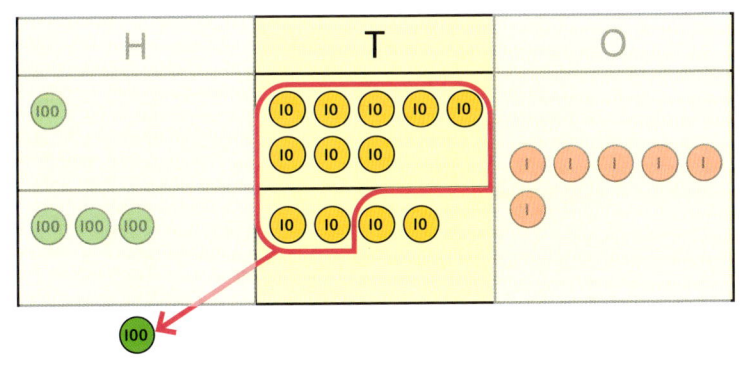

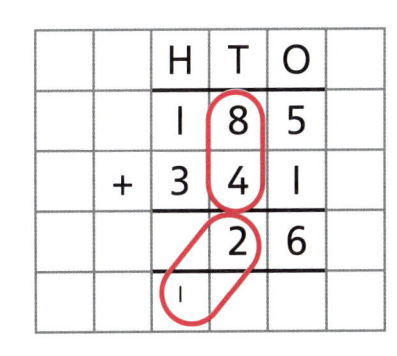

Add the hundreds.

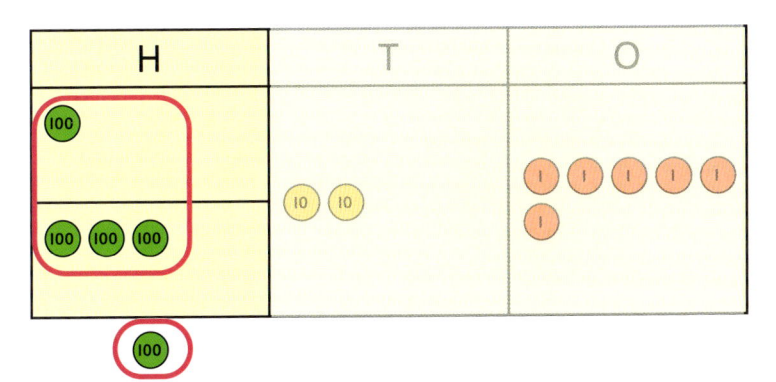

Unit 3: Addition and subtraction (2), Lesson 4

Think together

1 Work out the additions.

a)
	H	T	O
	4	9	5
+	3	8	4

b)
	H	T	O
	2	5	3
+	1	7	4

c)
	H	T	O
	1	2	1
	2	7	3
+	1	4	3

I wonder if adding 3 numbers is like adding 2 numbers.

2 Max is working out 184 + 217.

Max: I think I will only need to exchange the 1s because the 10s only add up to 9.

	H	T	O
	1	8	4
+	2	1	7

Is Max correct?

Test his idea by doing the calculation.

Unit 3: Addition and subtraction (2), Lesson 4

3 Here are some calculations.

253 + 174

253 + 123

253 + 179

253 + 188

253 + 149

Sort the calculations into the table.

No exchange	1 exchange	2 exchanges

I can tell where each calculation goes without doing any additions.

I will write a calculation of my own for each of the columns.

CHALLENGE

→ Practice book 3A p89

Unit 3: Addition and subtraction (2), Lesson 5

Subtract two numbers (across 10)

Discover

There are 361 steps to the top of the tower.

145, 146, 147

Olivia

Aki

1) a) Make the number 361 using base 10 equipment.

b) How many steps does Aki have left to climb?

Share

a) and **b)** 361 − 147 = ☐.

Exchange 1 ten for 10 ones.

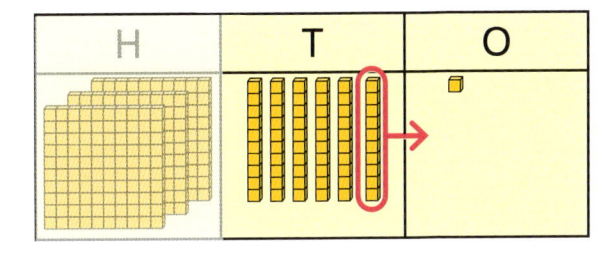

There are now 5 tens and 11 ones.

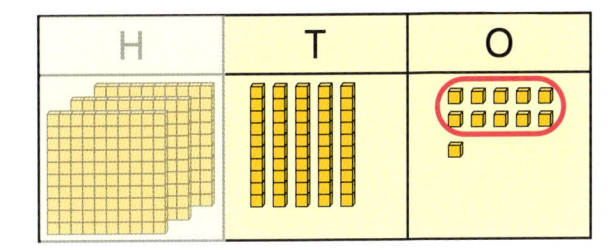

	H	T	O
	3	⁵6̸	¹1
−	1	4	7

Subtract the 1s.

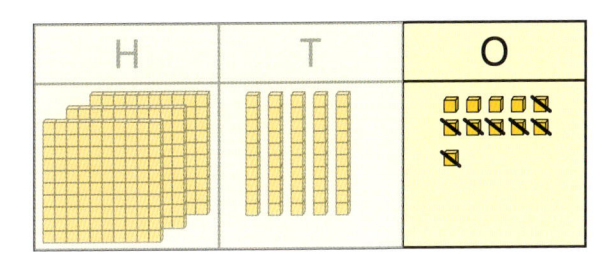

	H	T	O
	3	⁵6̸	¹1
−	1	4	7
			4

Then subtract the 10s

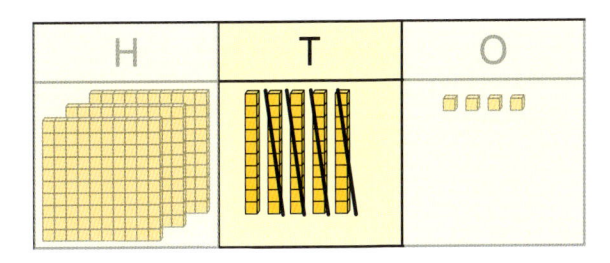

	H	T	O
	3	⁵6̸	¹1
−	1	4	7
		1	4

Then subtract the 100s.

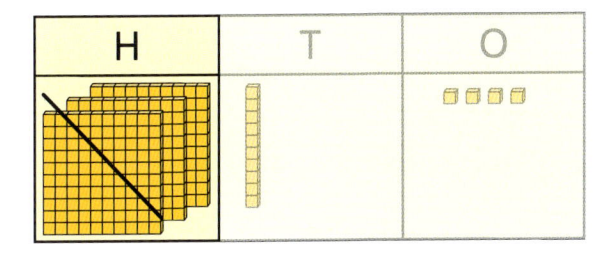

	H	T	O
	3	⁵6̸	¹1
−	1	4	7
	2	1	4

361 − 147 = 214

Aki has 214 steps left to climb.

Unit 3: Addition and subtraction (2), Lesson 5

Think together

1 There are 561 steps to the top of a skyscraper. Lexi has climbed 325.

How many steps does she still have to climb?

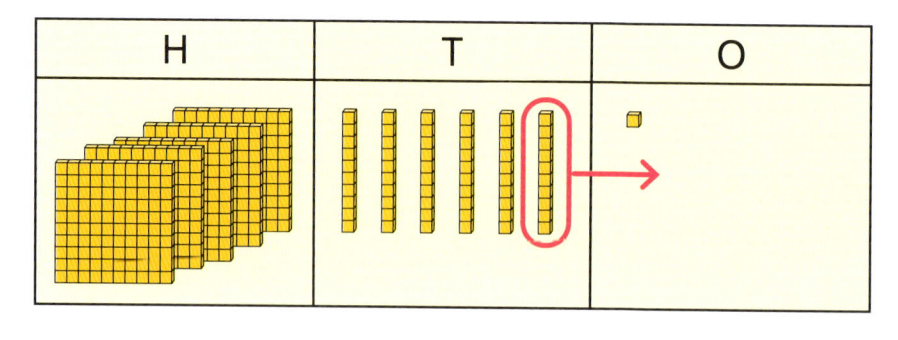

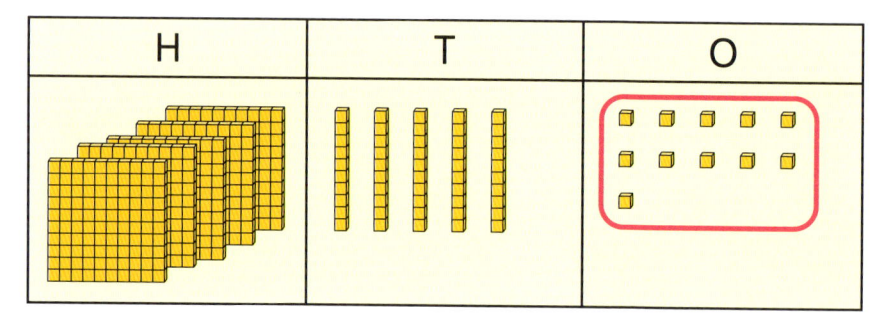

	H	T	O
	5	⁵6̸	¹1
−	3	2	5

2 Emma and Ebo have made some mistakes.

Explain what has happened.

Work out the correct answers.

a) 341 − 235 = ☐

	H	T	O
	3	4	1
−	2	3	5
	1	1	4

b) ☐ = 583 − 255

	H	T	O
	5	⁷8̸	¹3
−	2	5	5
	3	3	8

126

Unit 3: Addition and subtraction (2), Lesson 5

CHALLENGE

3 **a)** Amelia is working out the answer to this question.

> I know I am going to need to do an exchange.

Amelia

	H	T	O
	6	9	2
−	3	1	7

How does Amelia know this before answering the question?

b) Work out the missing digits.

482 − 13◯ = ◯◯7

482 − 13◯ = ◯◯6

482 − 13◯ = ◯◯9

> Is it something to do with the last number?

> It's easy to make a mistake with this sort of question.

127

→ Practice book 3A p92

Unit 3: Addition and subtraction (2), Lesson 6

Subtract two numbers (across 100)

Discover

Last year I took you to football practice on 184 days.

1 a) There are 365 days in a year.

Make the number 365 using place value counters.

b) Subtract 184 from 365 to work out the number of days that Alex did not go to football practice.

128

Share

a)

b) Subtract the ones.

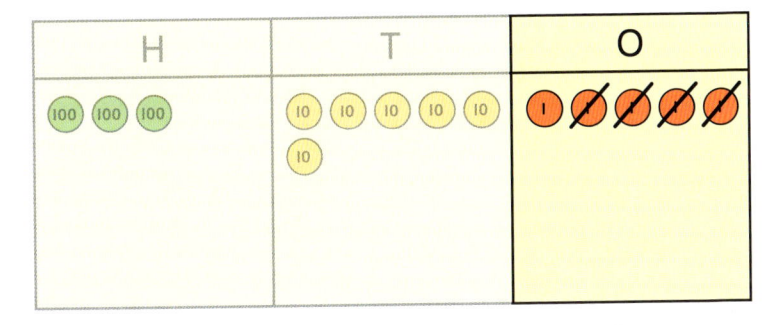

Exchange 1 hundred for 10 tens. Then subtract the 10s.

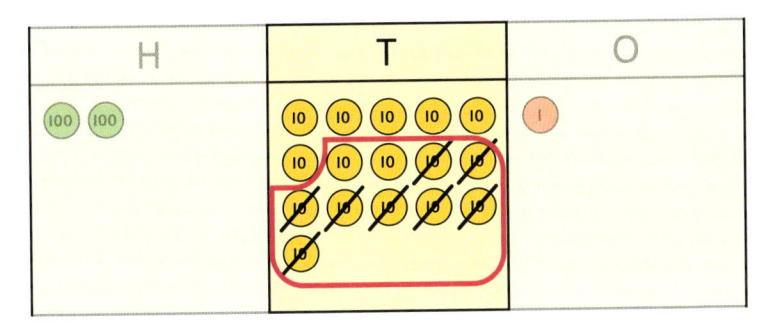

Subtract the 100s.

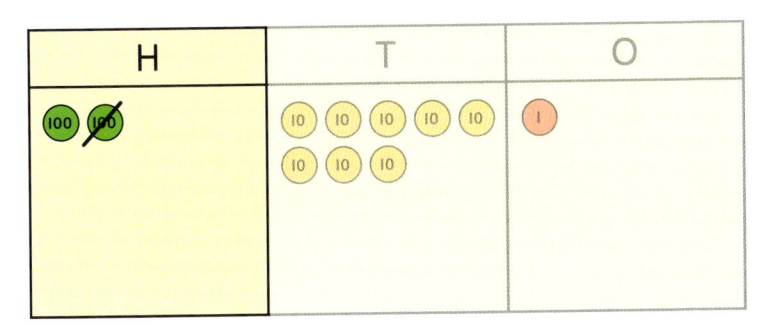

Unit 3: Addition and subtraction (2), Lesson 6

129

Unit 3: Addition and subtraction (2), Lesson 6

Think together

1 Work out 519 − 145.

H	T	O
100 100 100 100 100	10	1 1 1 1 1 1 1 1 1

	H	T	O
	5	1	9
−	1	4	5

2 Work out the following.

Do you notice any patterns?

What stays the same? What is different?

a)
	H	T	O
	8	2	7
−	1	4	4

b)
	H	T	O
	8	2	7
−	1	5	4

c)
	H	T	O
	8	2	7
−	1	7	4

d)
	H	T	O
	8	2	7
−	1	8	4

Unit 3: Addition and subtraction (2), Lesson 6

3 Max is working out this subtraction.

	H	T	O
	4	2	3
−	1	4	7

I think this needs more than one exchange.

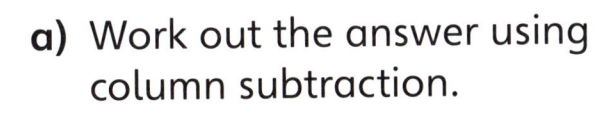

a) Work out the answer using column subtraction.

What do you notice?

b) Discuss how to solve this subtraction with a partner.

	H	T	O
	5	0	6
−	3	2	8

I know I need to exchange 1 ten for 10 ones, but there aren't any 10s.

I need to work out how this is possible.

131

→ Practice book 3A p95

Unit 3: Addition and subtraction (2), Lesson 7

Add a 3-digit and a 2-digit number

Discover

Large fish tank £275
Fish tank pump £16
Clownfish £61 each
Zebrafish £45 each

1 a) Zoe buys a large fish tank and a pump.

How much does Zoe spend altogether?

b) Aaron buys a zebrafish and a clownfish.

How much does this cost in total?

132

Unit 3: Addition and subtraction (2), Lesson 7

Share

a) The calculation is 275 + 16.

First add the 1s.

Exchange 10 ones for 1 ten.

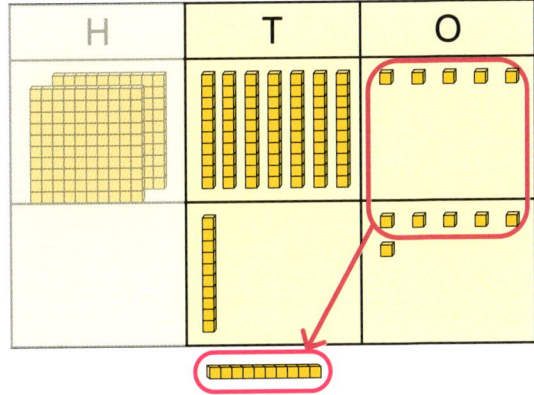

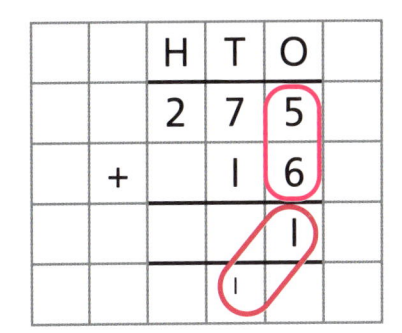

Then add the 10s.

Don't forget the exchanged 10.

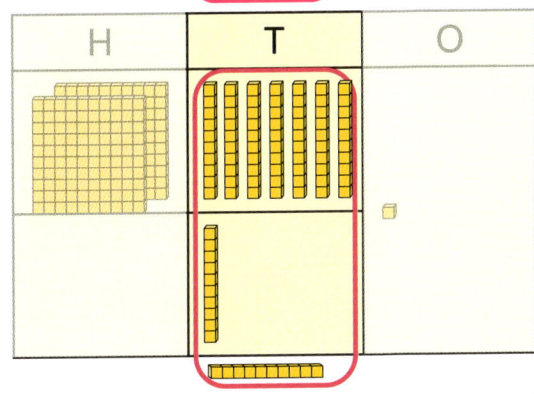

And then add the 100s.

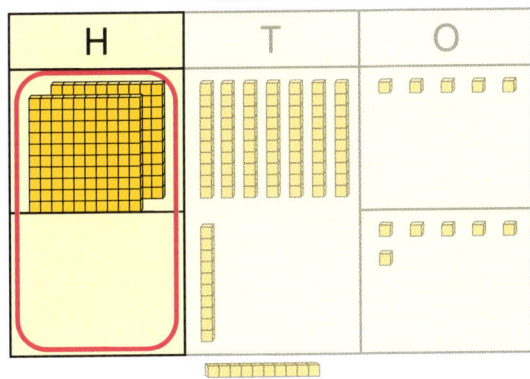

b) 45 + 61 = 106

The zebrafish and the clownfish cost £106 in total.

133

Unit 3: Addition and subtraction (2), Lesson 7

Think together

1 **a)** Work out 126 + 57.

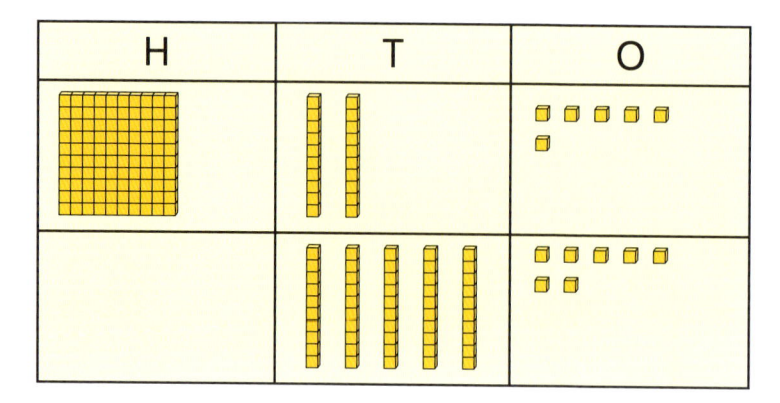

b) Work out 156 + 27.

c) What do you notice about your answers?

Why do you think this is?

2 Mark and Poppy wanted to write their additions in columns.

What mistakes did they make?

Mark's addition

	H	T	O
		1	5	4
+			7	2
		1	2	6
			1	

Poppy's addition

	H	T	O
		1	6	4
+			3	7
		1	9	11

134

Unit 3: Addition and subtraction (2), Lesson 7

CHALLENGE

3) Here are 5 number cards.

| 3 | 3 | 3 | 8 | 8 |

How many different additions can you make?

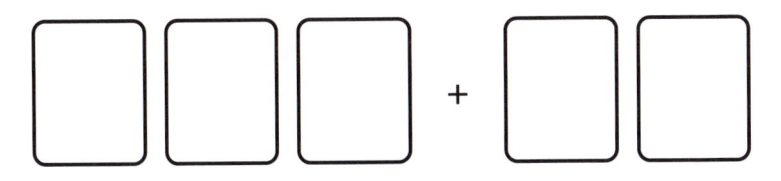

☐☐☐ + ☐☐

Do any of your calculations add to the same total?

Explain why.

Now I can solve any addition with 3 digits and 2 digits.

I will make up some additions where you exchange for both 10s and 100s.

135

→ Practice book 3A p98

Unit 3: Addition and subtraction (2), Lesson 8

Subtract a 2-digit number from a 3-digit number

Discover

We planted 175 new trees last year.

38 did not survive the winter.

1 a) Luis worked out how many new trees survived. What mistake did he make?

```
  H T O
  1 7 5
-   3 8
  ─────
  1 4 3
```

Luis

*7 tens – 3 tens = 4 tens
8 ones – 5 ones = 3 ones.
So 175 – 38 = 143.*

b) What is the correct answer?

Share

a)

> Luis has subtracted the 1s in the wrong order.

Luis needed to subtract 8 ones.

He should have exchanged 1 ten for 10 ones first.

b) 175 − 38 = ☐

First exchange 1 ten for 10 ones.

| H | T | O |

Then subtract the ones.

| H | T | O |

> I wrote it as columns. I remembered how to show the exchange of 1 ten.

Now subtract the tens.

| H | T | O |

	H	T	O
	1	⁶7̸	¹5
−		3	8
	1	3	7

There are no hundreds to be subtracted.

175 − 38 = 137

Unit 3: Addition and subtraction (2), Lesson 8

Think together

1 a) Work out

H	T	O
(2 hundreds blocks)	(4 tens)	(5 ones)

	H	T	O
		2	4	6
−			6	3

b)

	H	T	O
	3	9	5
−		8	7

c)

	H	T	O
	3	1	5
−		7	6

2 Annie is sorting objects to recycle.

Object	Number of items
Cans	43
Plastic bottles	271
Glass bottles	85

a) How many more plastic bottles than cans did Annie recycle?

b) How many more plastic bottles than glass bottles did she recycle?

138

Unit 3: Addition and subtraction (2), Lesson 8

3 Gio has made the number 405.

H	T	O
100 100 100 100		1 1 1 1 1

a) Explain how you would subtract each of these numbers from 405.

| 7 | 17 | 217 |

b) Gio subtracts a number from 405 and gets this number.

H	T	O
100 100 100	10 10 10 10 10 10	1 1 1

What number did Gio subtract?

I think the number must be less than 100.

I don't think I need to exchange any 1s.

→ Practice book 3A p101

Unit 3: Addition and subtraction (2), Lesson 9

Complements to 100

Discover

1 a) How many squares does Zac have to move to get to 100?

Complete the number sentence and the part-whole model.

87 + ☐ = 100

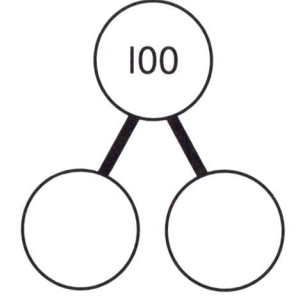

b) How many squares does Emma have to move to get to 100?

Complete the number sentence and the part-whole model.

51 + ☐ = 100

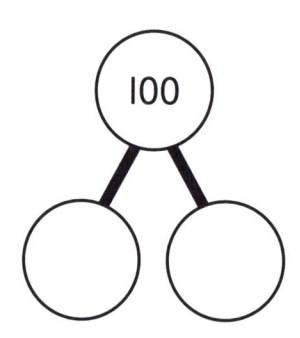

Unit 3: Addition and subtraction (2), Lesson 9

Share

a)

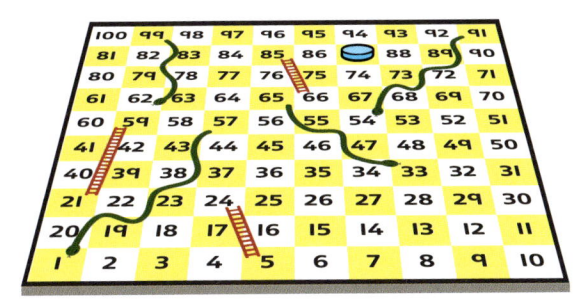

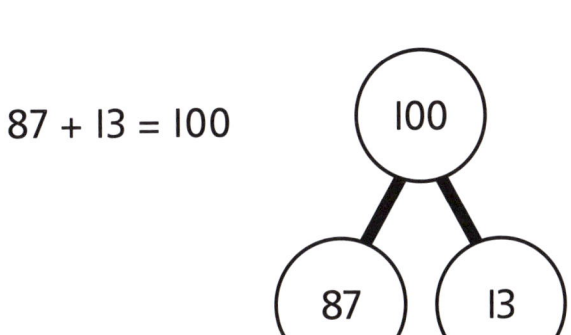

87 + 13 = 100

100
├ 87
└ 13

Zac has to move 13 squares.

"I counted the squares left."

b)

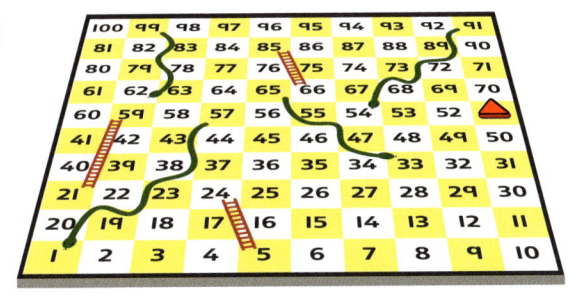

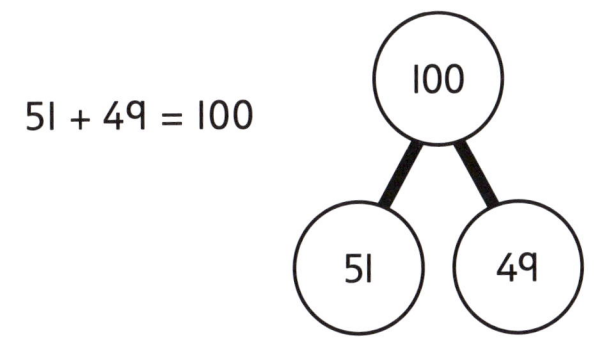

51 + 49 = 100

100
├ 51
└ 49

Emma has to move 49 squares.

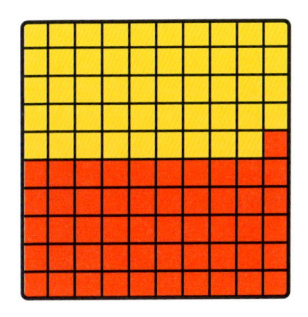

"I counted the 10s first. Then I counted the 1s needed to make 100."

141

Unit 3: Addition and subtraction (2), Lesson 9

Think together

1 Complete the part-whole model.

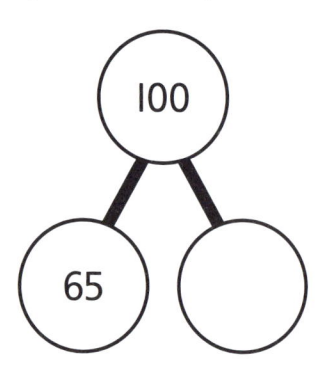

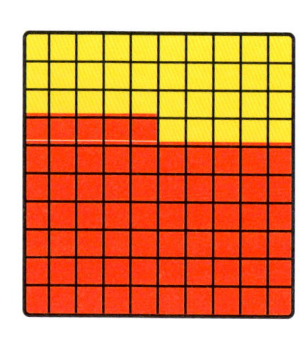

2 Find the missing numbers.

a)

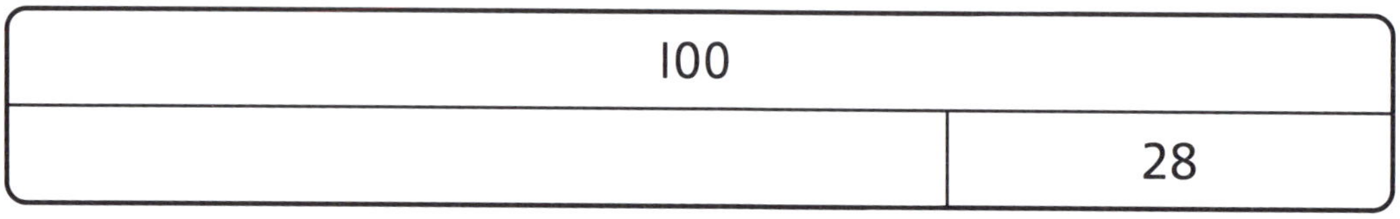

100	
	28

b)

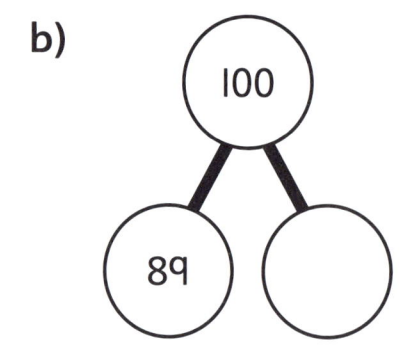

I used a 100 square to help me.

142

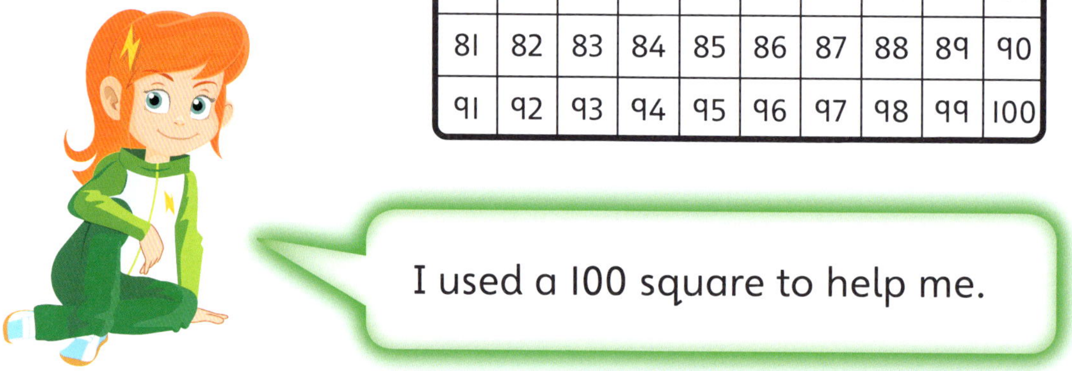

Unit 3: Addition and subtraction (2), Lesson 9

CHALLENGE

3 **a)** What is the missing number?

62 + ☐ = 100

Use the number line to help you.

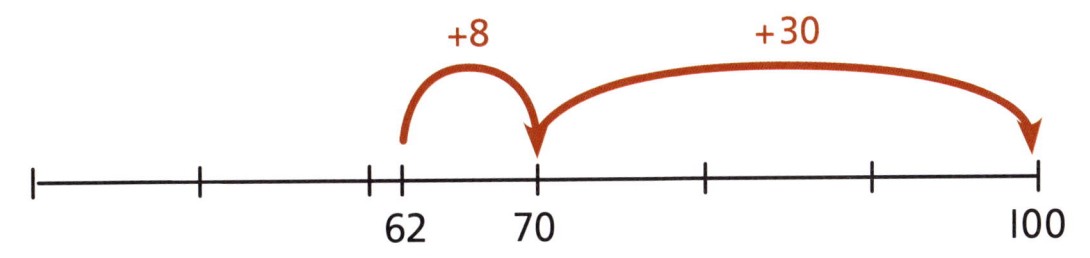

+8   +30

62   70   100

b) Work out the missing numbers.

37 + ☐ = 100

43 + ☐ = 100

☐ + 78 = 100

c) What mistake has been made?

44 + 66 = 100

First, I worked out what I needed to add to make the next 10.

→ Practice book 3A p104

143

Unit 3: Addition and subtraction (2), Lesson 10

Estimate answers

Discover

I need 595 matchsticks for my model.

Approx. 300 matchsticks

Approx. 200 matchsticks

Approx. 400 matchsticks

1 a) Ebo counts all of the matchsticks from one bag.
   There are exactly 211. Which bag did he count from?

   b) Ebo needs to use 2 bags to make his model.
   Which other bag should he use?

Share

a) Ebo has counted 211 matchsticks.

He has only used one bag.

I can use a number line to see that 211 is much closer to 200 than to 300.

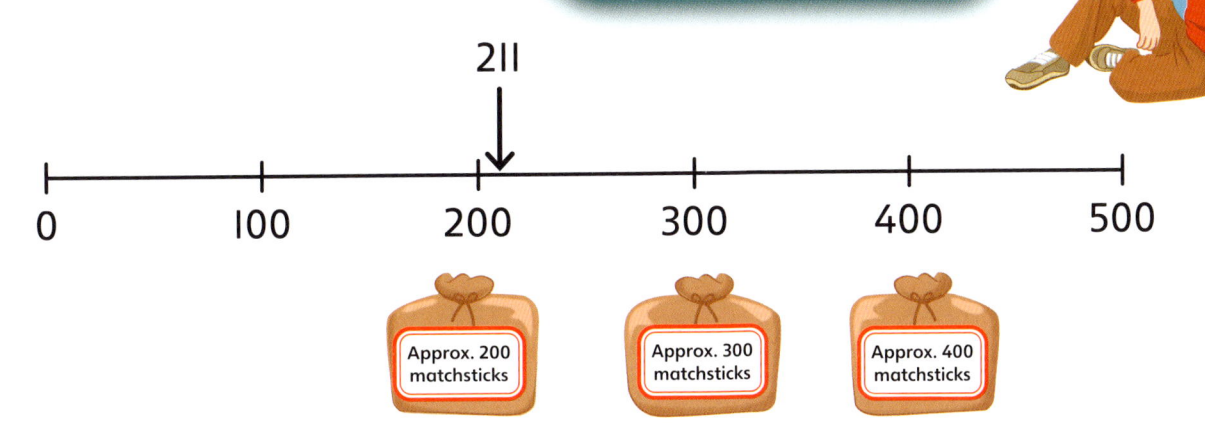

211

|—————|—————|—————|—————|—————|
0   100   200   300   400   500

Approx. 200 matchsticks   Approx. 300 matchsticks   Approx. 400 matchsticks

211 is **approximately** 200.

Ebo counted the bag that has approximately 200 matches.

'Approximately 200' means a number close to 200.

'Approx.' is short for 'approximately'.

b) Ebo needs 595 matchsticks, which is approximately 600. He already has approximately 200.

600 − 200 = 400.

Ebo needs 400 more.

He should use the bag with approximately 400 matchsticks.

145

Unit 3: Addition and subtraction (2), Lesson 10

Think together

1 Find an approximate answer to 381 + 398.

> I think the answer will be approximately 600, because I am adding 3 hundreds and 3 hundreds.

> I think the answer should be closer to 800, because both numbers are approximately 400.

Who do you agree with?

What approximation could you use to estimate the answer?

2

> I worked out 512 − 280 = 332
>
> Can I use approximation to check?

a) Is Alex's answer close to your estimate?

b) Should she try the calculation again?

146

Unit 3: Addition and subtraction (2), Lesson 10

3 There are two bags of flour.

Alex

"I estimate the total mass of the flour is 600 g."

"I estimate the difference in the masses is 200 g."

Alex has made some estimates about the masses of the bags of flour.

Which of the following could be the masses of the two bags of flour?

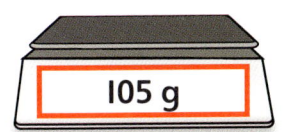

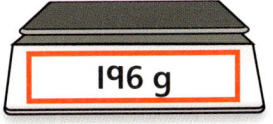

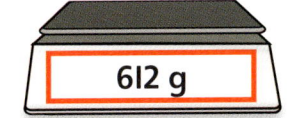

105 g   196 g   407 g   612 g

→ Practice book 3A p107

Unit 3: Addition and subtraction (2), Lesson 11

Inverse operations

Discover

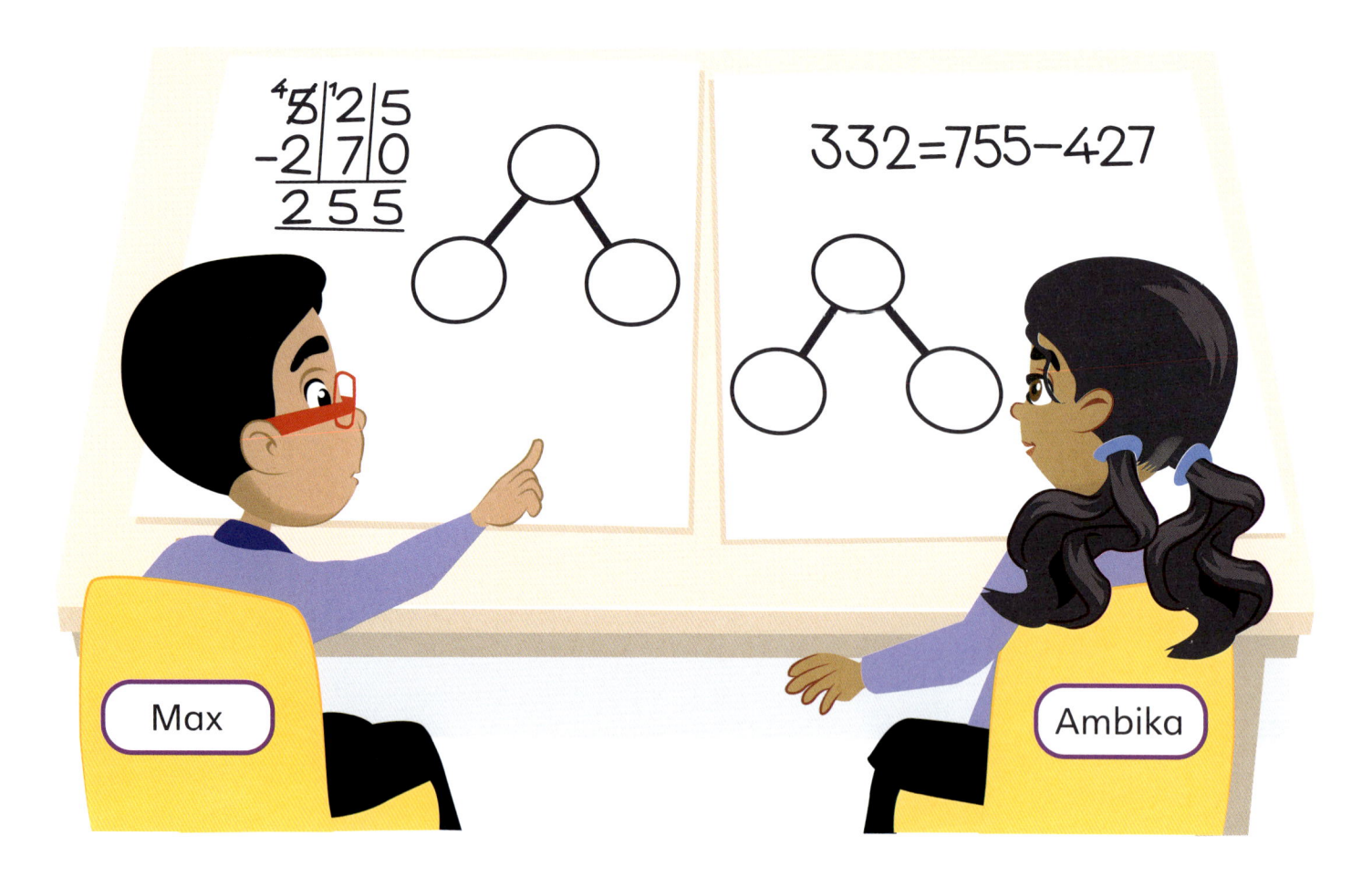

525 − 270 = 255

332 = 755 − 427

Max

Ambika

1 a) Use an addition to check Max's subtraction.

b) Use an addition to check Ambika's subtraction.

148

Share

a) 525 − 270 = 255

	H	T	O
	2	7	0
+	2	5	5
	5	2	5

525 → 270, 255

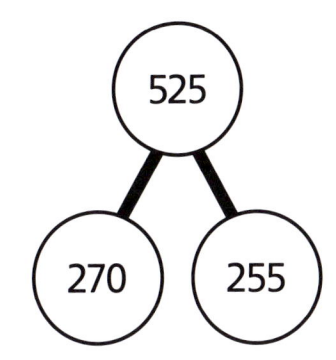

The addition for Max's calculation gives the same whole and parts. This shows it is correct.

b) Check Ambika's subtraction by adding.

	H	T	O
	4	2	7
+	3	3	2
	7	5	9

Ambika's subtraction is incorrect because when you add the parts you get a different whole.

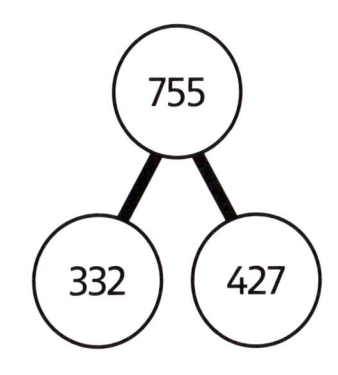

	H	T	O
	7	⁴5̸	¹5
−	4	2	7
	3	2	8

755 → 332, 427

755 − 427 = 328

so 328 = 755 − 427

149

Unit 3: Addition and subtraction (2), Lesson 11

Think together

1 One of these subtractions is incorrect.

Use an addition to check which one is correct.

a)
612 − 371 = 341

612 − 371 = 241

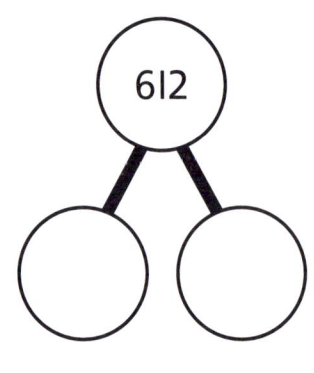

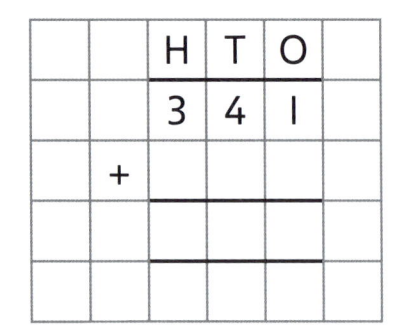

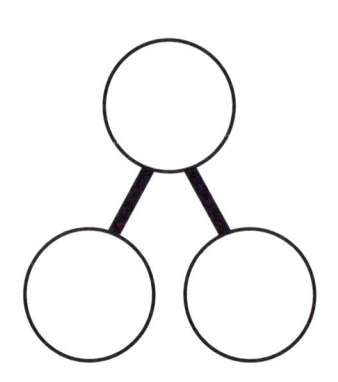

b) Use a subtraction to check this addition.

344 + 477 = 812

Unit 3: Addition and subtraction (2), Lesson 11

2. Emma has worked out 501 − 499 = 91.

	H	T	O
	⁴5̸	0	¹⁰1̸
−	4	9	9
	0	9	1

> That doesn't look right. 499 is approximately 500, so the answer should be close to 0.

a) What two mistakes has she made?

b) How could you work this out in your head?

CHALLENGE

3. Reena is working out this addition.

$$176 + 741$$

She gets the answer 917.

Discuss with a partner different ways you can check Reena's answer. Find as many ways as you can.

> I will look at what each number is close to and approximate.

> I will do a subtraction.

151

→ Practice book 3A p110

Unit 3: Addition and subtraction (2), Lesson 12

Problem solving (1)

Discover

1 a) Holly bought a racing bike and paid to have a service. How much did she spend in total?

b) Write an approximation to check the calculation.

Unit 3: Addition and subtraction (2), Lesson 12

Share

a) A bar model shows the parts and the whole clearly.

"I started by drawing a bar model to help see what I need to work out."

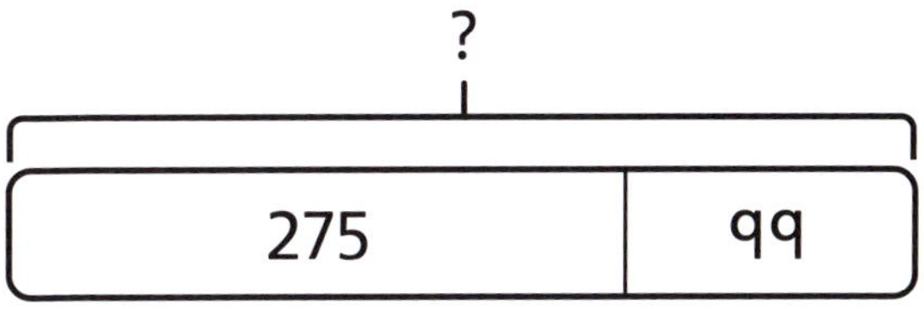

| 275 | 99 |

with ? above the whole.

```
  H T O
  2 7 5
+   9 9
  3 7 4
    1 1
```

"We know the parts but need to work out the whole. I added the parts together."

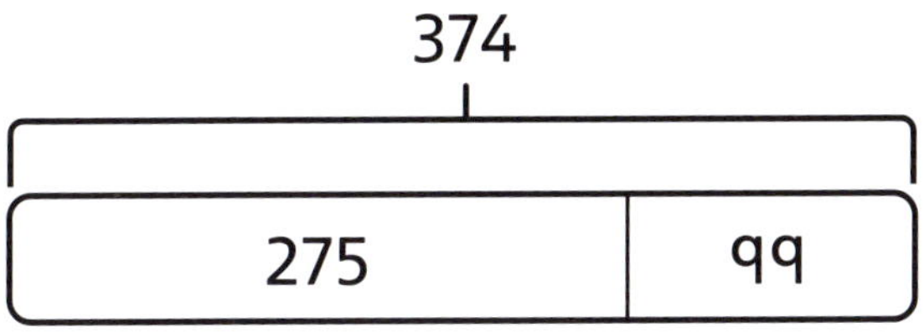

374
| 275 | 99 |

Holly spent £374 in total.

b) £99 is approximately £100.

£275 + £100 = £375

£375 is very close to £374.

The answer looks correct.

"I think I can approximate just one of the numbers."

153

Unit 3: Addition and subtraction (2), Lesson 12

Think together

1 At the same shop, Holly's dad bought her a mountain bike and a helmet.

How much did he spend?

Mountain bike £159

Helmet £25

	H	T	O
	1	5	9
+			

Holly's dad spent £☐.

2 A family bought a tandem and a child's bike. They spent £468.

How much did the child's bike cost?

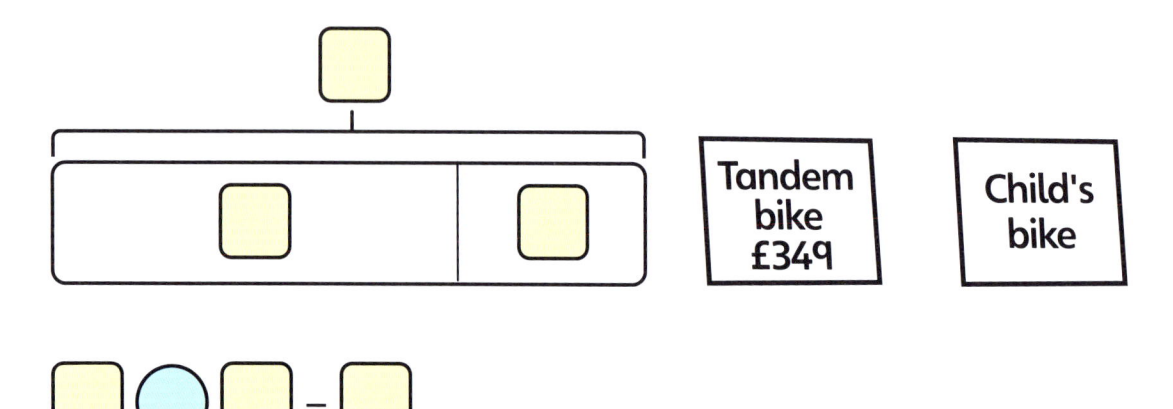

Tandem bike £349

Child's bike

☐ ◯ ☐ = ☐

The child's bike cost £☐.

Unit 3: Addition and subtraction (2), Lesson 12

CHALLENGE

3) a) Toshi bought a racing bike, a helmet and lights.

How much did he spend altogether?

Draw models to show the steps in this problem.

> Look at the picture of the bike shop to find the information you need.

> I think there are two steps, so I will try drawing two bar models.

> There are three numbers to add, so I will draw one bar model with three parts.

b) Sofia bought a bike and two helmets. The total was £399.

Which bike did she buy?

What models can you use to show the steps of this problem?

155

→ Practice book 3A p113

Unit 3: Addition and subtraction (2), Lesson 13

Problem solving (2)

Discover

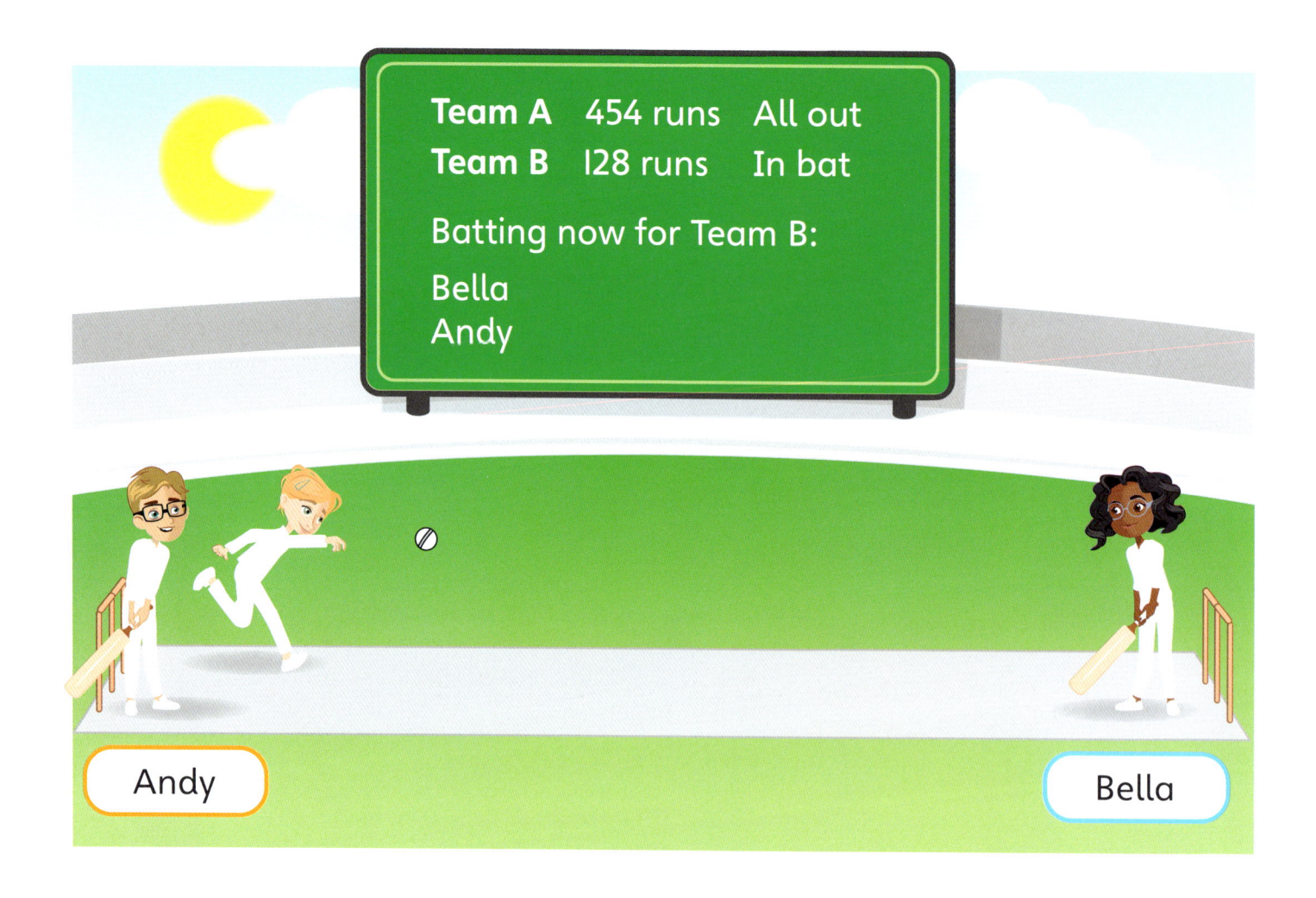

Team A   454 runs   All out
Team B   128 runs   In bat

Batting now for Team B:
Bella
Andy

Andy

Bella

1 a) How many more runs has Team A scored than Team B?

b) Bella and Andy start batting for Team B.

Bella scores 105 and Andy scores 83.

How many runs has Team B scored now?

Unit 3: Addition and subtraction (2), Lesson 13

Share

a) Team A has 454 runs. Team B has 128 runs.

I am comparing two numbers, so I drew two bars.

Team A: 454
Team B: 128 ⟵⟶ ?

	H	T	O
	4	⁴5̸	¹4
−	1	2	8
	3	2	6

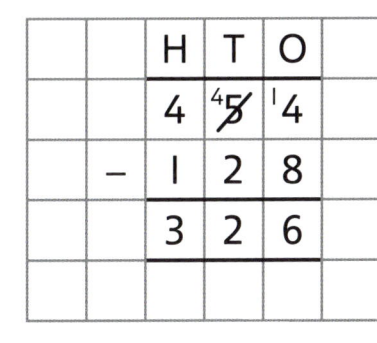

I needed to find the difference, so I subtracted.

454 − 128 = 326

Team A has scored 326 more runs than Team B.

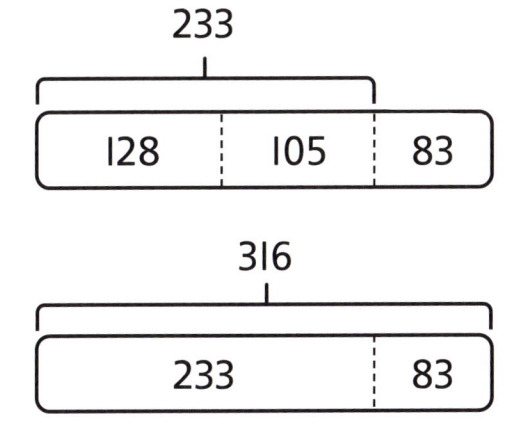

b) 128 + 105 = 233

233
| 128 | 105 | 83 |

316
| 233 | 83 |

I added in two steps. First, I added Bella's score. Then I added Andy's score to the total.

Team B has now scored 316 runs in total.

157

Unit 3: Addition and subtraction (2), Lesson 13

Think together

1 Aki's team scored 317 runs and Isla's team scored 451.

How many more runs did Isla's team score?

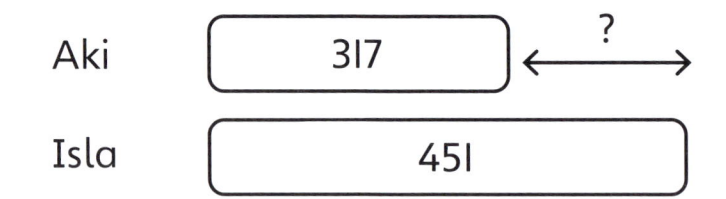

Aki | 317 | ⟷ ?

Isla | 451

Isla's team scored ☐ more runs than Aki's team.

2 Mo and Lexi scored 320 runs. Jamilla scores 165 and Emma scores 56.

How many more runs do Jamilla and Emma need in order to score the same as Mo and Lexi?

Mo and Lexi | 320

Jamilla and Emma | 165 | 56 | ⟷

Jamilla and Emma need ☐ more runs.

I wonder how I could check my answers on this page.

Unit 3: Addition and subtraction (2), Lesson 13

3 Richard scores 188 runs and Olivia scores 56 more than Richard.

How many runs do they score altogether?

I made a bar model with three parts.

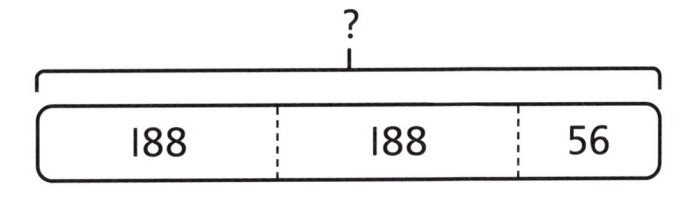

| 188 | 188 | 56 |

I made two bars to show that Olivia scored more than Richard.

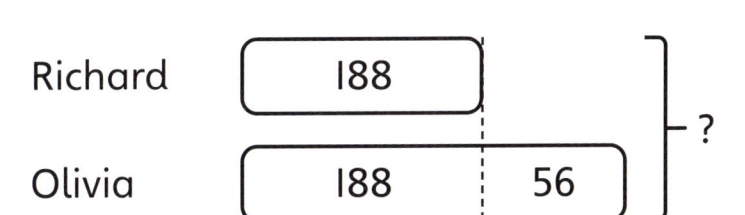

Richard | 188 |

Olivia | 188 | 56 | ?

Which bar model shows the problem better?

Copy the bar model and then solve the problem.

→ Practice book 3A p116

Unit 3: Addition and subtraction (2)

End of unit check

1 What is missing from this calculation?

333 ▢ = 353

A + 2   B + 200   C + 20   D − 20

2 Which addition exchanges 10 ones **and** 10 tens?

A
H	T	O
2	0	1
+3	0	9

B
H	T	O
4	1	0
+3	9	0

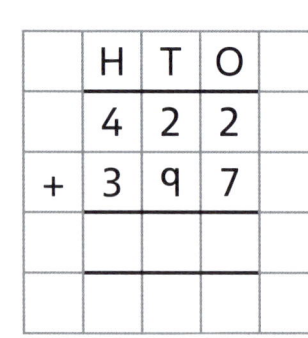

C
H	T	O
4	2	2
+3	9	7

D
H	T	O
4	1	2
+3	8	9

3 Which subtraction is not correct?

A
H	T	O
²3̸	¹5	0
− 1	8	0
1	7	0

B
H	T	O
²3̸	¹5	4
− 1	8	5
1	7	1

C
H	T	O
²3̸	¹5	5
− 1	8	4
1	7	1

D
H	T	O
3	8	5
− 2	1	5
1	7	0

160

Unit 3: Addition and subtraction (2)

4 Which calculation has an answer that is approximately 500?

A 901 – 399   B 401 + 198   C 350 + 248   D 999 – 598

5 Richard has done an addition to check his calculation.

325 + 476 =

Which calculation was he trying to solve?

A 476 – 325

B 325 – 476

C 801 – 325

D 801 – 376

6 Tim and Alanna each have a length of wool.

Tim's wool is 500 cm long.

Alanna cuts 175 cm off her wool. Now it is the same length as Tim's.

How long was Alanna's wool to start with?

161

→ Practice book 3A p119

Unit 4
Multiplication and division 1

In this unit we will …
- Recognise unequal groups
- Understand how an array can show two multiplications
- Work out multiples of 2, 5 and 10

In Year 2, we recognised when groups were equal and unequal.

Equal groups

Unequal groups

We will need some maths words. How many of these have you used before?

equal   multiply   divide   multiple

times-tables   sharing   grouping

array   bar model

repeated addition   commutative

You need to know that an array can tell you two different multiplication facts.

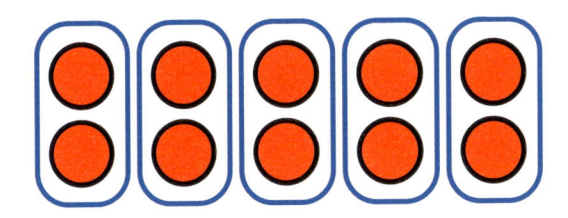

5 groups of 2

$5 \times 2 = 10$

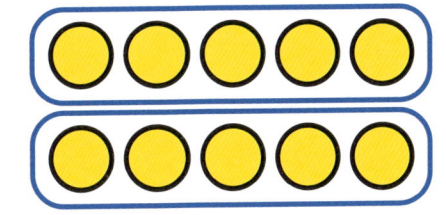

2 groups of 5

$2 \times 5 = 10$

Unit 4: Multiplication and division (1), Lesson 1

Multiplication – equal groups

Discover

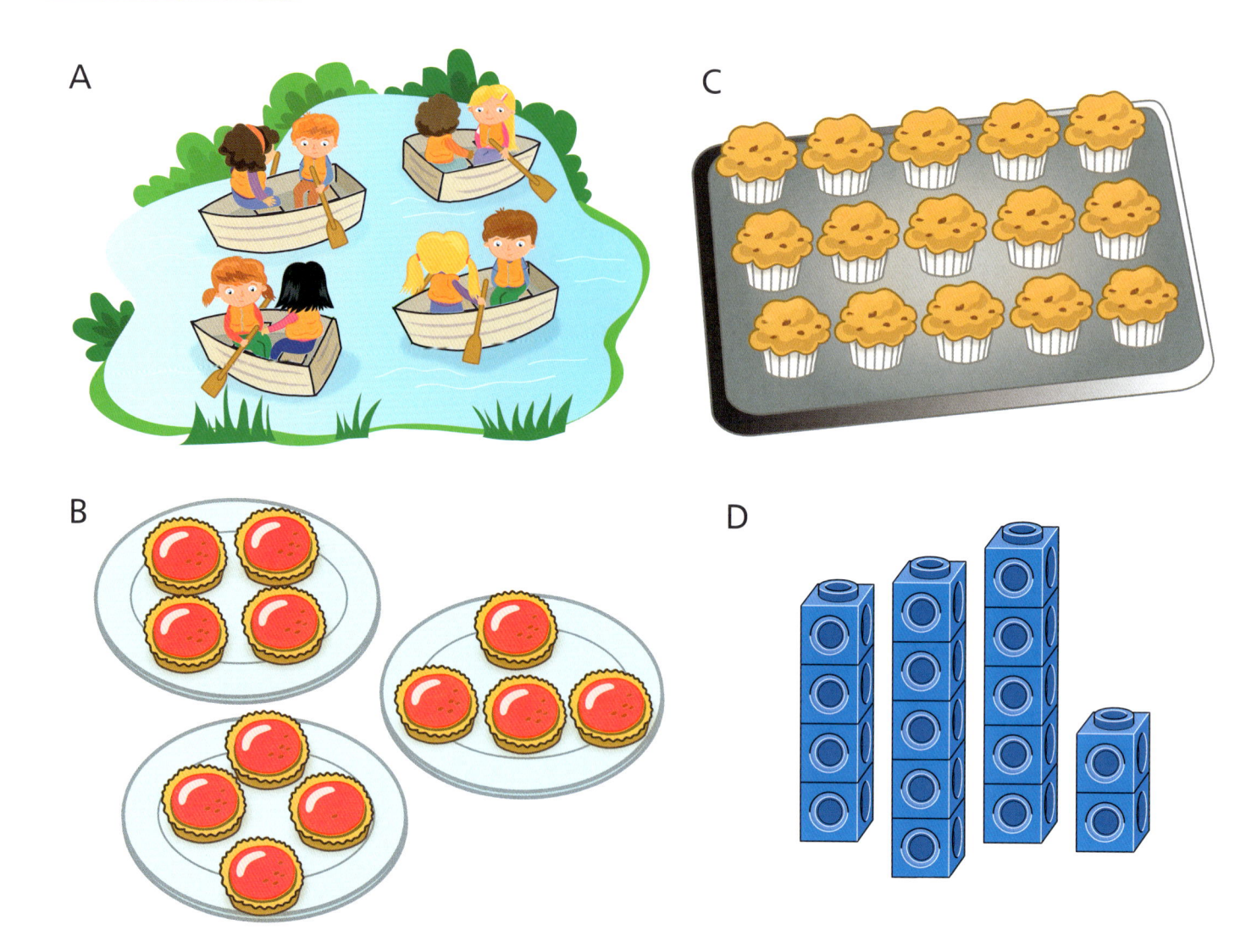

A

B

C

D

1 a) Can you see 4 groups of 2?

Write this as a **repeated addition** and multiplication.

b) Can you see 3 groups of 5?

Write this as a multiplication.

164

Share

a) There are 4 boats of children.

There is a group of 2 children in each boat.

There are 4 groups of 2.

2 + 2 + 2 + 2 = 8

4 × 2 = 8

I can see the total number of children is 8.

b) There are 3 groups (rows) of 5 muffins on the tray.

3 × 5 = 15

I can see 3 rows of 5 muffins. So the total is 15.

Unit 4: Multiplication and division (1), Lesson 1

Think together

1) How many counters are there in total?

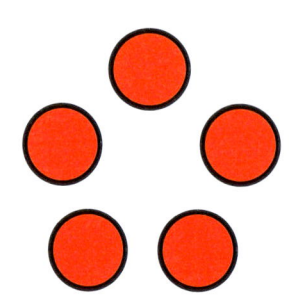

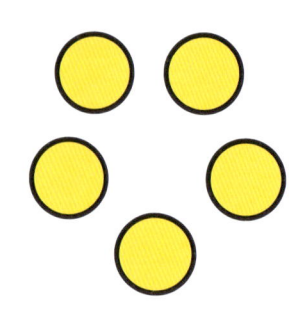

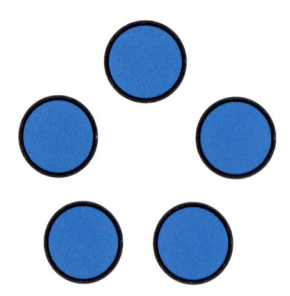

Write a multiplication to work out how many counters.

☐ × ☐ = ☐

2) Write a multiplication to work out how many jam tarts in total.

☐ × ☐ = ☐

The groups don't look the same, but are they *equal*?

Unit 4: Multiplication and division (1), Lesson 1

CHALLENGE

3

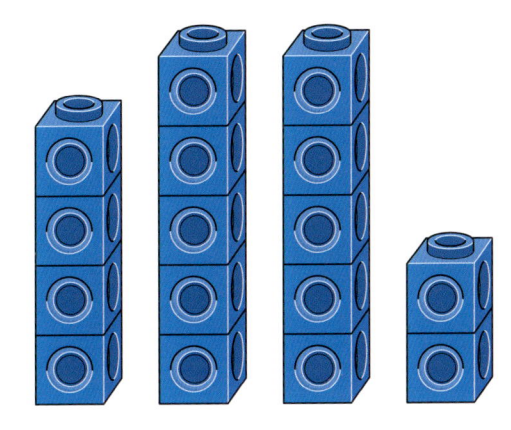

a) Explain why this does not show equal groups.

b) How can you make the groups equal?

I wonder if I can use the same number of cubes to make a different number of equal groups.

I am going to rebuild the towers and try to make them equal.

→ Practice book 3A p121

Unit 4: Multiplication and division (1), Lesson 2

Use arrays

Discover

"We both have 20 counters. We each need to make an array."

Aki   Max

1) a) Complete the array for Max.

   Write down a multiplication for the array.

   b) Arrange the same number of counters into a different array.

Share

a) There are 20 counters.

The counters can be arranged into a 4 rows of 5 counters. That's 4 lots of 5.

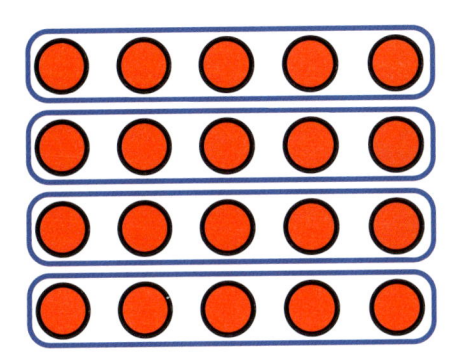

Multiplication is **commutative**. You can write the numbers in either order. You get the same answer.

You can also think of this as 5 columns of 4 counters.

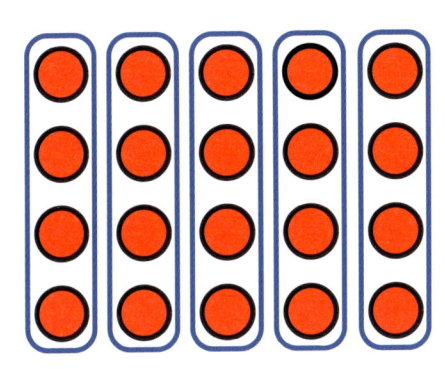

The array shows the multiplication 4 × 5 = 20 or 5 × 4 = 20.

I have arranged my counters in 2 rows of 10.

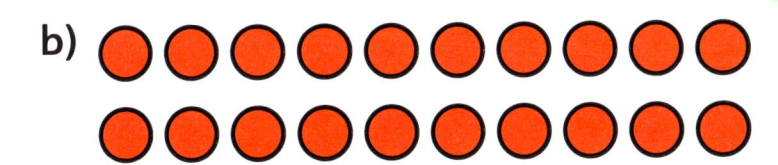

b)

This array shows 2 × 10 = 20 or 10 × 2 = 20.

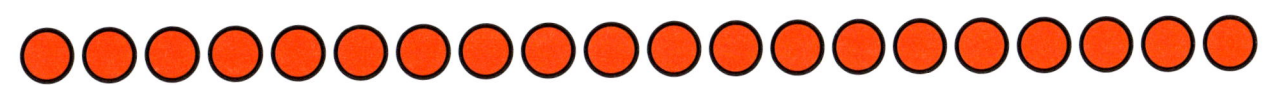

This shows 1 × 20 or 20 × 1 array.

169

Unit 4: Multiplication and division (1), Lesson 2

Think together

1 What two multiplications does this array show?

☐ × ☐ = ☐

☐ × ☐ = ☐

2 How many counters are there in total?

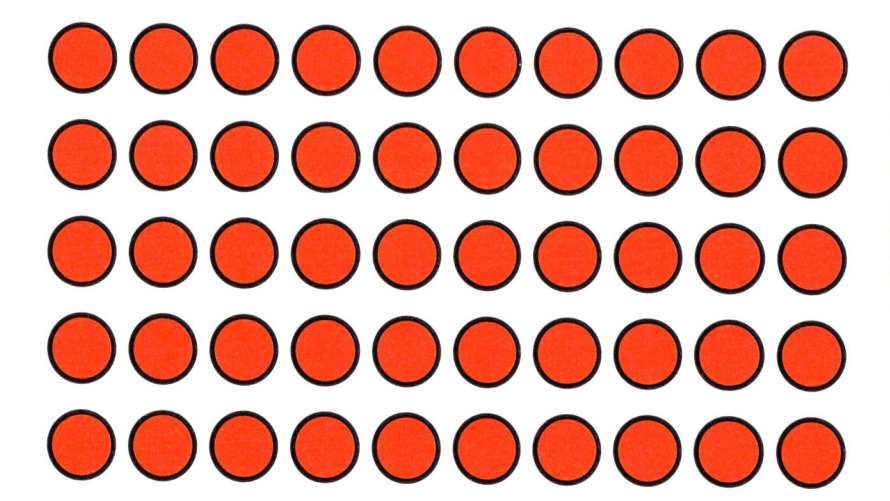

I think I can find the total with more than one multiplication.

Unit 4: Multiplication and division (1), Lesson 2

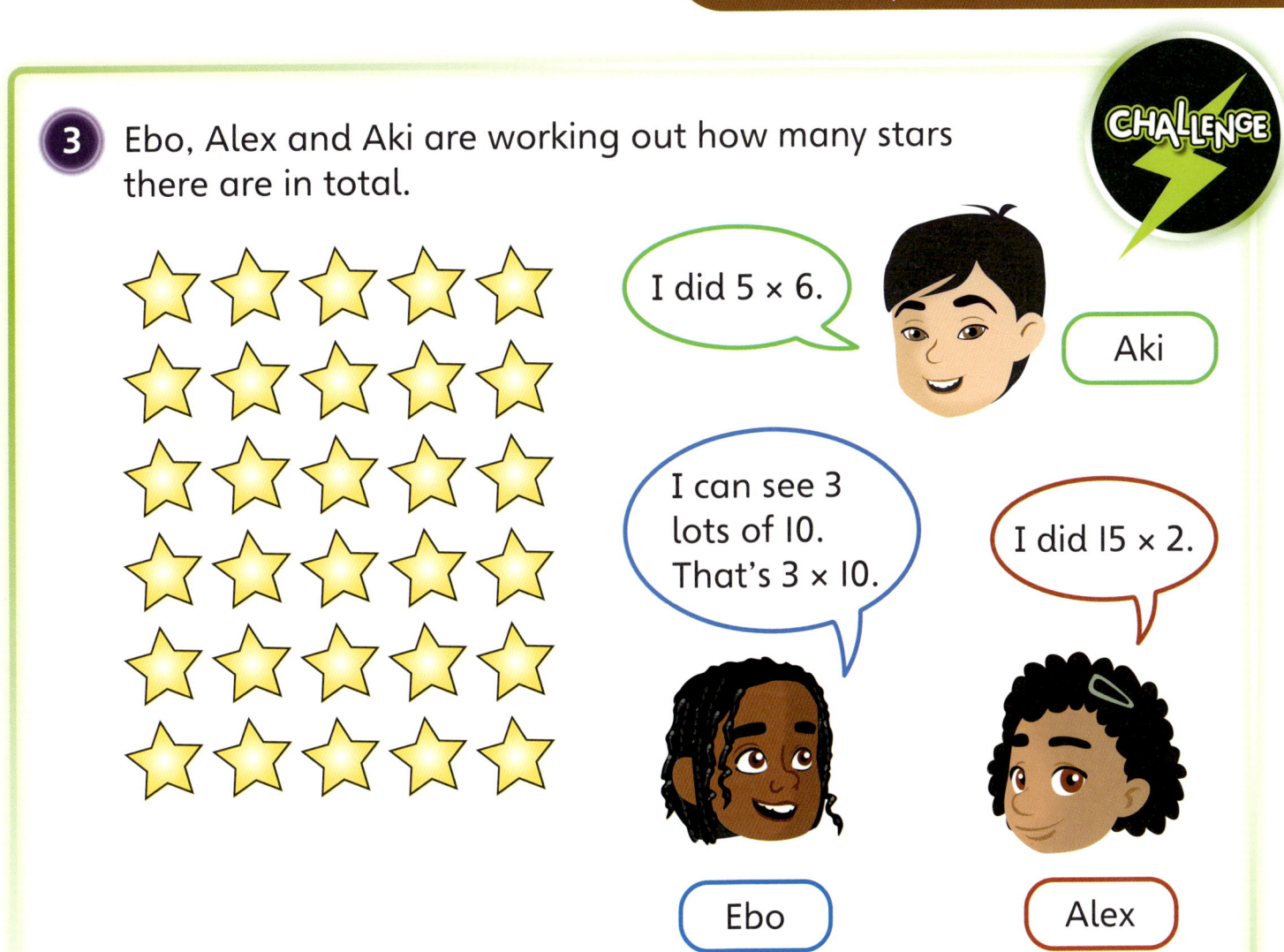

CHALLENGE

3) Ebo, Alex and Aki are working out how many stars there are in total.

Aki: "I did 5 × 6."

Ebo: "I can see 3 lots of 10. That's 3 × 10."

Alex: "I did 15 × 2."

For each person, circle the groups with your finger.

Can you see any other equal groups?

"I remember that 3 × 10 means 3 groups of 10. I can see 3 groups of 10."

"I wonder if they all get the same answer."

171

→ Practice book 3A p124

Unit 4: Multiplication and division (1), Lesson 3

Multiples of 2

Discover

Multiples of 2 are numbers that are in the 2 times-table.

1 a) Point to or colour in the first ten numbers in the 2 times-table.

b) Colour in all the multiples of 2 on a 100 square.
Use a different colour.

What do you notice?

Share

a)

1	2	3	4	5	6	7	8	9	10
11	12	13	14	15	16	17	18	19	20
21	22	23	24	25	26	27	28	29	30
31	32	33	34	35	36	37	38	39	40
41	42	43	44	45	46	47	48	49	50
51	52	53	54	55	56	57	58	59	60
61	62	63	64	65	66	67	68	69	70
71	72	73	74	75	76	77	78	79	80
81	82	83	84	85	86	87	88	89	90
91	92	93	94	95	96	97	98	99	100

I went through my 2 times-table, so $1 \times 2 = 2$ ...

b)

1	2	3	4	5	6	7	8	9	10
11	12	13	14	15	16	17	18	19	20
21	22	23	24	25	26	27	28	29	30
31	32	33	34	35	36	37	38	39	40
41	42	43	44	45	46	47	48	49	50
51	52	53	54	55	56	57	58	59	60
61	62	63	64	65	66	67	68	69	70
71	72	73	74	75	76	77	78	79	80
81	82	83	84	85	86	87	88	89	90
91	92	93	94	95	96	97	98	99	100

I can see that all the coloured numbers are in the same columns.

All the coloured numbers end with 0, 2, 4, 6 or 8.

Unit 4: Multiplication and division (1), Lesson 3

Think together

1) What are the missing numbers?

| 12 | 14 | 16 | | | | | | |

| 72 | 74 | 76 | | | | | | |

2) Which number cards show multiples of 2?

56   30   ☒8   87   134

One of the numbers has a digit covered. I'm not sure I can tell if it's a multiple of 2.

But we can still see the 1s digit.

Unit 4: Multiplication and division (1), Lesson 3

CHALLENGE

3) Here are some digit cards.

| 4 | 7 | 8 |

Remember, an even number is a multiple of 2.

a) Mo uses two of the cards to make a 2-digit number.

How many even 2-digit numbers can Mo make?

b) Mo now uses all three cards to make a 3-digit number.

How many even numbers can he make?

There might be an easy way to check if a number is even.

I will check the last digit I used.

175

→ Practice book 3A p127

Unit 4: Multiplication and division (1), Lesson 4

Multiples of 5 and 10

Discover

1 a) Where are all the multiples of 10?

What do you notice about the multiples of 10?

b) The numbers covered with stars all come from the same times-table. Which one?

Share

a)

1	2	3	4	5	6	7	8	9	**10**
11	12	13	14	15	16	17	18	19	**20**
21	22	23	24	25	26	27	28	29	**30**
31	32	33	34	35	36	37	38	39	**40**
41	42	43	44	45	46	47	48	49	**50**
51	52	53	54	55	56	57	58	59	**60**
61	62	63	64	65	66	67	68	69	**70**
71	72	73	74	75	76	77	78	79	**80**
81	82	83	84	85	86	87	88	89	**90**
91	92	93	94	95	96	97	98	99	**100**

I can see that the numbers in the last column end in 0. They are all multiples of 10.

b)

1	2	3	4	5	6	7	8	9	10
11	12	13	14	★	16	17	18	19	20
21	22	23	24	★	26	27	28	29	★
31	32	33	34	35	36	37	38	39	★
41	42	43	44	★	46	47	48	49	50
51	52	53	54	★	56	57	58	59	★
61	62	63	64	65	66	67	68	69	★
71	72	73	74	75	76	77	78	79	80
81	82	83	84	★	86	87	88	89	90
91	92	93	94	95	96	97	98	99	★

Numbers that end in 0 and 5 are all in the 5 times-table.

The covered numbers are 15, 25, 30, 40, 45, 55, 60, 70, 85 and 100.

All the numbers end in 0 or 5.

Unit 4: Multiplication and division (1), Lesson 4

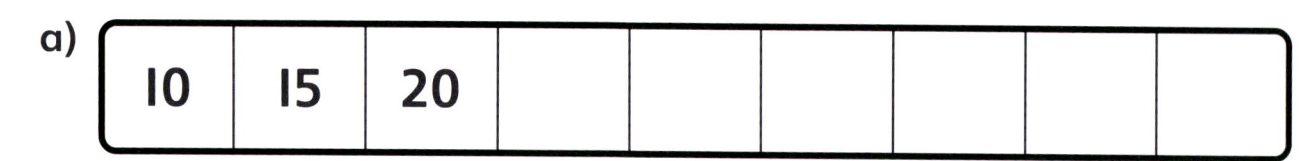

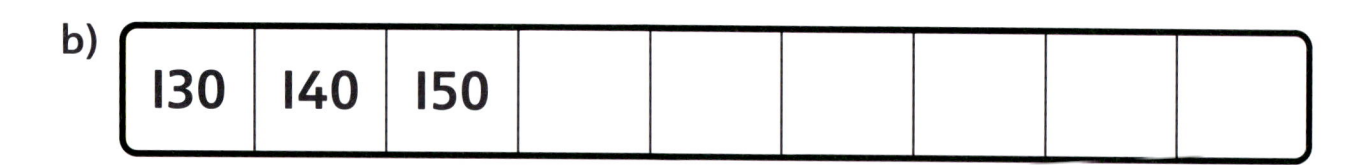

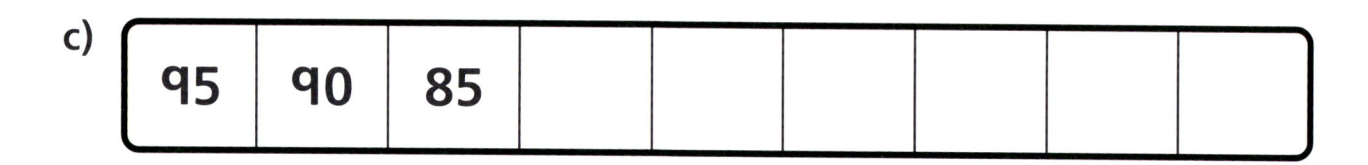

Think together

1 What are the missing numbers?

a) | 10 | 15 | 20 | | | | | | |

b) | 130 | 140 | 150 | | | | | | |

c) | 95 | 90 | 85 | | | | | | |

2 Emma has these digit cards.

| 0 | | 5 | | 8 |

a) How many 2-digit multiples of 5 can she make?

b) How many 2-digit multiples of 10 can she make?

c)
> I can make more 3-digit multiples of 10 than 2-digit multiples of 10.

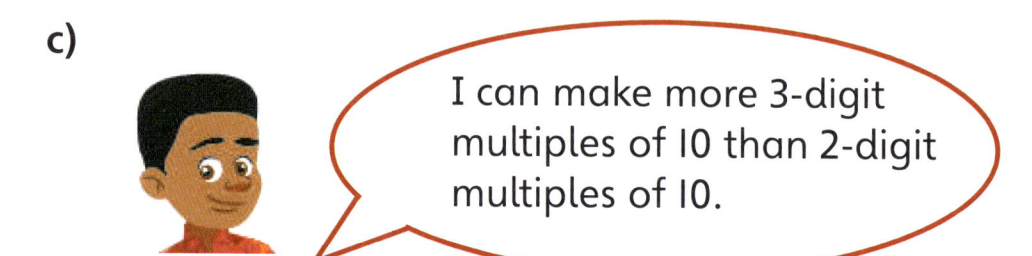

Do you agree with Lee? Explain your answer.

178

Unit 4: Multiplication and division (1), Lesson 4

CHALLENGE

3) Here are some number cards.

| 63 | 70 | 95 | 120 | 158 | 300 |

Put the numbers into the correct part of the table.

	Multiple of 5	Not multiple of 5
Even numbers		
Odd numbers		

I'm going to try to write my own cards to put in the table.

I wonder if there are any multiples of 5 that are not multiples of 10.

179

→ Practice book 3A p130

Unit 4: Multiplication and division (1), Lesson 5

Share and group

Discover

Amal

1 **a)** Amal has 20 flowers.

He shares the flowers equally between the 5 vases.

How many flowers are in each vase?

b) Write this as a division.

Share

a) **Method 1**

I took 20 flowers and 5 vases. I put 1 flower in each vase. Then I repeated this until I had no flowers left.

Method 2

20

There are 5 flowers in each vase.

I used a bar model. I shared 20 into 5 equal parts.

These are both examples of division by sharing.

b) There are 20 flowers and there are 5 vases.

To work out how many are in each vase we do 20 ÷ 5.

There are 4 flowers in each vase, 20 ÷ 5 = 4.

Unit 4: Multiplication and division (1), Lesson 5

Think together

1 Danny has 10 apples.

He shares them with his friend Bella.

How many apples do they have each?

2 Danny has another 10 apples.

He puts the apples into bags.

He puts 2 apples in each bag.

How many bags does he need?

Unit 4: Multiplication and division (1), Lesson 5

CHALLENGE

3) Lee is making up two word problems for this division.

15 ÷ 3 = 5

What does each number in the division represent for each problem? Lee's first word problem is:

> Paul has 15 sweets.
> He shares them between 3 children.
> How many sweets do they each get?

Lee's second word problem is:

> Paul has 15 sweets.
> He puts them into groups of 3.
> How many groups are there?

Work out the answers to Lee's word problems.

I think one of these is an example of sharing and one is an example of grouping.

I am going to use a bar model to solve each problem. Then I will see the difference between them.

→ Practice book 3A p133

Unit 4: Multiplication and division (1)

End of unit check

1 Which image does not show equal groups?

A

B

C

D

2 Which multiplication is represented by the array?

A 5 × 2
B 4 × 5
C 20 × 0
D 4 × 6

3 Which of these is not a multiple of 2?

A 6
B 12
C 20
D 21

4 What number should be in the square marked with a triangle?

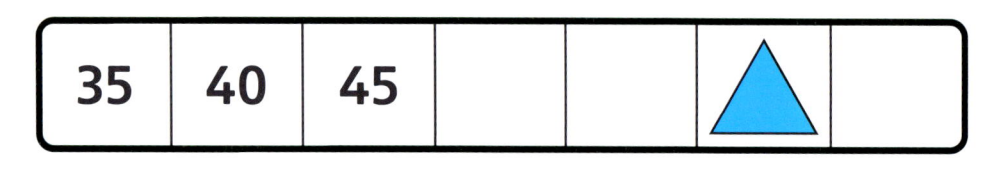

| 35 | 40 | 45 | | | △ | |

A 5
B 6
C 50
D 60

184

Unit 4: Multiplication and division (1)

5 Apples are packed into bags of 5.

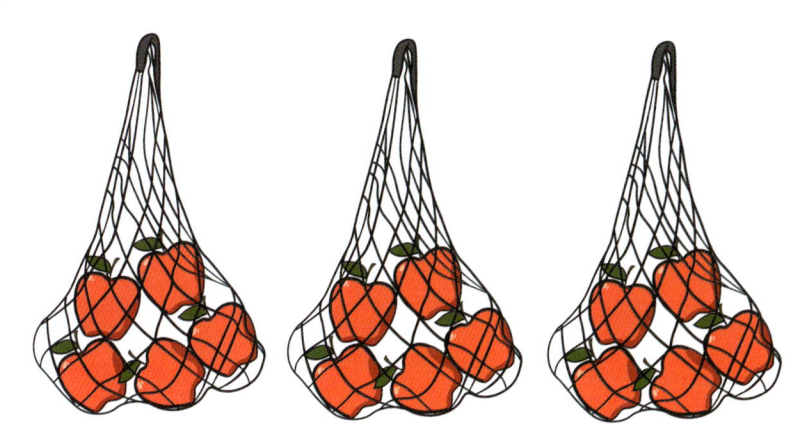

How many apples are there in total?

- **A** 3
- **B** 5
- **C** 8
- **D** 15

6 Max has 10 pencils.

He shares the pencils equally between 5 of his friends.

How many pencils do each of his friends get?

7 Isla is making 3-digit numbers using the digit cards below.

| 5 | 3 | 8 |

a) What is the largest 3-digit even number Isla can make?

b) What is the largest 3-digit multiple of 5 Isla can make?

c) Can Isla make a 3-digit number that is a multiple of 10?

➔ Practice book 3A p136

Unit 5
Multiplication and division ➋

In this unit we will …

- ⚡ Learn the 3, 4 and 8 times-tables
- ⚡ Find a simple remainder when a number is divided
- ⚡ Use a bar model to solve multiplication and division problems

We will use bar models to help solve multiplication and division problems.

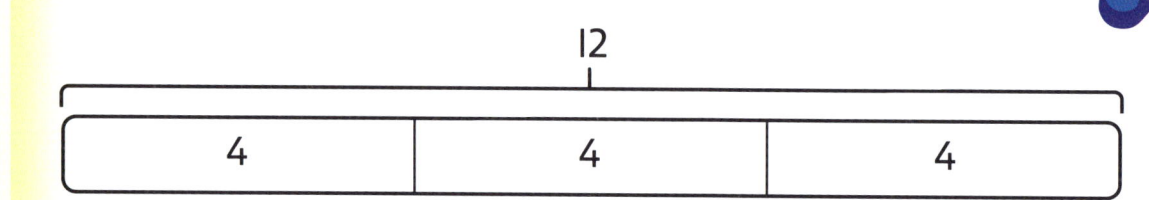

12
4	4	4

"We will need some maths words. How many of these have you used before?"

- equal
- multiply
- divide
- multiple
- times-tables
- sharing
- grouping
- array
- bar model
- repeated addition
- multiplication sentence
- multiplication fact
- division sentence
- division fact
- remainder

"We need to use number lines too. These will help us understand multiplication and division."

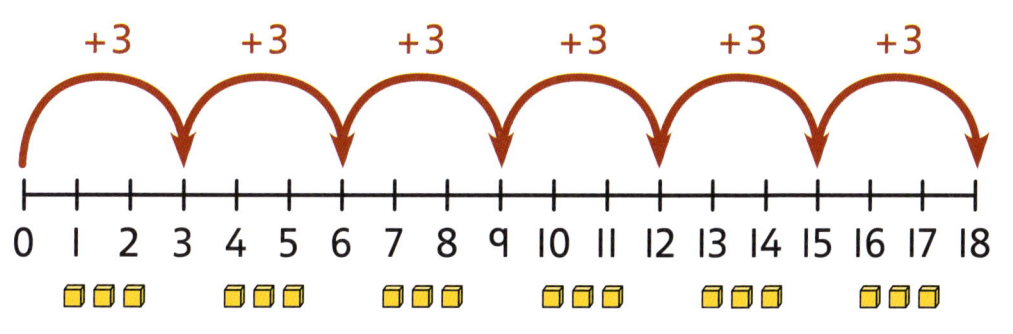

+3 +3 +3 +3 +3 +3

0 1 2 3 4 5 6 7 8 9 10 11 12 13 14 15 16 17 18

187

Unit 5: Multiplication and division (2), Lesson 1

Multiply by 3

Discover

1 a) There are 3 balls under each cup.

How many balls are there in total?

Write down a **multiplication sentence** to work out the answer.

b) Work out 8 × 3.

Share

I could count them one by one.

a) Under each cup there are 3 balls.

I did a repeated addition, using a number line to help me.

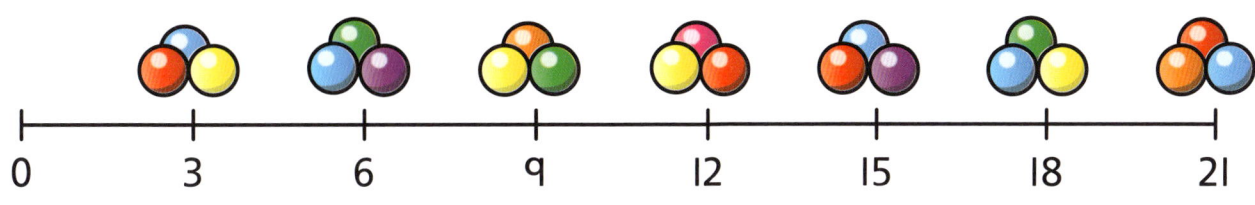

3 + 3 + 3 + 3 + 3 + 3 + 3 = 21

7 × 3 = 21

There are 21 balls in total.

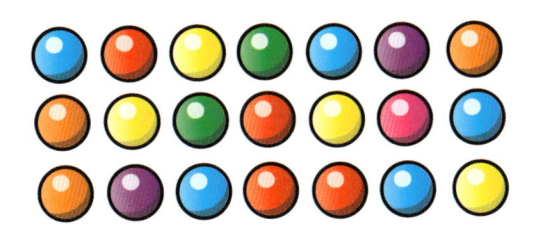

Now I know 7 groups of 3, I can easily work out 8 groups of 3.

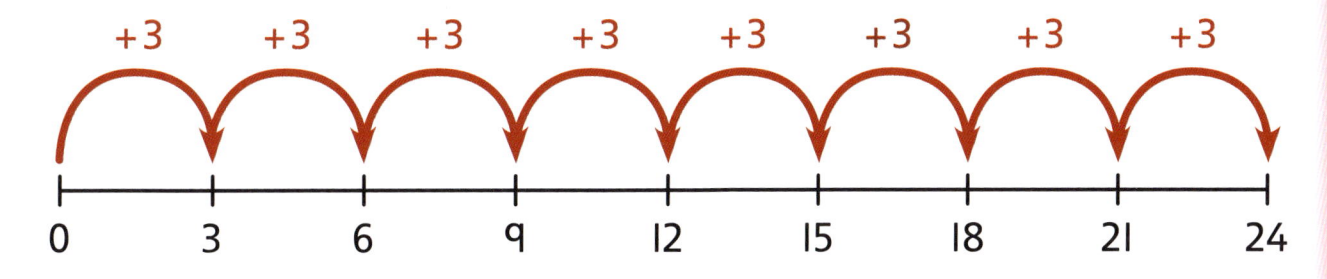

This is a 7 × 3 array. 7 × 3 = 21

b) 8 × 3 = 24

189

Unit 5: Multiplication and division (2), Lesson 1

Think together

1 There are 3 balls under each cup.

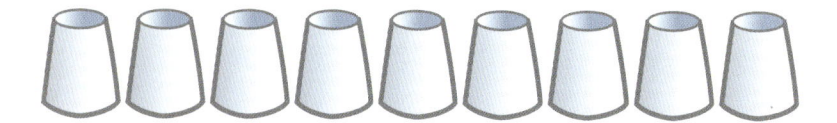

How many balls are there?

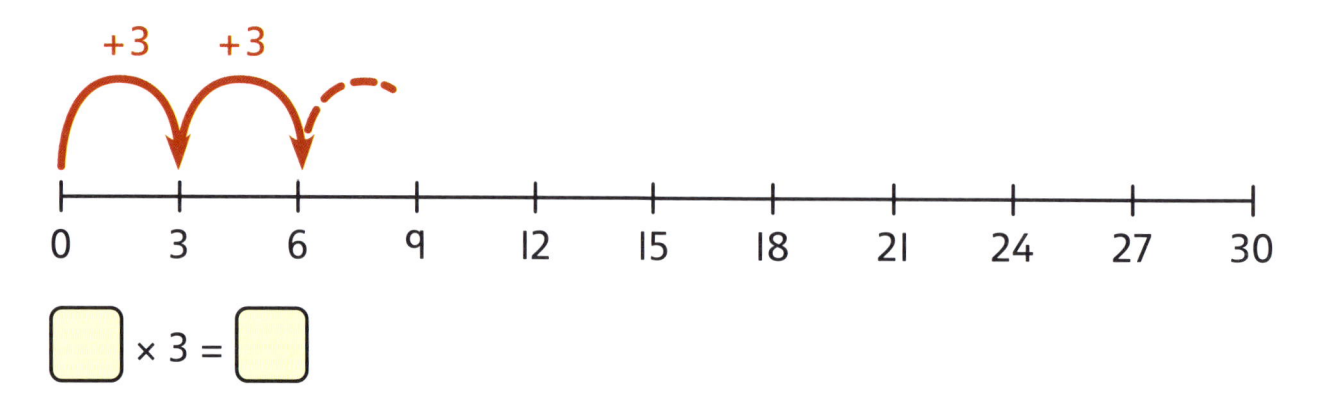

☐ × 3 = ☐

2 How many hats are there?

☐ × ☐ = ☐

190

Unit 5: Multiplication and division (2), Lesson 1

CHALLENGE

3) What is the same? What is different?

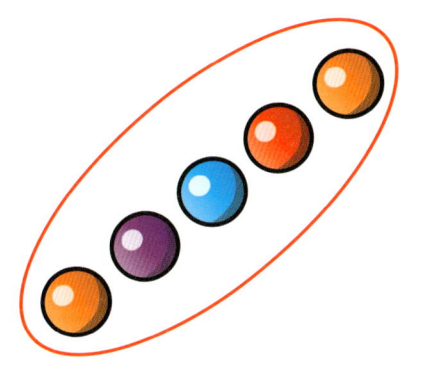

Discuss with a partner.

> I think they all have the same number of objects.

> There are 3 groups of 5 marbles. I wonder if they could make equal groups a different way.

→ Practice book 3A p138

Unit 5: Multiplication and division (2), Lesson 2

Divide by 3

Discover

1 a) Each box holds 3 cupcakes.

How many boxes are needed for all the cupcakes?

Work this out by writing a **division sentence**.

b) David buys 27 cakes. He shares them equally between 3 people.

How many cakes do they get each?

Unit 5: Multiplication and division (2), Lesson 2

Share

a) There are 18 cupcakes.

Each box holds 3 cupcakes.

If I put 3 cupcakes into each box, I have 3 fewer each time. I will use a number line to jump back.

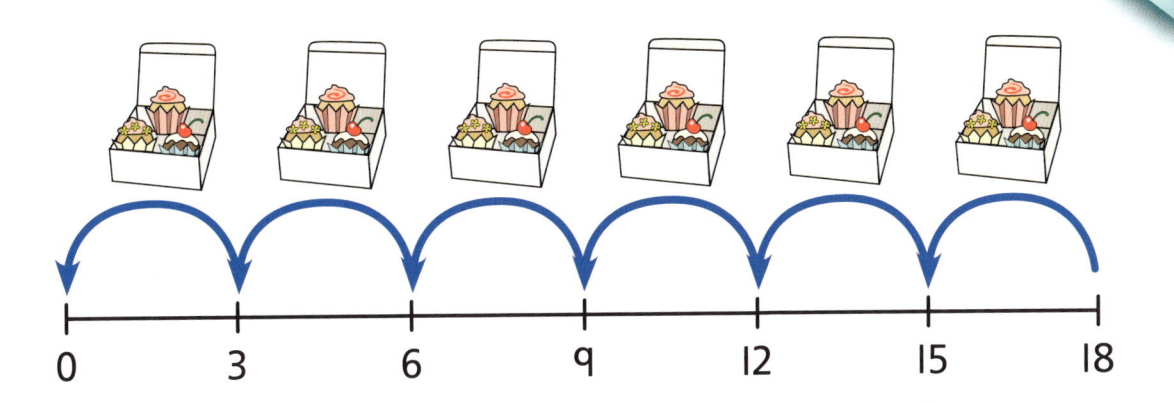

18 ÷ 3 = 6

6 boxes are needed.

I shared them out 1 at a time. I could have shared them 3 at a time.

b)

There are 27 cakes.

There are 3 people.

Each person gets 9 cakes.

27 ÷ 3 = 9

193

Unit 5: Multiplication and division (2), Lesson 2

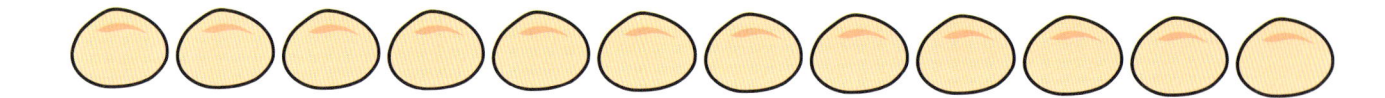

Think together

1) Bread rolls are packed in 3s.

How many packs can be made?

There are ☐ bread rolls.

There are 3 bread rolls in each pack.

☐ ÷ 3 = ☐

2) 21 doughnuts are shared equally between 3 plates.

How many doughnuts will go on each plate?

☐ ÷ ☐ = ☐

Unit 5: Multiplication and division (2), Lesson 2

CHALLENGE

3 Class 3A have been set a question.

$$33 \div 3$$

Here are three different methods.

Zac: I took 33 counters and put them into groups of 3.

Olivia: I drew an array to help me.

Lee: I am going to use a multiplication fact that I know off by heart to get the answer.

Explain how each child got the answer.

Which method do you prefer? What other method could you use?

I prefer Zac's method because you have to make groups of 3 for division.

I wonder if you could also use sharing.

195

→ Practice book 3A p141

Unit 5: Multiplication and division (2), Lesson 3

The 3 times-table

Discover

36 ÷ 3 = 12   12 × 3 = 36
33 ÷ 3 = 11   11 × 3 = ☐
30 ÷ 3 = 10   10 × 3 = 30
27 ÷ 3 = 9   9 × 3 = 27
24 ÷ 3 = 8   8 × 3 = 24
21 ÷ 3 = 7   7 × 3 = 21
18 ÷ 3 = ☐   6 × 3 = 18
15 ÷ 3 = 5   5 × 3 = 15
12 ÷ 3 = 4   4 × 3 = ☐
9 ÷ 3 = ☐   3 × 3 = 9
6 ÷ 3 = 2   2 × 3 = 6
3 ÷ 3 = 1   1 × 3 = 3

1. a) What are the missing answers?
How did you work them out?

b) Which multiplication fact can help you work out the total number of bananas shown?

196

Share

a) First look at the multiplications.

I will draw each as an array to help me work them out.

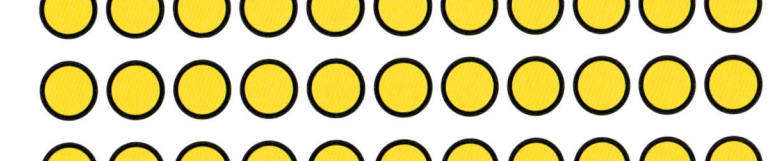

4 × 3 = 12   11 × 3 = 33

Now look at the divisions.

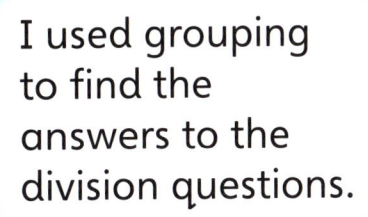

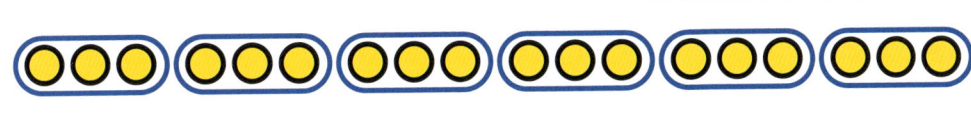

I used grouping to find the answers to the division questions.

9 ÷ 3 = 3

18 ÷ 3 = 6

You can use multiplication facts to help you. If 6 × 3 = 18, then 18 ÷ 3 = 6. Can you see the link?

b)

5 × 3 = 15

Unit 5: Multiplication and division (2), Lesson 3

Think together

1 Use multiplication facts to work out how many items there are in each picture.

Which fact did you use to find each total?

a)

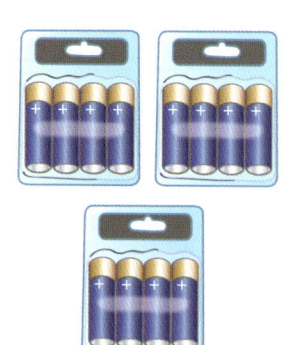

☐ ◯ ☐ = ☐

b)

☐ ◯ ☐ = ☐

2 How many of these can you work out in one minute?

11 × 3	9 × 3	0 × 3	12 ÷ 3
3 × 7	8 multiplied by 3	☐ × 3 = 36	multiply 2 by 3
divide 30 by 3	3 × ☐ = 18	24 ÷ 3	number of questions in this grid

It is not always important to be quick, but knowing your multiplication facts can help save time.

198

Unit 5: Multiplication and division (2), Lesson 3

3 **a)** Find two different methods to work out 12 × 3.

CHALLENGE

Emma: I know 6 × 3 = 18, but I don't know 12 × 3 in my head.

Luis: I know how you can work it out.

Which method do you prefer?

Which method is quicker?

If Emma already knows 6 × 3 = 18, then I think she can work it out.

b) How can you work these out using the 3 times-table?

3 × 3 × 3 = ☐

13 × 3 = ☐

3 × 20 = ☐

I wonder how many 3 times-table facts I know off by heart. I will cover them up and see if I can remember them.

→ Practice book 3A p144

Unit 5: Multiplication and division (2), Lesson 4

Multiply by 4

Discover

1. a) There are 6 donkeys.

    How many donkey legs are there in total?

    Write a multiplication sentence to work out the answer.

   b) A family of 5 people are going donkey trekking.

    Mr Peters pays 20 £1 coins in total for him and his family.

    Is this the correct amount?

Share

a) There are 6 donkeys.

Each donkey has 4 legs.

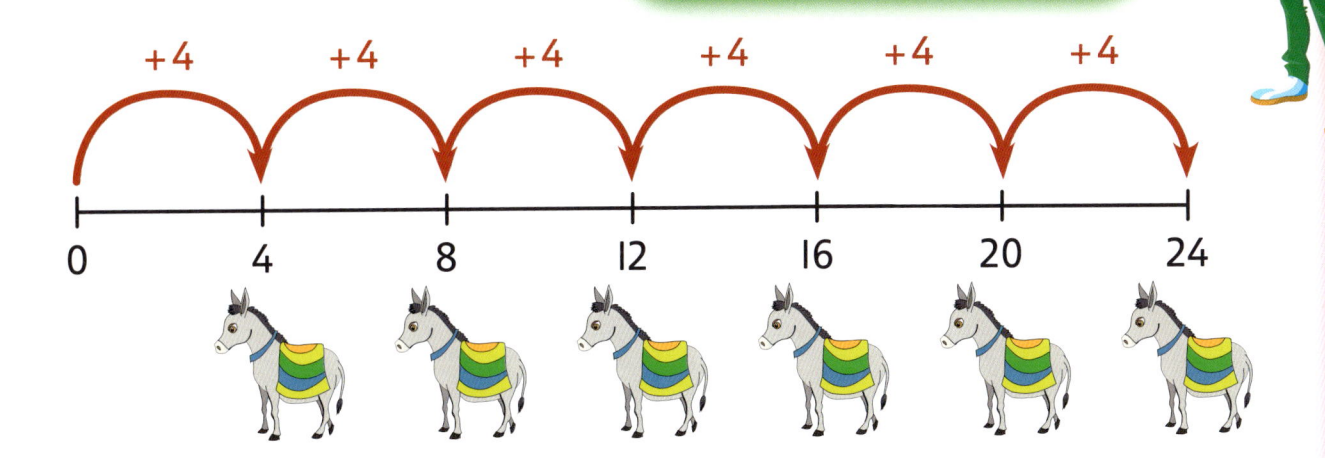

6 × 4 = 24

There are 24 donkey legs in total.

Instead of counting the legs in 1s, I am going to count up in 4s.

Remember, we can think of 6 × 4 as meaning 6 groups of 4, which is what we have.

b) There are 5 people in the family.

The cost for each person is £4.

The total cost is 5 × £4 = £20.

Mr Peters pays the correct amount.

Unit 5: Multiplication and division (2), Lesson 4

201

Unit 5: Multiplication and division (2), Lesson 4

Think together

1 **a)** There are 7 donkeys.

How many donkey legs are there in total?

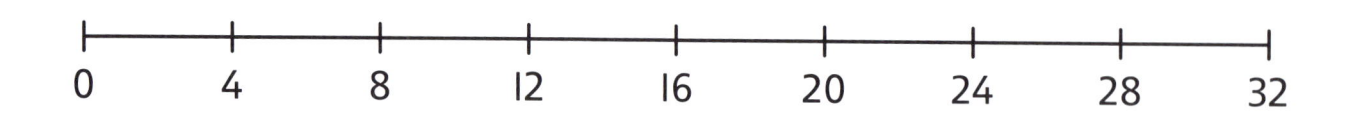

0 4 8 12 16 20 24 28 32

☐ × 4 = ☐

b) How much does it cost in total for 4 people to go donkey trekking?

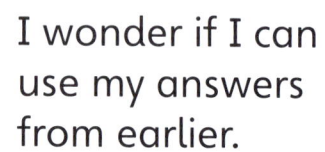

☐ × ☐ = ☐

I wonder if I can use my answers from earlier.

2 There are 32 donkey legs.

How many donkeys are there?

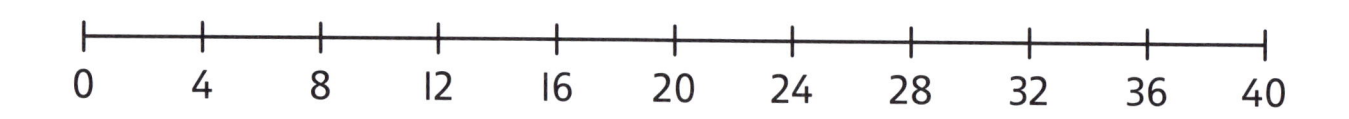

0 4 8 12 16 20 24 28 32 36 40

There are ☐ donkeys because ☐ × ☐ = ☐.

Unit 5: Multiplication and division (2), Lesson 4

CHALLENGE

3 A box contains 4 apples.

How many apples are there in 9 boxes?

> To work this out you have to do 9 × 4.

Jamie

> I have a different way of multiplying by 4. You can multiply by 2 and then multiply by 2 again.

Ebo

Ebo did the following working.

$$9 \times 2 = 18$$
$$18 \times 2 = 36$$
$$\text{So, } 9 \times 4 = 36$$

Does this work for 10 × 4?

What about 6 × 4?

Check it with your own numbers.

Use equipment to show why this works.

> I can show this using a picture or cubes.

> That's interesting! To multiply by 4, I can double and then double again!

203

→ Practice book 3A p147

Unit 5: Multiplication and division (2), Lesson 5

Divide by 4

Discover

1 a) 20 cards are dealt equally between 4 players.

How many cards does each player get?

Write this as a division sentence.

b) The 28 left over cards are put into piles of 4.

How many piles are there?

Share

a) 20 cards are dealt out.

There are 4 players.

Each player gets 5 cards.

"I will give the cards out 1 at a time."

20 ÷ 4 = 5

"I grouped them into 4s until there were none left."

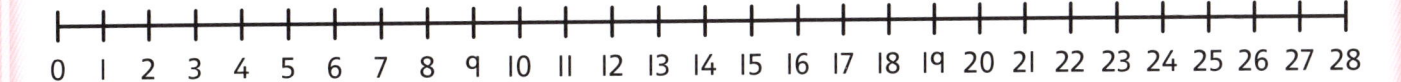

b)

There are 28 cards.

There are 4 cards in each group.

28 ÷ 4 = 7

There are 7 piles.

Unit 5: Multiplication and division (2), Lesson 5

Think together

1) 12 coins are shared between 4 money boxes.

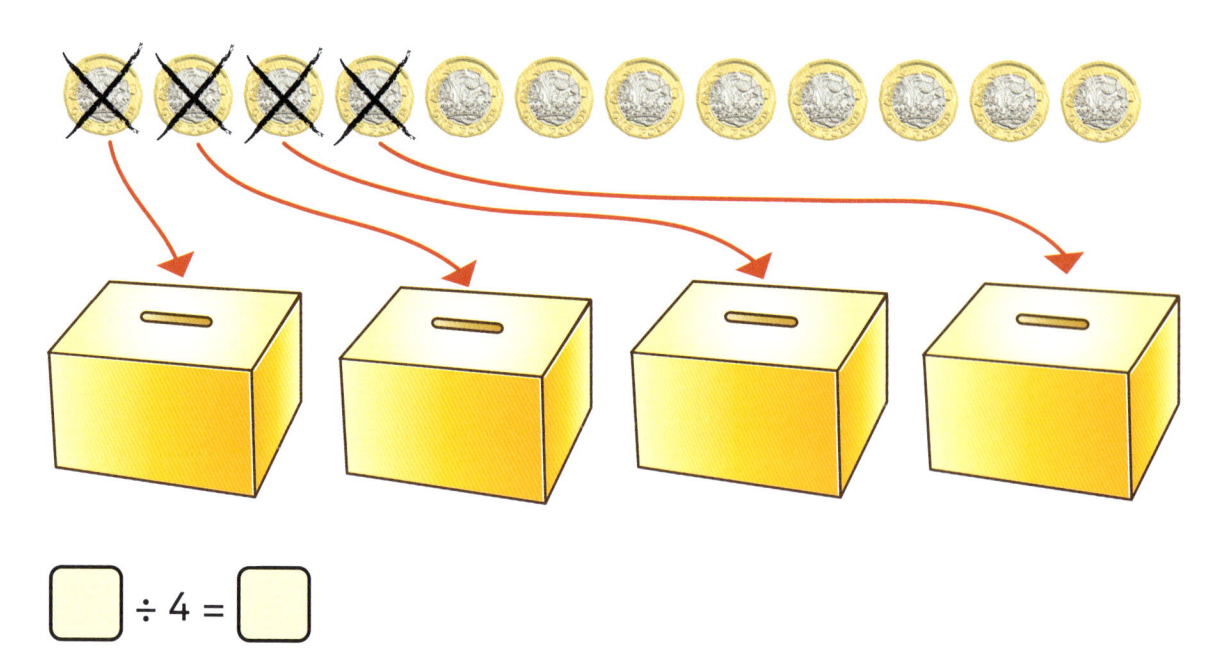

☐ ÷ 4 = ☐

2) There are 32 flowers.

The flowers are put into bunches of 4.

How many bunches are there?

☐ ÷ ☐ = ☐

Unit 5: Multiplication and division (2), Lesson 5

3 **a)** 44 marbles are shared equally between the boxes.

I have 44 marbles. I know I need to divide by 4. I can divide by 2 and by 2 again. This will tell me how many I should put in each box.

Jamie

How many marbles are there in each box?

b) Is it possible to divide 22 marbles equally between 4 boxes? Discuss this with a partner.

I think Jamie's method works every time.

I wonder which numbers can be divided by 4 and which cannot. Is there any way of telling?

→ Practice book 3A p150

207

Unit 5: Multiplication and division (2), Lesson 6

The 4 times-table

Discover

0 × 4 = 0
1 × 4 = 4
2 × 4 = 8
3 × 4 = 12
4 × 4 = 16
5 × 4 = 20
6 × 4 =
7 × 4 = 28
8 × 4 =
9 × 4 = 36
10 × 4 = 40
11 × 4 = 44
12 × 4 = 48

1 **a)** What numbers are the children covering?

How did you work them out?

b) Which multiplication facts will help you work out these calculations?

4 × 7 = ☐   48 ÷ 4 = ☐

Work out the answers.

208

Share

a) Create arrays using counters to find the answers.

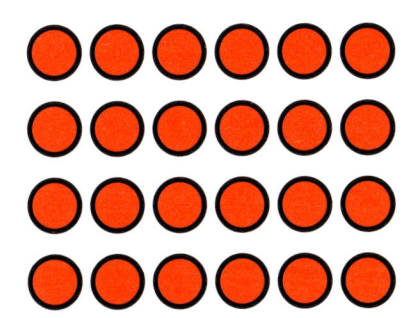

6 × 4 = 24

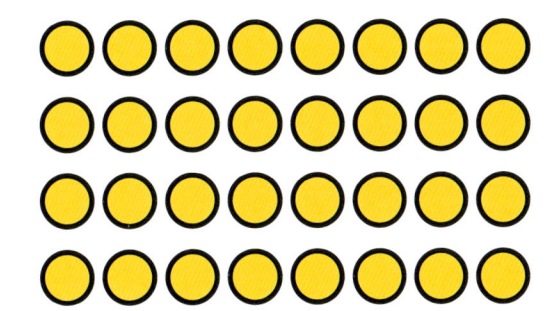

8 × 4 = 32

The children are covering 24 and 32.

b)

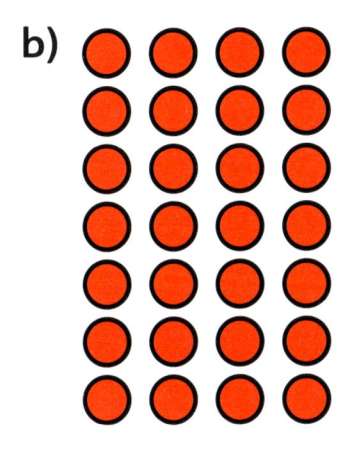

4 × 7 = 28

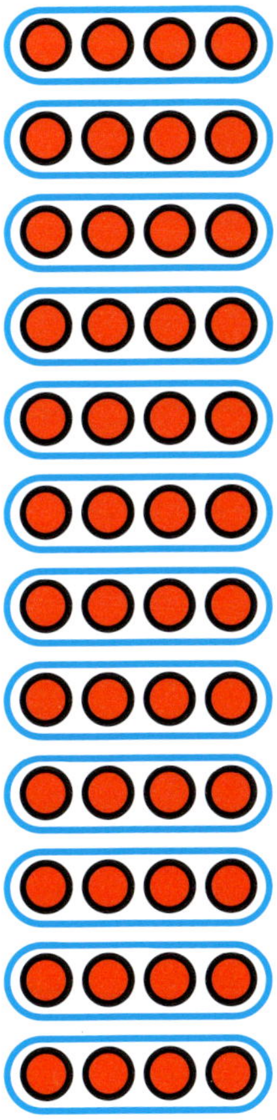

48 ÷ 4 = 12

I know that 4 × 7 is the same as 7 × 4.

If I know 12 × 4 = 48, I also know 48 ÷ 4 = 12.

Unit 5: Multiplication and division (2), Lesson 6

Think together

1) Use multiplication facts to work out how many there are of each item in total.

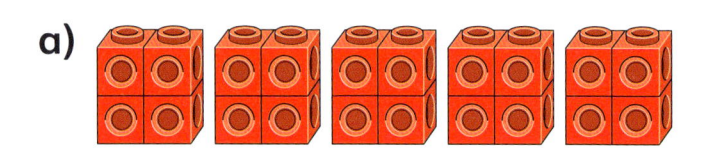

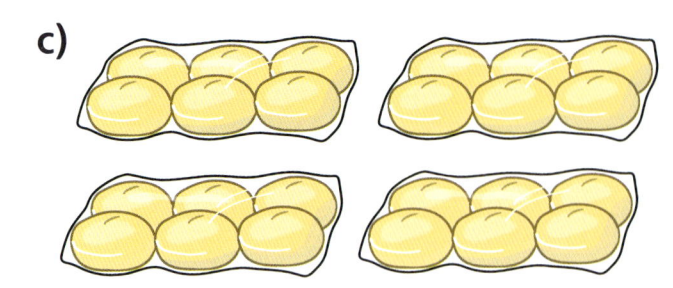

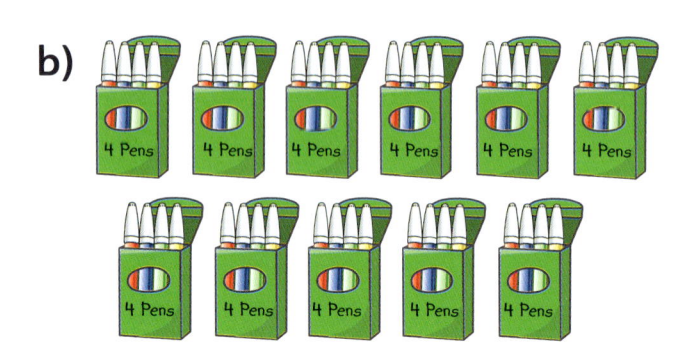

a)

b)

c)

2) Mary has been asked some questions.

Which questions has Mary got right?

7 × 4 = 28
4 × 9 = 36
4 × 1 = 4
0 × 4 = 4
10 × 4 = 43

12 ÷ 4 = 3
4 ÷ 4 = 0
8 ÷ 4 = 32
24 ÷ 4 = 8
44 ÷ 4 = 11

I can tell straight away that at least one of the multiplication answers is wrong!

Unit 5: Multiplication and division (2), Lesson 6

CHALLENGE

③ Put a counter on all the numbers in the 4 times-table.

1	2	3	4	5	6	7	8	9	10
11	12	13	14	15	16	17	18	19	20
21	22	23	24	25	26	27	28	29	30
31	32	33	34	35	36	37	38	39	40
41	42	43	44	45	46	47	48	49	50
51	52	53	54	55	56	57	58	59	60
61	62	63	64	65	66	67	68	69	70
71	72	73	74	75	76	77	78	79	80
81	82	83	84	85	86	87	88	89	90
91	92	93	94	95	96	97	98	99	100

What patterns do you notice?

What do the numbers have in common?

You could go on finding numbers even bigger than 100 that are in the 4 times-table.

All the numbers so far are even. I wonder if that is true for any number in the 4 times-table.

I know how the 4 times-table relates to the 2 times-table. I will use a different colour for the 2 times-table.

211

→ Practice book 3A p153

Unit 5: Multiplication and division (2), Lesson 7

Multiply by 8

Discover

1 a) Each pie has been cut into 8 slices.

How many slices are there in total?

Write down a multiplication sentence to work out the answer.

b) 5 × 2 = ☐   5 × 4 = ☐   5 × 8 = ☐

What do you notice?

Share

a) Each pie is cut into 8 slices.

There are 4 pies.

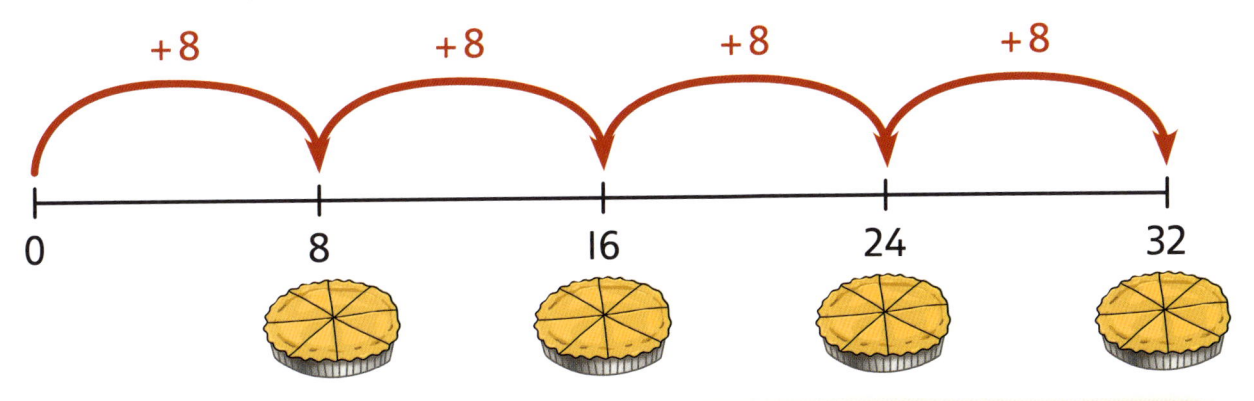

$4 \times 8 = 32$

There are 32 slices in total.

> Remember, we can think of 4×8 as meaning 4 groups of 8, which is what we have.

b) 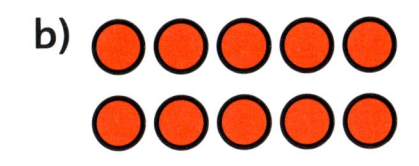 $5 \times 2 = 10$

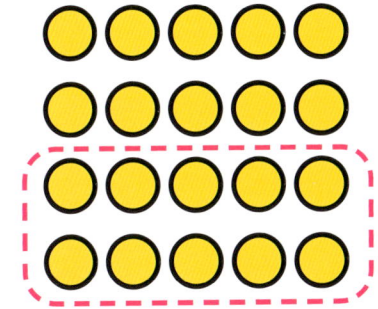

$5 \times 4 = 20$

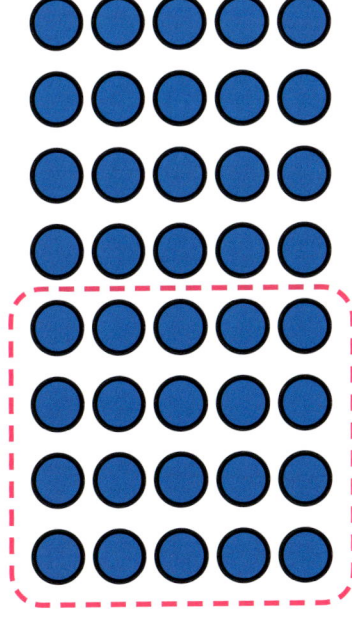

$5 \times 8 = 40$

> The answer doubles each time. I wonder if this works if I change the 5 to any other number.

Unit 5: Multiplication and division (2), Lesson 7

Think together

1) A spider has 8 legs.

How many legs are there altogether?

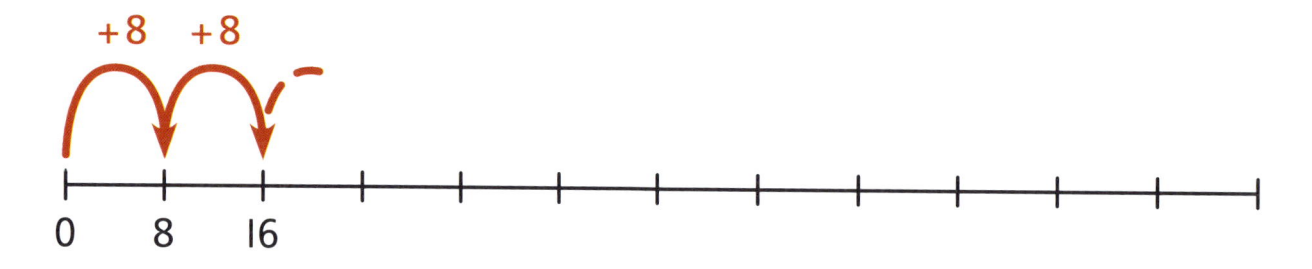

6 × 8 = ☐

2) A ticket to see a play is £8.

11 people are waiting to buy tickets.

How much will it cost them in total?

☐ × ☐ = ☐

Unit 5: Multiplication and division (2), Lesson 7

3 Here are two methods for multiplying.

Luis: Here is my method for multiplying by 4.

Isla: Here is my method for multiplying by 8.

To multiply by 4

First, double your number (multiply by 2).

Then double your answer (multiply by 2 again).

To multiply by 8

First, double your number (multiply by 2).

Then double your answer (multiply by 2 again).

Then double your answer again (multiply by 2 again).

a) Use Luis's method to work out 9 × 4.

b) Use Isla's method to work out 9 × 8.

c) Work out 15 × 4, and 15 × 8.

Did you have to start again to work out part b)?

I wonder if this works for any number.

If so, I wonder why it works.

215

→ Practice book 3A p156

Unit 5: Multiplication and division (2), Lesson 8

Divide by 8

Discover

1 a) Each ice lolly mould uses 8 lollipop sticks.

Mr Jones has 24 sticks.

How many moulds can he fill?

b) Miss Hall has 38 sticks.

How many moulds can she fill?

Share

a) Mr Jones has 24 lollipop sticks.

Each mould uses 8 sticks.

I will put the sticks into groups of 8.

I can use a number line to record what I am doing.

24 ÷ 8 = 3

Mr Jones can fill 3 moulds.

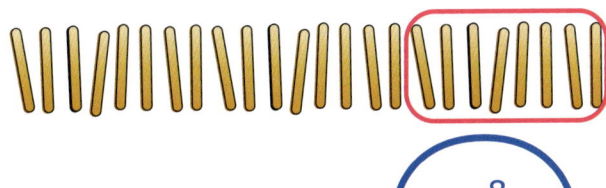

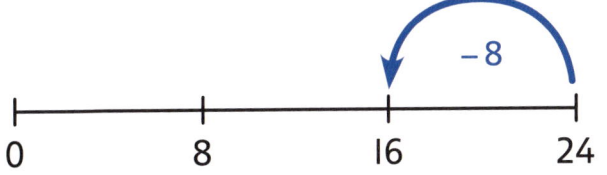

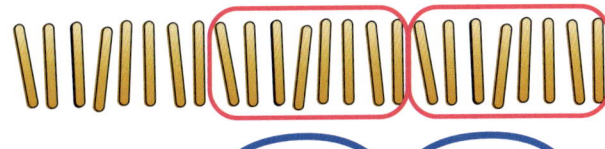

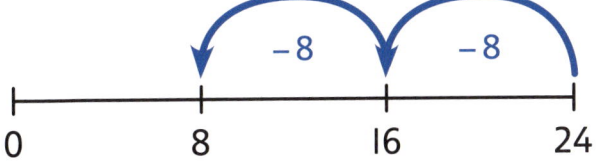

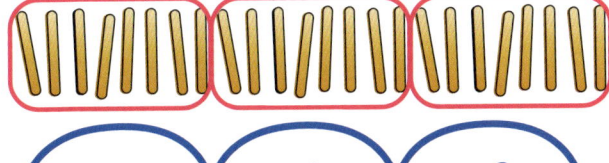

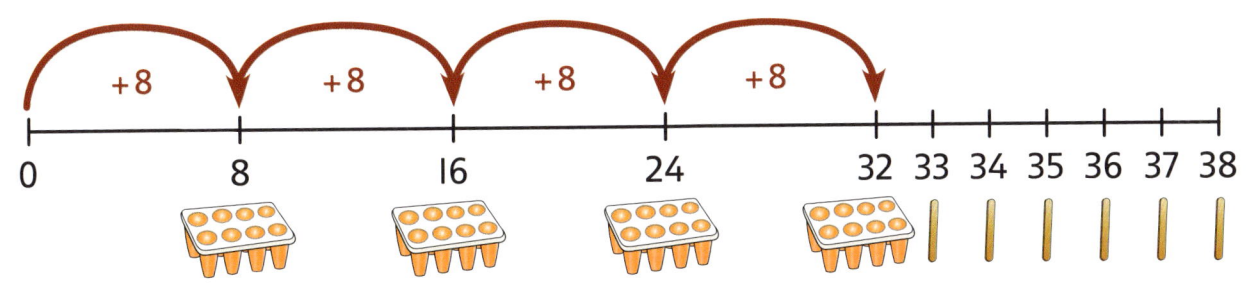

b) Miss Hall has 38 sticks.

Miss Hall can fill 4 moulds.

There aren't enough sticks left to fill a fifth mould.

Unit 5: Multiplication and division (2), Lesson 8

217

Unit 5: Multiplication and division (2), Lesson 8

Think together

1 Alex has baked 8 cupcakes.

She has 40 chocolate chips to share equally between the cupcakes.

How many chocolate chips can she use on each cupcake?

40 ÷ 8 = ☐

2 Use the diagrams to work out the divisions.

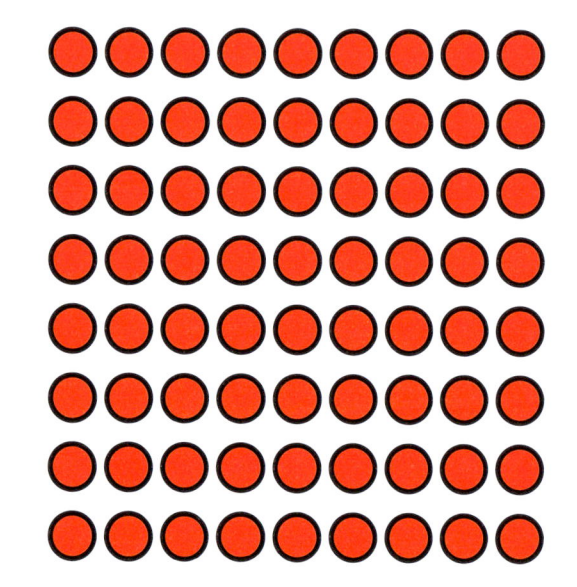

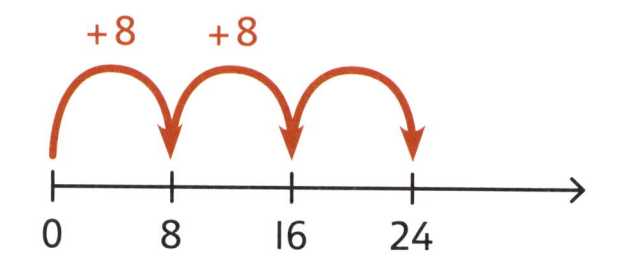

a) 72 ÷ 8 = ☐

b) 48 ÷ 8 = ☐

3 Lexi is cutting a cake.

First she cuts it in half.

Then she cuts each piece in half.

Then she cuts each new piece in half.

a) How can Lexi use what she has done to work out:

16 ÷ 2, 16 ÷ 4 and 16 ÷ 8?

b) Write a rule to divide by 8.

Use your rule to work out 88 ÷ 8.

I used the candles to help me work out each calculation.

I wonder what Lexi is doing to each piece of cake each time. I think this will help me find a rule I can use.

→ Practice book 3A p159

Unit 5: Multiplication and division (2), Lesson 9

The 8 times-table

Discover

12 × 2 = 24   12 × 4 = 48   12 × 8 = 96
11 × 2 = 22   11 × 4 = 44   11 × 8 = 88
10 × 2 = 20   10 × 4 = 40   10 × 8 = 80
9 × 2 = 18   9 × 4 = 36   9 × 8 =
8 × 2 = 16   8 × 4 = 32   8 × 8 = 64
7 × 2 = 14   7 × 4 = 28   7 × 8 = 56
6 × 2 = 12   6 × 4 = 24   6 × 8 =
5 × 2 = 10   5 × 4 = 20   5 × 8 = 40
4 × 2 = 8   4 × 4 = 16   4 × 8 = 32
3 × 2 = 6   3 × 4 = 12   3 × 8 = 24
2 × 2 = 4   2 × 4 = 8   2 × 8 =
1 × 2 = 2   1 × 4 = 4   1 × 8 = 8
0 × 2 = 0   0 × 4 = 0   0 × 8 = 0

1 a) What answers are missing?

b) What is the connection between the 2, 4 and 8 times-tables?

Share

a) You need to work out 2 × 8, 6 × 8 and 9 × 8.

2 × 8 = 16   6 × 8 = 48   9 × 8 = 72

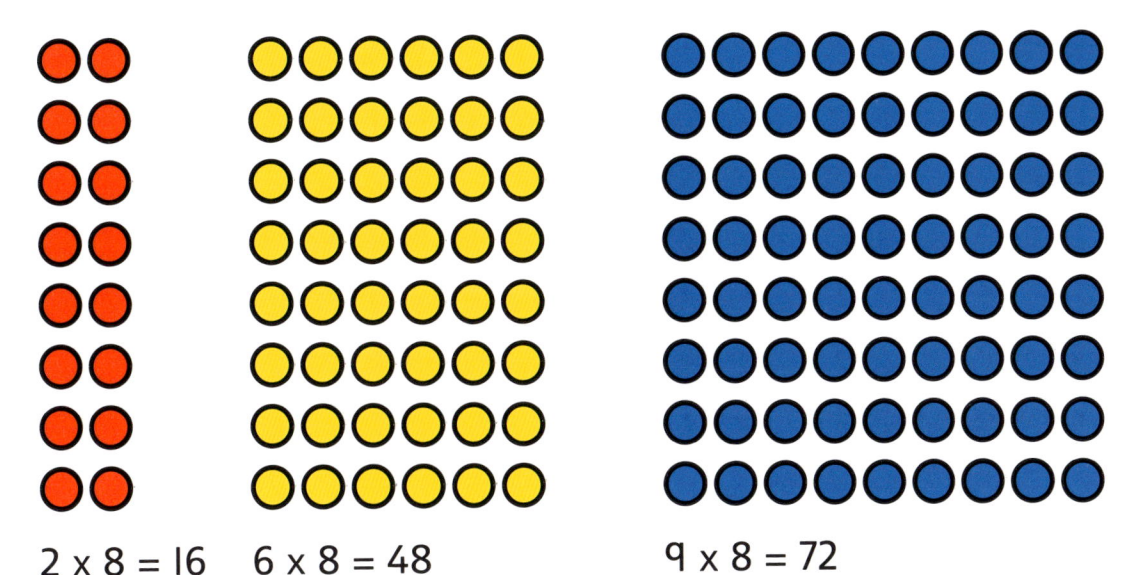

I used arrays to work out the answers. Now I need to try to remember these facts.

b) Compare the times-tables using arrays.

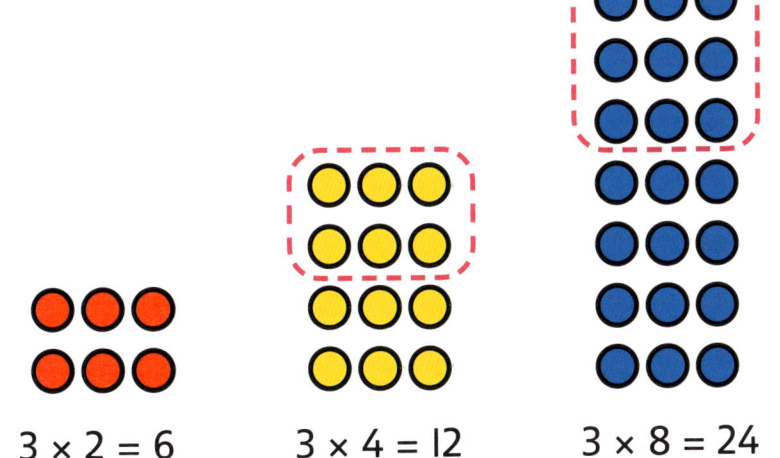

3 × 2 = 6   3 × 4 = 12   3 × 8 = 24

I can see a pattern. The answers double each time.

Unit 5: Multiplication and division (2), Lesson 9

Think together

1 How many of each object are there in total?

What multiplication fact can you use to work out each total?

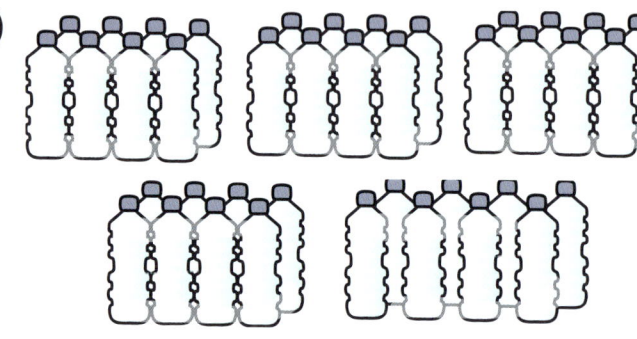

a)

☐ × ☐ = ☐

b)

☐ × ☐ = ☐

c)

☐ × ☐ = ☐

2 How many of these do you know off by heart?

a) 3 × 8 = ☐

b) 10 × 8 = ☐

c) ☐ × 8 = 8

d) ☐ = 12 × 8

e) 40 ÷ 8 = ☐

f) 5 × 8 = ☐

g) 8 × 2 = ☐

h) ☐ ÷ 8 = 0

222

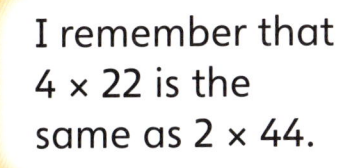

Unit 5: Multiplication and division (2), Lesson 9

CHALLENGE

3) Find all the matching answers.

What is the pattern?

| 5 × 8 |
| 3 × 8 |
| 1 × 8 |
| 8 × 11 |
| 8 × 10 |
| 8 × 8 |

| 2 × 4 |
| 4 × 20 |
| 10 × 4 |
| 4 × 22 |
| 6 × 4 |
| 16 × 4 |

| 12 × 2 |
| 32 × 2 |
| 2 × 40 |
| 4 × 2 |
| 2 × 44 |
| 20 × 2 |

I have found some matches without working out any of the calculations.

I remember that 4 × 22 is the same as 2 × 44.

223

→ Practice book 3A p162

Unit 5: Multiplication and division (2), Lesson 10

Problem solving – multiplication and division ①

Discover

Amal

1) a) The plants are planted in rows of 4.

There are 24 to plant.

How many rows of plants will there be?

b) Amal has some bunches of flowers.

There are 10 flowers in each bunch.

How many flowers does he have in total?

Share

a) There are 24 plants.

I will put them into groups of 4.

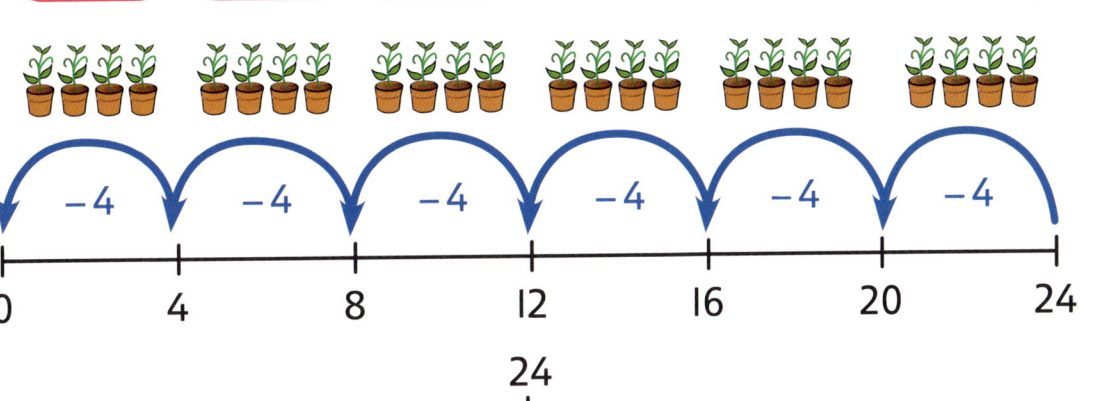

$24 \div 4 = 6$

There will be 6 rows of 4 plants.

I put them into groups of 4 using a bar model.

b) Amal has 2 bunches of flowers.

$2 \times 10 = 20$

There are 10 flowers in each bunch.

$2 \times 10 = 20$

Amal has 20 flowers in total.

We can use bar models to help us see when to divide and when to multiply.

Unit 5: Multiplication and division (2), Lesson 10

Think together

1) How many plants are there in total?

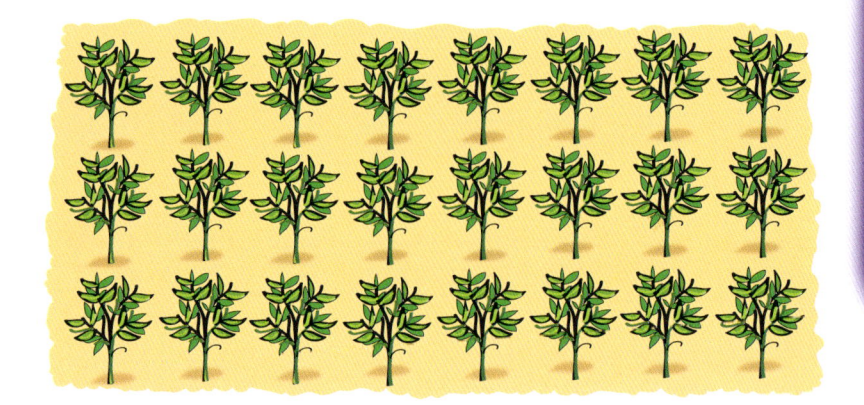

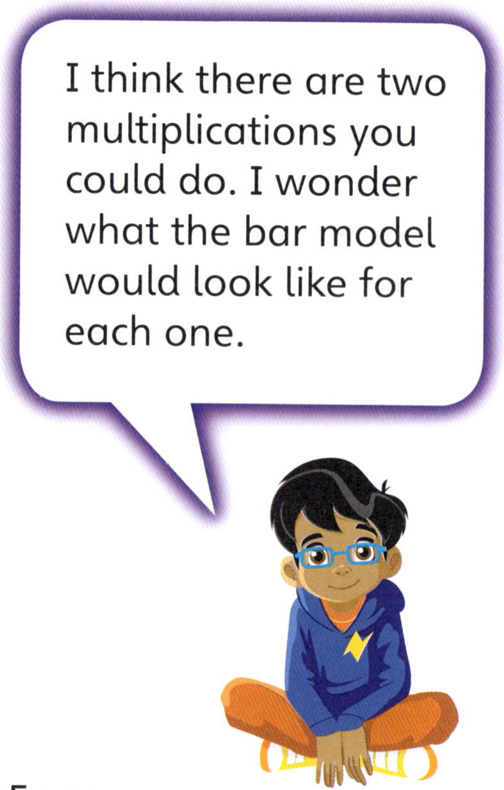

☐ ◯ ☐ = ☐

There are ☐ plants in total.

> I think there are two multiplications you could do. I wonder what the bar model would look like for each one.

2) 30 flowers are shared equally between the 5 vases.
How many flowers in each vase?

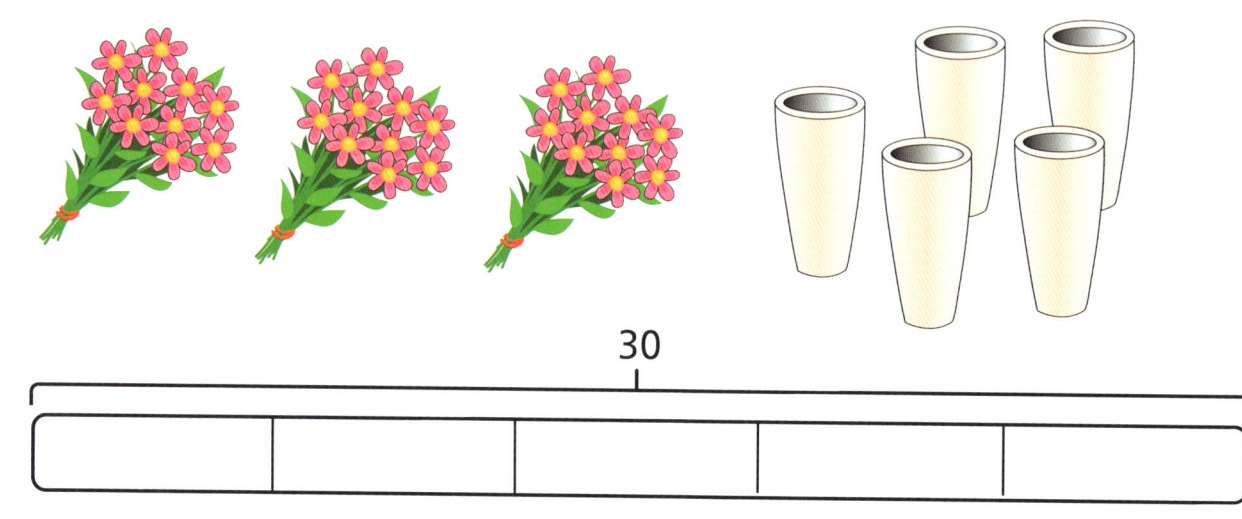

30

☐ ◯ ☐ = ☐

There are ☐ flowers in each vase.

226

Unit 5: Multiplication and division (2), Lesson 10

3 Clare buys 8 small plant pots and 4 large plant pots.

PLANT POT SALE

£3

The 4 large plant pots cost the same as 8 small plant pots.

How much does 1 large plant pot cost?

Write down all your steps.

> I think this question involves a multiplication and a division.
>
> I need to draw two bar models.

> I might be able to do this without doing two calculations.
>
> A bar model may help me.

CHALLENGE

227

→ Practice book 3A p165

Unit 5: Multiplication and division (2), Lesson 11

Problem solving – multiplication and division 2

Discover

1. a) Andy has put 3 blocks end to end to make a new shape.

   What is the length of Andy's shape?

   b) Isla makes a shape that is 32 cm long.

   How many blocks does she use?

Share

a) Andy puts down 3 blocks.

I will use a bar model to help me see what I should do.

I need to multiply to work out the total length.

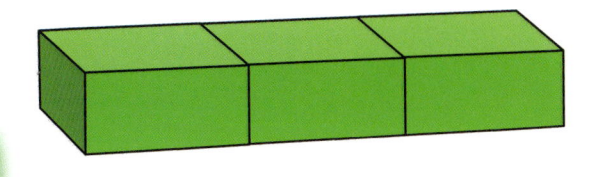

Total length

| 8 | 8 | 8 |

3 × 8 = 24

The length of Andy's shape is 24 cm.

b) Isla's shape is 32 cm long.

4 × 8 = 32

I laid the blocks down and kept adding on until I got to 32 cm.

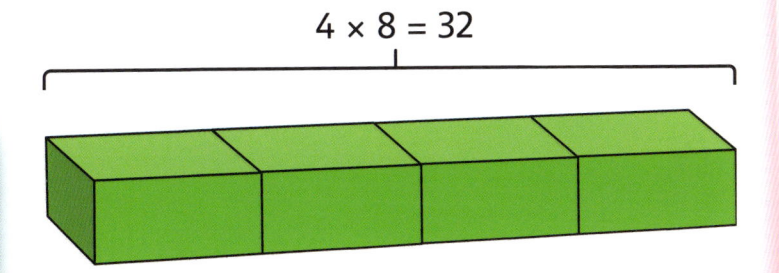

I used division. I think this is a quicker way.

32 ÷ 8 = 4

Isla uses 4 blocks.

There is another possible answer.

32 ÷ 4 = 8

Isla uses 8 blocks.

229

Unit 5: Multiplication and division (2), Lesson 11

Think together

1 This shape has been made with the same blocks.

How long is the new shape?

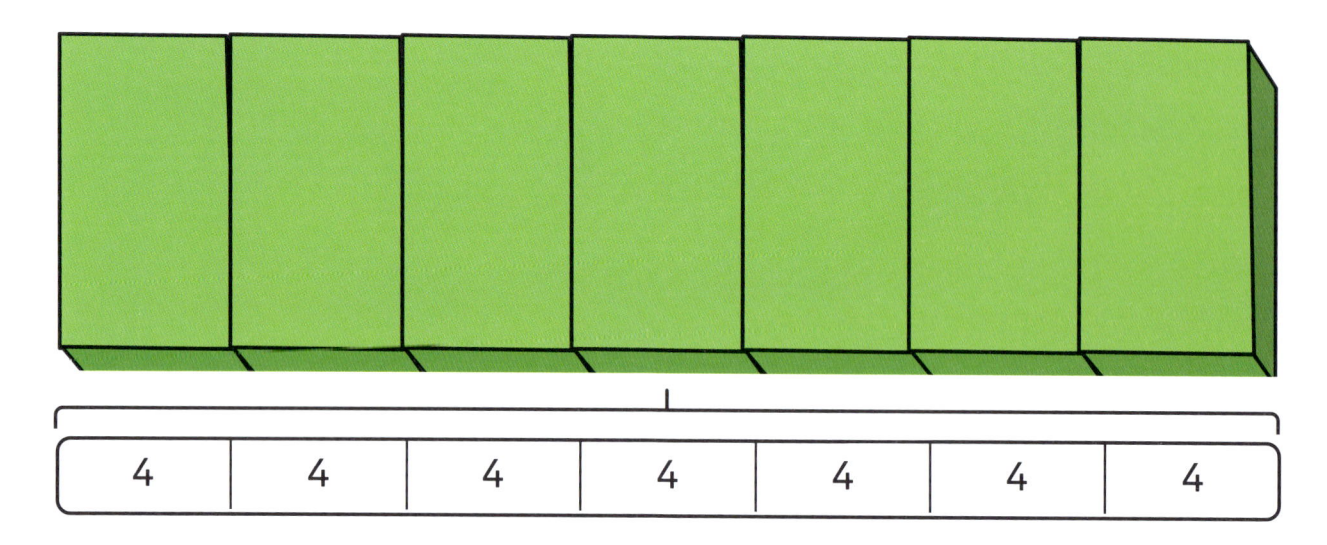

| 4 | 4 | 4 | 4 | 4 | 4 | 4 |

☐ × ☐ = ☐

The new shape is ☐ cm long.

2 Which tower is taller?

How much taller is it?

Tower A: ☐ × ☐ = ☐ cm tall.

Tower B: ☐ × ☐ = ☐ cm tall.

Tower ☐ is the taller tower.

It is ☐ cm taller.

A   B

230

Unit 5: Multiplication and division (2), Lesson 11

3 Isla makes this pattern using 7 wooden blocks.

How long is the new pattern?

CHALLENGE

I think I need to work out two multiplications and then add.

These are the same blocks that the children used in the Discover activity.

→ Practice book 3A p168

Unit 5: Multiplication and division (2), Lesson 12

Understand divisibility ①

Discover

① a) Lexi and Zac are using lollipop sticks to make squares.
How many squares can they make?
How many lollipop sticks are left over?

b) How would the answer change if they had 14 lollipop sticks?
What about 15, 16 or 17 lollipop sticks?

Unit 5: Multiplication and division (2), Lesson 12

Share

a) 4 lollipop sticks make 1 square.

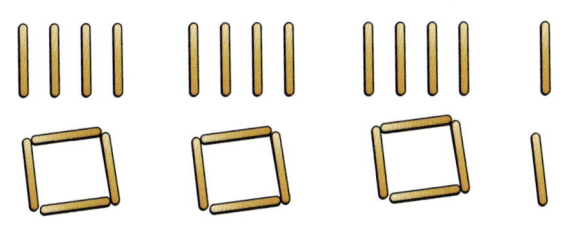

13 lollipop sticks make 3 squares with 1 stick left over.

We call the amount left over the **remainder**.

I will try organising my work in a table.

b)

Number of sticks	Working	Number of squares	Number of sticks left over
14		3	2
15		3	3
16		4	0
17		4	1

233

Unit 5: Multiplication and division (2), Lesson 12

Think together

1) Lexi and Zac use more lollipop sticks.

How would you complete the table?

Number of sticks	Working	Number of squares	Number of sticks left over
18		4	
19			
20			

2) a) Describe the pattern that Lexi can see.

Lexi: I can see a pattern in the number of lollipop sticks left over.

b) Is Zac correct?

Zac: I don't think you can have more than 3 lollipop sticks left over.

Unit 5: Multiplication and division (2), Lesson 12

CHALLENGE

③ Lexi and Zac are now making triangles using lollipop sticks.

Complete the table.

Number of sticks	Working	Number of triangles	Number of sticks left over
10	△△△ /	3	1
11			
12			
13			
14			
15			

There is a similar pattern to last time.

I wonder what the greatest number of lollipop sticks you can have left over is.

235

→ Practice book 3A p171

Unit 5: Multiplication and division (2), Lesson 13

Understand divisibility ②

Discover

1 a) There are 22 apples.

They are packed in bags of 5.

How many full bags are made?

How many apples are left over?

b) Write the calculation as a division.

☐ ÷ ☐ = ☐ remainder ☐

Share

a) Start with 22 apples.

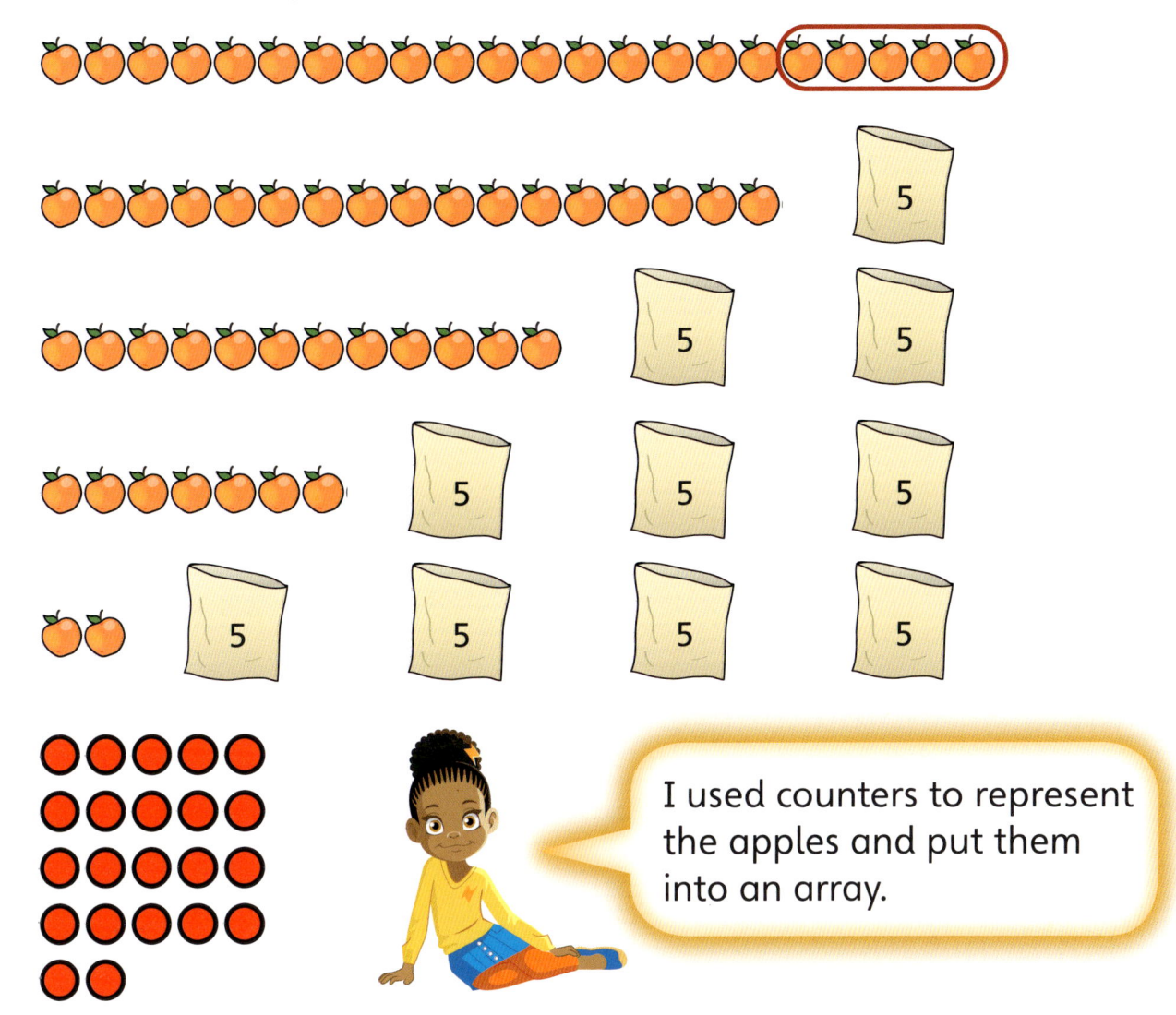

I used counters to represent the apples and put them into an array.

4 full bags are made and 2 apples are left over.

b) This is grouping.

There are 22 apples. There are 5 apples in each bag.

There are 4 full bags and 2 apples left over.

22 ÷ 5 = 4 remainder 2

Unit 5: Multiplication and division (2), Lesson 13

Think together

1 Here are some oranges.

The oranges are shared between 2 bowls.

Can they be shared equally?

☐ ÷ ☐ = ☐ remainder ☐

2 14 cubes are put into towers of 3.

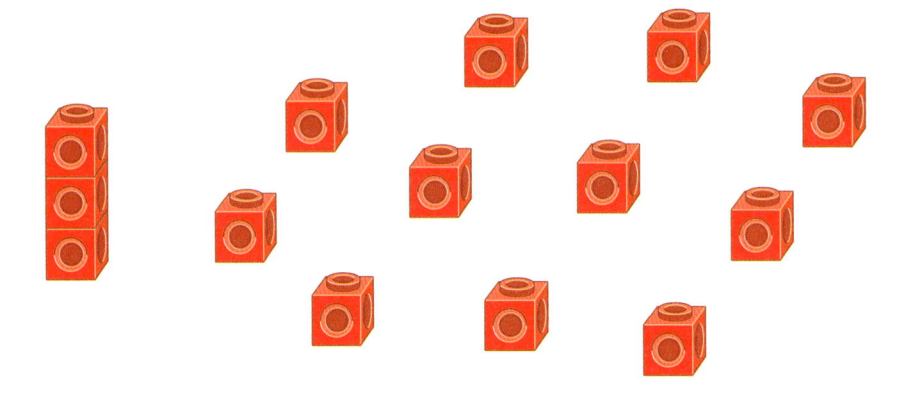

How many complete towers can be made?

How many cubes are left over?

☐ ÷ ☐ = ☐ remainder ☐

238

Unit 5: Multiplication and division (2), Lesson 13

3 Explore the division calculations.

CHALLENGE

a) For each one, how many wholes are there and what is the remainder?

12 ÷ 5 = ☐ remainder ☐   17 ÷ 4 = ☐ remainder ☐

13 ÷ 8 = ☐ remainder ☐   51 ÷ 10 = ☐ remainder ☐

> I know 2 × 5 = 10 and I know 3 × 5 = 15. This will help me work out 12 ÷ 5.

> I wonder if I can use times-tables to help solve these.

b) Alex divides a number by 3. There is no remainder.

What could the number be? Where have you seen these numbers before?

239

→ Practice book 3A p174

Unit 5: Multiplication and division (2)

End of unit check

1 David shares 24 grapes between 3 people.

How many grapes does each person get?

A 21   B 6   C 8   D 72

2 Which calculation will **not** work out the total number of cakes?

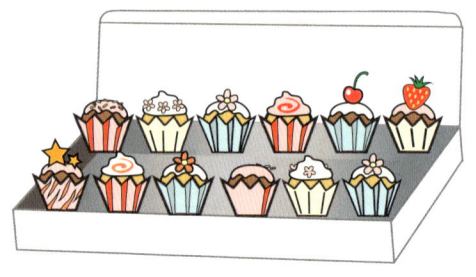

A 12 + 12 + 12 + 12   C 4 × 12

B 12 × 4   D 4 + 4 + 4 + 4

3 Which multiplication gives the greatest answer?

A 7 × 3   B 8 × 2   C 6 × 4   D 0 × 10

Unit 5: Multiplication and division (2)

4 Which multiplication gives the same answer as 6 × 8?

   A 3 × 8
   B 12 × 4
   C 9 × 5
   D 12 × 16

5 A pack contains 4 bread rolls.

   How many bread rolls are there in 7 packs?

   A 11   B 35   C 28   D 24

6 Lexi shares 16 cubes equally between 3 people.

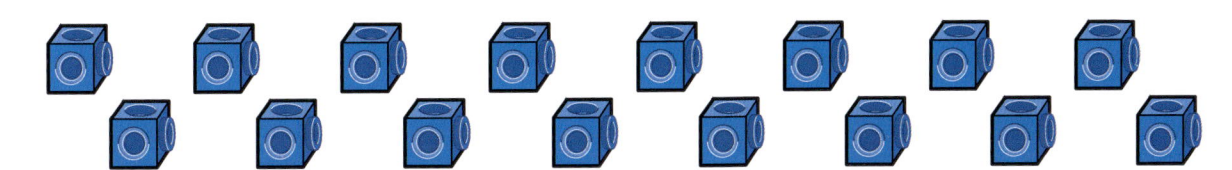

   How many cubes do they each get? How many cubes are left over?

   A 1 cube, 5 left over
   B 4 cubes, 3 left over
   C 6 cubes, 0 left over
   D 5 cubes, 1 left over

7 What is the missing value?

   ☐ × 4 = 24 ÷ 3

→ Practice book 3A p177

Practice helps us get better!

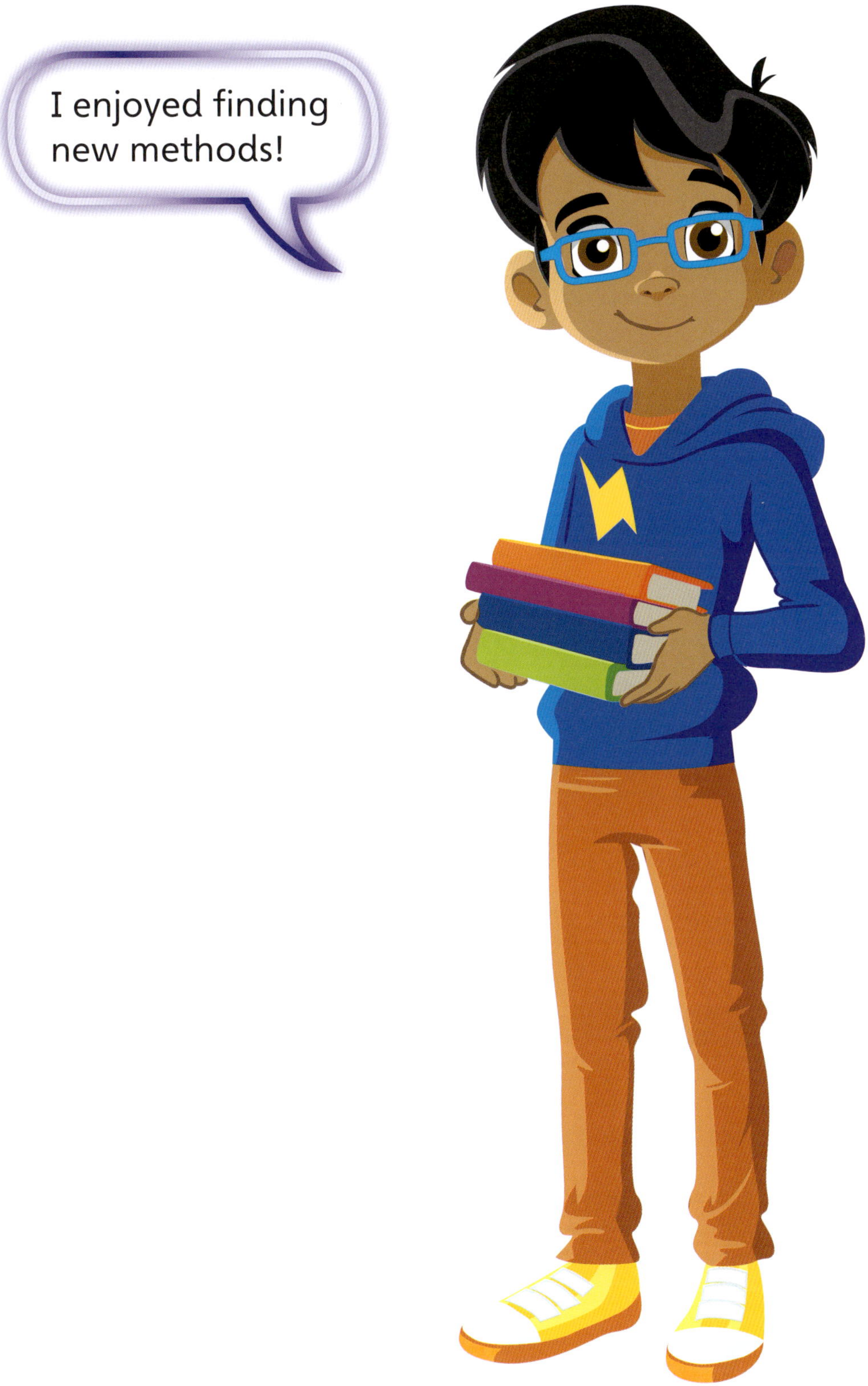
I enjoyed finding new methods!

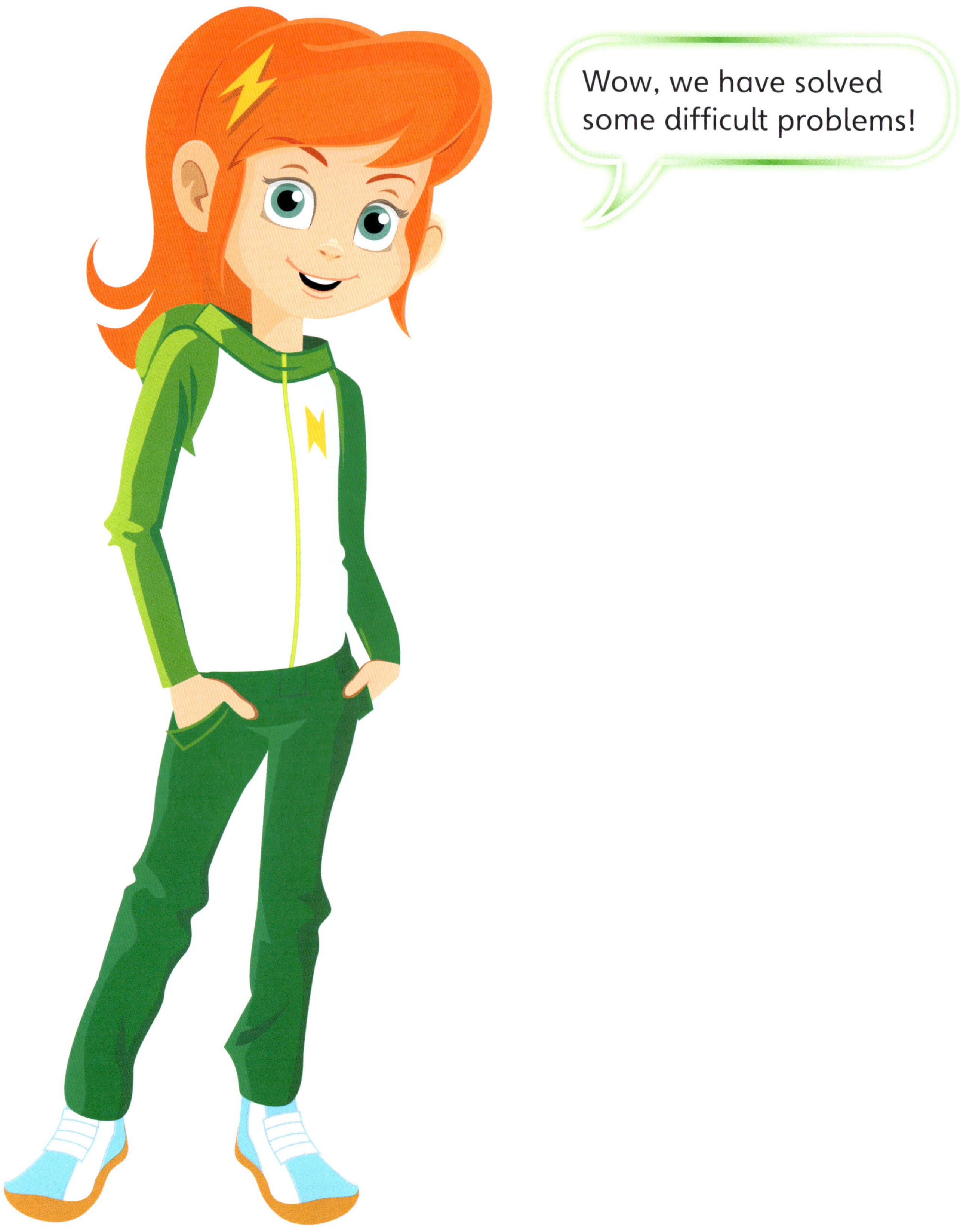
Wow, we have solved some difficult problems!

Yes, we have! Can we find even better ways to solve problems?

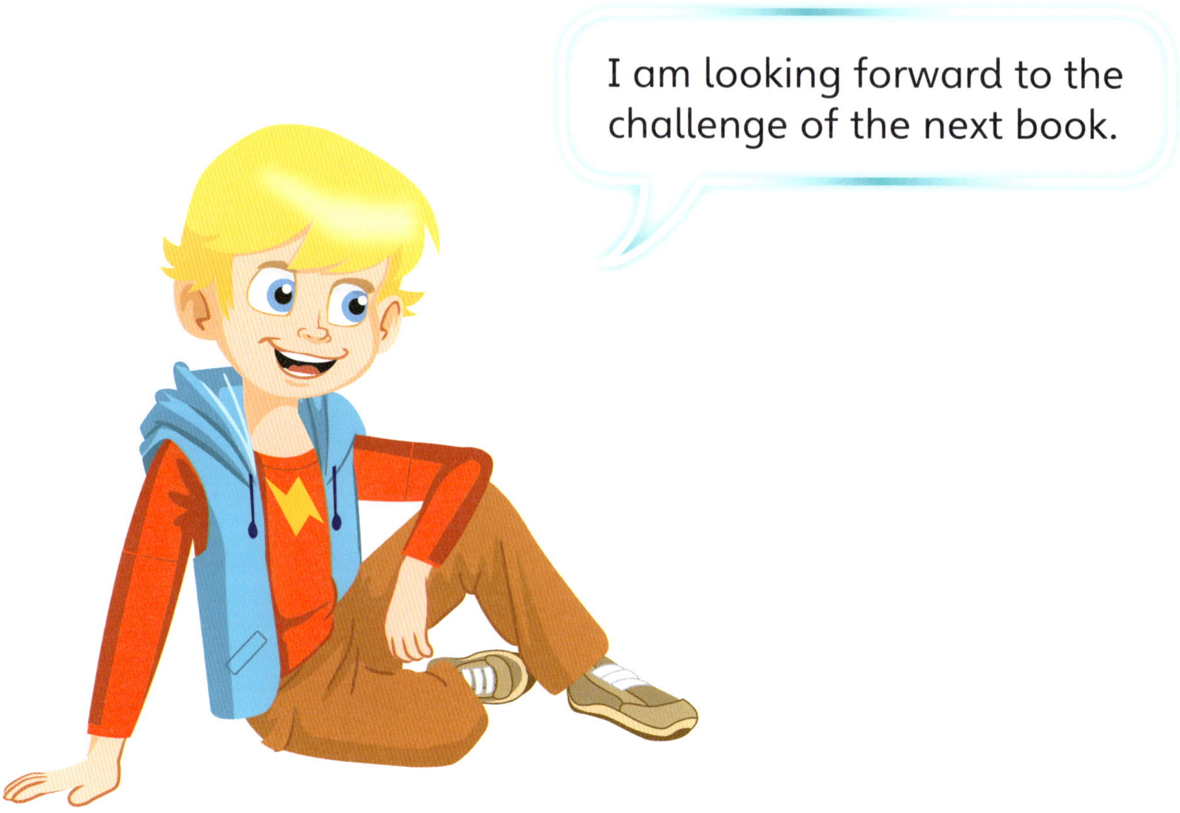
I am looking forward to the challenge of the next book.

What do we know now?

Can you do all these things?

- Count in 100s
- Explain when to exchange 1s, 10s and 100s
- Add and subtract using mental and written methods
- Check answers in different ways
- Work out multiples of 2, 5 and 10

Some of it was difficult, but we did not give up!

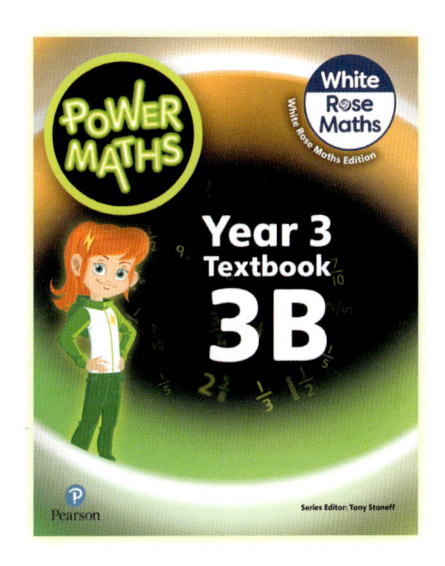

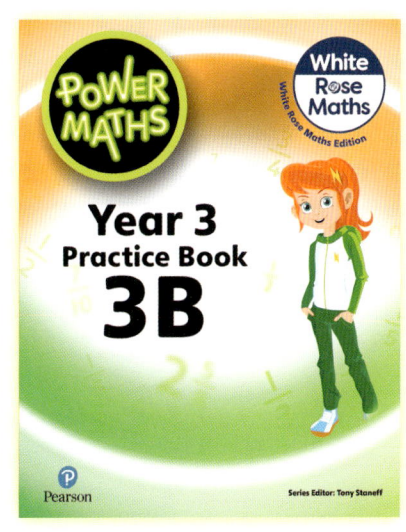

Now you are ready for the next books!

Published by Pearson Education Limited, 80 Strand, London, WC2R 0RL.

www.pearsonschools.co.uk

Text © Pearson Education Limited 2018, 2022
Edited by Pearson and Florence Production Ltd
First edition edited by Pearson, Little Grey Cells Publishing Services and Haremi Ltd
Designed and typeset by Pearson and Florence Production Ltd
First edition designed and typeset by Kamae Design
Original illustrations © Pearson Education Limited 2018, 2022
Illustrated by Nigel Dobbyn, Virginia Fontanabona, Paul Moran, Nadene Naude at Beehive Illustration, Emily Skinner at Graham-Cameron Illustration, Florence Production Ltd and Kamae Design
Images: The Royal Mint, 2017: 201, 206
Cover design by Pearson Education Ltd
Front and back cover illustrations by Diego Diaz and Nadene Naude at Beehive Illustration
Series editor: Tony Staneff; Lead author: Josh Lury
Authors (first edition): Tony Staneff and Josh Lury
Consultants (first edition): Professor Liu Jian and Professor Zhang Dan

The rights of Tony Staneff and Josh Lury to be identified as authors of this work have been asserted by them in accordance with the Copyright, Designs and Patents Act 1988.

This publication is protected by copyright, and permission should be obtained from the publisher prior to any prohibited reproduction, storage in a retrieval system, or transmission in any form or by any means, electronic, mechanical, photocopying, recording, or otherwise. For information regarding permissions, request forms and the appropriate contacts, please visit https://www.pearson.com/us/contact-us/permissions.html Pearson Education Limited Rights and Permissions Department

First published 2018
This edition first published 2022

26 25 24 23 22
10 9 8 7 6 5 4 3 2 1

British Library Cataloguing in Publication Data
A catalogue record for this book is available from the British Library

ISBN 978 1 292 41951 0

Copyright notice
All rights reserved. No part of this publication may be reproduced in any form or by any means (including photocopying or storing it in any medium by electronic means and whether or not transiently or incidentally to some other use of this publication) without the written permission of the copyright owner, except in accordance with the provisions of the Copyright, Designs and Patents Act 1988 or under the terms of a licence issued by the Copyright Licensing Agency, Barnards Inn, 86 Fetter Lane, London EC4A 1EN (http://www.cla.co.uk). Applications for the copyright owner's written permission should be addressed to the publisher.

Printed in the UK by Bell & Bain Ltd, Glasgow

For Power Maths online resources, go to:
www.activelearnprimary.co.uk

Note from the publisher
Pearson has robust editorial processes, including answer and fact checks, to ensure the accuracy of the content in this publication, and every effort is made to ensure this publication is free of errors. We are, however, only human, and occasionally errors do occur. Pearson is not liable for any misunderstandings that arise as a result of errors in this publication, but it is our priority to ensure that the content is accurate. If you spot an error, please do contact us at resourcescorrections@pearson.com so we can make sure it is corrected.